D0706828

THE FAILURES OF PHILOSOPHY

The Failures of
Philosophy

A HISTORICAL ESSAY

Stephen Gaukroger

PRINCETON UNIVERSITY PRESS

PRINCETON & OXFORD

Copyright © 2020 by Princeton University Press

Requests for permission to reproduce material from this work
should be sent to permissions@press.princeton.edu

Published by Princeton University Press
41 William Street, Princeton, New Jersey 08540
6 Oxford Street, Woodstock, Oxfordshire OX20 1TR

press.princeton.edu

All Rights Reserved

ISBN 9780691207506
ISBN (e-book) 9780691209579
LCCN 2020940121

British Library Cataloging-in-Publication Data is available

Editorial: Ben Tate and Josh Drake
Production Editorial: Debbie Tegarden
Jacket/Cover Design: Layla Mac Rory
Production: Danielle Amucci
Publicity: Alyssa Sanford and Amy Stewart
Copyeditor: Francis Eaves

This book has been composed in Miller

Printed on acid-free paper. ∞

Printed in the United States of America

10 9 8 7 6 5 4 3 2 1

We need history, but not in the way that the spoiled loafer in the garden of knowledge needs history.

—NIETZSCHE, 'OF THE USE AND ABUSE OF HISTORY'

CONTENTS

THE HISTORY OF PHILOSOPHY has typically been written as the history of its achievements. Philosophy is not an unqualified success story, however, and its failures—not the failures of particular philosophical theories or programmes, but the failures of philosophy itself—reveal as much to us as do its successes. Examination of these failures prompts us to ask what the alternatives to philosophy have been, whether these proved more satisfactory than philosophy, and if so why. This in turn allows us to gain some insight not only into the limits of philosophical enquiry, but, more importantly, into whether there are basic features of philosophy that hinder its treatment of many of the questions to which it has directed its attention.

As histories of philosophy go, the present treatment is both compact and selective. Compact, because a compact account is better able to bring an urgency and sharp focus to the issues. Selective, because the narrative has been shaped by historiographical considerations, and these have yielded a different story from the usual one. Many developments that figure in histories of the discipline are absent here, while others that appear only rarely if at all will be explored. As regards the degree of novelty of the approach that I am taking, the influence of Hume's reflections on the limits and limitations of philosophy, at least as I read them, will be evident: philosophy is indispensable if we are to subject the things we believe to critical reflection, but at the same time we need to exercise judgement on its capacities, since it is a resource that can fall out of control and become self-perpetuating, leading us up blind alleys.

THE FAILURES OF PHILOSOPHY

Introduction

WHAT IS IT THAT we want out of philosophy? In considering their discipline, whether in historical or contemporary terms, few philosophers have raised the question, other than at a perfunctory level, of what the point of philosophy is, what it sets out to achieve. Part of the problem has been that the history of philosophy has been treated as a story of progress, with Thomas Stanley, in the first history of philosophy in English (1655), describing his project as looking 'down to the bottom from which philosophy first took her rise', so that we might see 'how great a progresse she hath made'.[1] Yet difficulties arise once one tries to identify such progress. At the beginning of the seventeenth century, Stanley's predecessor Francis Bacon remarked that whereas science began slowly and then over a long period gradually came of age, philosophy burst onto the scene and delivered its most profound insights immediately, and has been inexorably in decline ever since. Two centuries later, Kant, in the Preface to the *Critique of Pure Reason*, offered an equally deflationary account, remarking that the history of philosophy had not been one of continuous progress, but rather a cycle of dogmatic assertions followed by sceptical refutations. And as regards the contributions to learning and wisdom that philosophy can currently take credit for, scientists for one have often been sceptical. The physicists John Barrow and Frank Tipler write that whereas many philosophers and theologians (a worrying association for many philosophers) 'appear to possess an emotional attachment to their theories and ideas which requires them to believe them, scientists tend to regard their ideas differently . . . leaving any judgement regarding their truth to observation'.[2] The geneticist Francis Crick is even more dismissive: 'If you ask how many cases in the past has a philosopher been successful at solving a problem, as far as we can say there are no such cases.'[3]

Before we can ask whether philosophy has made any progress, we need to be able to identify properly philosophical problems. There is an assumption among philosophers that, throughout its history, philosophy has engaged a number of perennial substantive questions. Daniel Stoljar, in a recent attempt to establish progress in the history of philosophy, has, for example, identified a number of what we might term core philosophical issues, not necessarily issues that every species of philosophical enquiry will concern itself with, and not necessarily exclusive, but representing a common conception of what issues philosophy deals with: the mind–body problem; free will and determinism; the basis and scope of human knowledge; the nature of morality; the existence of God; and 'the roots of being', that is, metaphysics and ontology.[4]

But can we assume that these questions capture perennial concerns, that the various contextualizations that enable us to go beyond labelling do not in fact yield something quite different from one another? Is there really a continuity between classical, early modern, Enlightenment, and modern analytic notions of the nature of the mind, or the nature of knowledge, or morality? Properly contextualized, not only does the labelling of questions fall apart in many cases, but we need to understand what prompts particular worries to arise, what allows their translation into philosophical problems, what counts as their resolution, and what constraints are operative: for example, whether a successful account of the mind has to secure the possibility of personal immortality; whether it is appropriate for an account of the mind to consider only an idealized healthy mind; whether moral philosophy should account for courage, humility, loyalty, or friendship as central virtues. Whether one of the aims (and one of the criteria of success) of metaphysics should be to rationalize religious beliefs, or whether it should be reconciliation of science and common sense; whether an account of free will must provide a basis for the understanding of morality; whether the paramount aim of ethics should be to induce us to behave morally: whether philosophy should prepare us for death; whether it should prepare us for life. At the same time, we need to clarify what progress, and failure, might consist in. Otherwise progress, particularly in the case of a university discipline, will just be a matter of the value that the practitioners of that discipline—theologians, cultural theorists, philosophers— place on it. After all, it is not as if theologians and cultural theorists, for example, are any less able than philosophers to point to a sequence of questions and answers, to what they identify as lasting results, and to their ability to constantly go beyond what their predecessors have achieved.

Accordingly, in what follows, we shall not be concerned with the progress or otherwise of philosophy as such. I cannot see that this is a well-formed question, a worry reinforced by Stoljar's statement that 'the level of progress in a field such as physics is extremely high by any standard',[5] for I cannot imagine that there could be such a standard or, if there were, how we would be able to judge the progress of physics against it.[6] But the deeper worry is that physics is being made the measure of all things, a wholly unexamined view that under-lies much modern analytic philosophy. And of course it is the tendency in analytic philosophy to assume that it can model itself on the sciences that allows it to imagine itself to be closer to a path of progress than other disciplines in the humanities. By assimilating philosophy to science, philosophers blithely assume that they have done enough to take the question of the value of philosophy out of the realm of mere self-assessment, at the same time significantly lessening the relevance of any understanding of its history.

By contrast, we shall be using its history to problematize philosophy, and since this is an enquiry into the failures of phi-losophy, it will be helpful to clarify from the outset what I mean by failures and what I mean by philosophy. The kind of 'failure' with which we shall be concerned involves not just the collapse of a substantive philosophical project, but the consequent replacement of a philosophical approach to the questions by something different. That is, we shall be concerned with cases where the issues at stake are considered sufficiently basic that, if philosophy has shown itself unable to solve them, something else needs to take over. We shall be looking at the failures, in this sense, of three major philosophical projects. The first is the attempt of philosophy in antiquity to provide an account of the good life, which we shall see is the defining project of classical philosophy. We shall be exploring the collapse of such attempts and their replacement by a theological—Christian—account which provided what was widely considered to be a more satisfactory non-philosophical treatment of the worries that had motivated philosophical enquiry. The second, which derives from a re-purposing of philosophy, is the attempt to devise a metaphysics that is able to stand over all other kinds of account, including accounts of natural phenomena, and offer a rationale and assessment of these. The collapse of this project took several different forms in the mid-eighteenth century, and this is especially interesting because the proposals that were offered for its replacement were very different from one another: a form of common sense in Hume, a translation of philosophical problems into medical ones in France, and an abandonment of philosophy in favour of literary forms in Germany. Here we witness a general agreement on both the failure of philosophy and the need for its replacement, but no consensus on what was needed to replace it. The third failure is the attempt of Kant and his immediate followers to a construct a philosophical 'theory of everything', renouncing metaphysics as traditionally conceived, but uniting epistemology, aesthetics, morality, science, religion, and law into a single 'transcendental' philosophy. Despite its unparalleled combination of rigour and imagination, this project collapsed more quickly than the other two, and it was replaced by a scientific theory of everything, which has subsequently become well entrenched. But rather than spelling an end to philosophical enquiry, it transformed the nature of philosophy, which was now turned into a metatheory of science, a shadow of its former self.

The other preliminary question concerns the 'philosophy' that underlies these three different substantive enterprises. Given their individual projects are so different, what is it that makes them all philosophy? Philosophy is generally taken to be essentially a 'second-order' exercise, something that transforms questions into a philosophical form through a process of abstraction. This characterization certainly fits the kinds of issue that we shall be concerned with, but we need to say more: we need to explore, within the philosophical projects themselves, how the commitment to abstract investigation arises, what its advantages over other forms of enquiry were conceived to be, and what problems it engendered. How the commitment to abstraction arises in the first place, and how it defines philosophical enquiry in antiquity, are explored in some detail in chapter 1. It is a crucial part of the exercise that our understanding of 'philosophy' derive from the specific projects themselves, not from some prior assumption about what constitutes philosophy, for in that case we would face the intractable problem of steering a path between fiat (e.g., by ruling out anything that fails to match current philosophical concerns) and allowing anything at all (Scientology, New Age philosophy) simply on the grounds that it styles itself philosophy and can be considered an abstract probing of conceptual issues on natural and human questions, however manifestly misguided this probing might be.

In short, we shall be pursuing a historical enquiry into philosophical programmes in terms of specific self-identified goals, examining their successes and particularly their failures to achieve those goals. The combination of the identification of particular substantive questions and a specific kind of abstract approach whose origins and rationale we can trace, limit the subject matter of this book to 'Western philosophy'. This is not the only way in which to explore the question of the point of the philosophy. We can, for example, look at the way in which abstract philosophical ideas have permeated national cultures, how they have provided, or failed to provide, fruitful vehicles for addressing or promoting local issues of social, political, and religious concern.[7] At the other end of the scale, we could compare philosophy in the West, from Plato to the present, with non-European forms of reflection, and ask what this comparison reveals about the nature of philosophy. The route that I shall be following is different from either of these. It is designed to investigate the aims and development of what has been identified as philosophy in the West, and to ask what the point of the exercise has been. The argument will be that the point has in fact changed on a number of occasions, partly in response to new challenges, but also in response to collapses in the philosophical enterprise provoked by other forms of discourse offering something more satisfactory than philosophical enquiry.

The failure of philosophical enquiry at crucial stages in European history tells us a great deal about what philosophy is. But such an investigation conflicts with the prevailing assumption among philosophers, that there are no intrinsic weaknesses in thinking philosophically, that any weaknesses can only be weakness of particular philosophical viewpoints or theories, and as such can be resolved within philosophy, by moving to a different philosophical viewpoint or theory. On such a view, philosophy has no 'outside', as it were: it is the most abstract discipline possible, something under which any form of reflection can be subsumed. It is effectively the canonical form of reflection on the world. One consequence of this is that reflective thought outside the West is always automatically a form of philosophy, because it couldn't be anything else. The fact that such thought invariably turns out to be relatively impoverished compared to mature Western thought, which might lead one to question the point of placing it in a tradition that is in many respects alien to it is instead taken to indicate the primitive and misguided nature of many of its forms. There is a clear risk here in holding up one's own activity as the model, and this prompts the question as to whether there is something fundamentally wrong with incorporating other forms of enquiry under the rubric of philosophy.

Justin Smith offers a more considered exercise in his *The Philosopher: A History in Six Types*.[8] The explicit aim is to provide a model for the investigation of practices that have not been carried out under the banner of philosophy, yet are, in other cultures, analogous to it, having developed autonomously. To this end, he distinguishes a number of what might be termed philosophical archetypes. The 'Curiosus' is someone interested in everything, whether empirical or conceptual. The 'Sage' is a model of the philosopher that is the most long-standing notion of the philosopher in the West, but also fits Indian philosophy particularly well. Third, there is the 'Gadfly', like Socrates, someone who wants to replace ill-conceived beliefs without necessarily proposing any of his own. Fourth, there is the 'Ascetic', common in Western medieval philosophy, but also in Buddhism, for example. Fifth there is the 'Mandarin', based on the Chinese elite class of bureaucrats. Mandarins are characterized as highly professionalized groups of elites who jealously guard disciplinary boundaries, among whom Smith identifies a number of modern elites, notably the French system of *normaliens* and the system of Oxbridge/Ivy League education, out of which the great majority of successful careers in philosophy take shape. Finally, there is the 'Courtier', in its modern form the public intellectual.

If one's aim is to ask to what extent forms of reflection outside the Western tradition, or prior to it, can be counted as philosophy, then there is much to be said for this approach, asking where philosophy fits into reflective enquiry in a way that brings no unwarranted assumptions about how easily various ways of tackling the issues can be assimilated to those of Western philosophy. But my aim in what follows is something that engages entirely different kinds of question. Restriction of the category of philosophy to the Western tradition is designed to reflect the fact that philosophy, as conceived in the West, is not some universal form of wholly abstract thought oblivious to the circumstances in which it has emerged, something that would automatically be attractive to, or even make sense to, thoughtful people anywhere. Rather, it comprises culturally specific modes of engaging with the world which have their own unique difficulties and weaknesses, and their own unique achievements.

Philosophy is a distinctive way of engaging the issues, and my aim is to identify and explore this distinctiveness by localizing the traditions of Western philosophy, so that their distinguishing features can be opened up to examination. And the plural form is especially important here, because we shall see that radical shifts in the aim of philosophy, between classical antiquity and the modern era for example, throw into question the extent to which there is sufficient affinity between philosophical movements throughout the history of Western thought to establish a substantive common project, something that goes beyond just a commitment to abstract enquiry, for example.

Examination of the history of philosophy provides a crucial tool here. Exploration of the fissures that its history reveals is the best way to expose the soft underbelly of philosophy. The history of philosophy, properly carried out, is its most powerful and dangerous tool, and the sign reportedly on a Princeton philosopher's door—'History of Philosophy, Just Say No'—reveals a more troubling warning than its author could have realized. To get a sense of the issues, consider the contrast between two opposing ways of thinking about what the history of philosophy reveals. On the first, it is assumed that the developments in philosophy since its beginnings in classical antiquity are the result of an evolution of the discipline towards ever deeper understanding. On the second, it is a case of philosophy failing to live up to different sets of historical promises, the victim of takeovers by other disciplines showing themselves to be demonstrably better at doing what it was trying to do, and philosophy, at crucial junctures, having to close down and start with a new set of aims. This un-nuanced contrast is sharper than is needed, and it does not exhaust the issues, but it does give one a sense of the magnitude of what is at stake.

Centrally in question is how the aims of philosophy have been thought of at different periods, how philosophers have set out to achieve these aims, and how failure in this regard has resulted in philosophical enquiry simply disappearing and being replaced by something with different aims, which in some cases has nevertheless retained the name 'philosophy' or been resumed in a different form as a self-styled 'philosophical' exercise. That is to say, we shall not simply be assuming a continuity in philosophy from antiquity to the present, but will rather be concerned to identify cases where philosophy has failed to deliver the goods, as it were, and has collapsed as a result, and to explore what has happened in the wake of these failures. Such an approach conflicts with the prevailing view, according to which philosophy is the most abstract discipline possible, something under which any form of reflection can be subsumed. If, on the contrary, we make no such assumptions, then we can engage the specifics of developments in the Western 'philosophical tradition' and reveal discontinuities that show up the limits of philosophical enquiry.

In particular, we are going to be concerned with something that histories of philosophy egregiously fail to notice, namely the drawbacks of thinking philosophically about a question. We shall encounter a number of historical cases of this, on the nature of the relation between mind and body, for example, and on the nature of scientific enquiry; but it is ethics that stands out. Philosophy is formed in the first place, as we shall see, not through reflection on metaphysical, natural-philosophical, or epistemological questions, but on questions of morality and virtue. In the origins of philosophy in Plato, ethics is constitutive of philosophical enquiry. Getting ethics right, so to speak, and getting people to behave accordingly was the whole point of the philosophical exercise. It was what drove the philosophical project in its origins, and it has always remained central to philosophy. Yet throughout its history, the complaint has been raised that philosophy is actually useless as far as morality is concerned, and the reason lies in the abstract nature of philosophical enquiry. Unlike, say, religion or literature, which can move us to reflect on our behaviour and act morally as a result, philosophy has no practical effects of this kind. Its abstraction has caused it to be disengaged from the very behaviour that it has set out to describe and evaluate. This is despite the fact that philosophers from classical antiquity onwards have been fully aware that ethics is not like other parts of philosophy (with some exceptions for theories of scientific method): it is supposed to have some impact on the way we behave. There is no point in a form of reflection on morality that does not, or could not, have consequences for behaviour. Philosophers have occasionally grappled with this question, with the sentimentalist philosophers of the eighteenth century such as Smith and Hume, for example, attempting to get to the core of the problem by renouncing abstract considerations in moral motivation. But whatever the strategy, there is no doubt that there is here something that raises problems for the abstract, second-order nature of the discipline of philosophy. Is philosophical enquiry actually well suited to dealing with such questions; and more generally, is philosophy by its very nature as a second-order discipline an inconsequential exercise?

In what follows, we shall be directing attention to something that histories of philosophy generally refuse to recognize, namely the way in which philosophy keeps encountering the limits of a second-order enquiry. It is only with Hume that these limits are recognized as such, at least in any sustained way, but in treatments of Hume the issues have been sidestepped and neutralized by treating what is actually a fundamental insight as a form of tired old scepticism: assimilating it, in a tried and tested philosophical way, to a species of problem that one knows all about and hence need not worry about. In this way, a pressing fundamental problem about the nature

and scope of philosophy is accommodated into the philosophical repertoire, de-fanged so that it can be considered as yet
another episode in the continuous history of the discipline.

∾

It is an important element in what follows that the contextualization I shall be pursuing is one that is designed to bring
to the surface the non-philosophical factors that lie behind
particular intellectual positions. In particular, whereas histories of philosophy set out what might be termed the doctrines
of philosophers, we shall be equally concerned with what, at
different times, shapes the discipline of philosophy: with the
question of what it is to think philosophically about a question. The project can also be described in another way. Many
philosophers have construed the history of Western philosophy as making a gradual progress towards current concerns.
By contrast, many historians of philosophy have now largely
abandoned such a genealogical approach. This prompts the
question as to just what kind of historical development philosophy exhibits. Hegel, one of most committed defenders of the
intrinsic progress view, brought sophisticated historiographical considerations to bear, enhanced by his ability to draw on a
deep understanding of historical and cultural questions. There
is no such level of sophistication in modern advocates of this
approach, who typically see the development of philosophy
on purely internal lines, very much on the model of how they
think that science develops. The most cursory investigation of
the linear progress view reveals its inadequacy, but such investigation does not tell us what an adequate account might look
like; still less does it offer a historiographical understanding.

It is such an understanding that I am proposing to offer,
and there are three core questions on which everything else

hinges. These are the question of the nature of philosophy, that of how to identify and assess both its successes and its failures, and the question of the appropriate periodization of philosophy for this project.

The first topic is that of what philosophy is. This is a pressing question for us, because a core part of the project is to argue that the goals of philosophy, goals that shape the direction of philosophical enquiry, change so significantly that tracing a continuous philosophical heritage becomes fraught. We cannot assume from the outset that there is a perennial philosophical tradition that stretches from antiquity to the present in any substantive sense. More specifically, we cannot assume that there is a form of activity beginning with the Presocratics which, by being continuously reworked—having the weeds removed, as it were, and the new shoots gradually cultivated—has led to current forms of philosophical enquiry. On the other hand, this in itself should not incline us in favour of a Hegelian account of the history of philosophy, despite Hegel's emphasis on the successive rise and decline of philosophical systems. What marks his teleological approach out from ours is that it is central to Hegel's conception that there is an overall philosophical goal that regulates the succession of systems, and the new developments that follow a decline are thought of as a rebirth or renewal of the broader project. Once we abandon Hegelian teleology, the main motivation for seeking some overarching, supra-historical form of philosophical enterprise disappears. We can treat the rise and fall of particular projects in their own terms. And, importantly, although these projects may use some of the resources of older ones, such as particular styles of reasoning, and may trace a genealogy to older projects, we are not obliged thereby to proceed as if these were part of the same continuous enterprise. Nevertheless, deciding between continuity and discontinuity is not an end in itself.

The point is rather that, if it turns out that the projects are significantly discontinuous, this has consequences for our understanding of the nature of philosophical thought, and we will need to enquire to what degree philosophical thought is not something that embodies perennial concerns, but rather is subject to historical contextualization.

What is at issue here are the aims of philosophy, and the task is to identify fault lines that generate fundamental changes in these aims. Classical, Hellenistic, and Roman philosophers, for example, had considered the ultimate aims of knowledge to be wisdom, happiness, and well-being. But Christianity transferred such aims into a purely spiritual realm, so that they could only be attained in a union with God, with the result that, in incorporating it into Christian teaching, they believed philosophy finally realized its true standing. When an autonomous form of philosophy re-emerged, from the thirteenth century onwards, this required a major realignment of the goals of philosophical enquiry. Despite an attempt to revive the original conception of philosophical understanding by Renaissance humanists, knowledge had been transformed in the process of Christianization, and the notion that, in pursuing philosophy, one was pursuing wisdom and happiness now had a decidedly naive and unworldly ring to it. Indeed, in the wake of Francis Bacon's criticism of a purely contemplative conception of philosophy, this came to be seen as the result of a profoundly mistaken understanding of what philosophy should be doing. Philosophy could no more produce wisdom and happiness than could mathematics or medicine. It was not that wisdom and happiness were not worthwhile goals, nor even that they were not the ultimate human goals, but rather that they were not to be realized through philosophy.

There is a crucial, if largely unappreciated, point here. These philosophical aims, and changes in philosophical aims, do not in themselves take the form of philosophical doctrines. In a crucial respect, they are extra-philosophical: they work at the level of shaping what one does with philosophy, how one pursues it, and how one conceives of what it is to be a philosopher. Investigating them tells us something about the discipline, about the point of the exercise. Particularly in an era in which philosophy has become subservient to science in many respects, there is a pressing need to stand back in order to understand the point of the exercise.

⁂

On the second question, that of success and failure of philosophy, it is absolutely crucial that we distinguish between the questions that motivate a philosophical programme on the one hand, and, on the other, the philosophical arguments used to realize the aims of that programme. Analytic philosophy in the twentieth century increasingly became a matter of resolving self-generated problems, so that motivation collapsed into the philosophical programme itself, as the exercise became increasingly remote and fruitless, and increasingly removed from effective engagement with concerns outside its own quasi-Platonic realm. But this is not how philosophy had traditionally proceeded. Throughout its history, it has dealt with pressing problems generated outside philosophy and subjected them to philosophical enquiry as a means of clarifying, reformulating, and resolving them. Coming to terms with the issues this raises is a distinctive feature of the approach we shall be taking. These issues are complex, but without addressing them, we cannot begin to identify the successes and failures of philosophical programmes, for these are successes and failures in achieving goals, which means that we must identify the goals, and this will only make complete sense if we understand what they derive from and why they arise in the first place.

The crucial point here is that success can be a matter of meeting extra-philosophical goals and imperatives. The most pressing problem is how we decide what resources we draw on in order to identify such extra-philosophical goals, and under what conditions we can rely on them. It is rare to find any recognition of these questions in histories of philosophy, and without this one proceeds as if it were simply a question of whether, taking goals as given, the premises and arguments based on them can successfully deliver these goals. On the other hand, to explore the extra-philosophical goals that motivate such arguments—and in the process determine what kinds of answers are going to be satisfying and compelling, something that philosophical questioning is not necessarily able to circumscribe—cannot involve bypassing the arguments entirely and substituting new questions. To the extent that we are dealing with *philosophical* projects, what gives these projects their philosophical identity is the nature of the arguments deployed. This leaves two questions. First, what resources do we have for exploring the extra-philosophical goals of philosophical programmes? Second, can we deploy these in a way that preserves the philosophical character of the programmes?

A good example of the difficulties is provided by the work of Pierre Hadot on 'ways of life' and 'spiritual exercises' in Hellenistic and Neoplatonist philosophy.[9] Hadot developed these ideas from Wittgenstein's idea of 'forms of life', and construed different philosophical programmes on the model of different forms of life. Rather than looking at the doctrines of the philosophical programmes in antiquity, he examined what can broadly be considered the training of the philosopher in these different programmes, under the rubric of 'spiritual exercises': what it was that one had to do to be a philosopher, how one had to behave. One valuable aspect of this approach is the elaboration of a conception of philosophy according to which there is a way of engaging intellectual, cultural, moral, scientific, and aesthetic problems which is not only distinctive, marking out the philosophical treatment of these problems from that of the theologian or statesman or the artist, for example, but one whereby the philosopher is someone who has a particular standing, a particular claim to be heard. Although the scientist has now usurped much of this role from the philosopher, in historical terms such questions were shaped around the philosopher, and questions can still be asked of the philosopher. The overriding issue here is: on what does the standing of the philosopher depend? Hadot's approach provides us with a crucial resource in understanding the shifting personae of the philosopher, for these correlate directly with the shifting nature of the philosophical enterprise. At the same time, it allows us to think through the way in which initially non-philosophical goals are translated into a philosophical form, especially in those cases where there remains something that cannot be accommodated in the philosophical formulation, but where the success of the enquiry depends on its ability to provide a comprehensive account. We shall see that ancient philosophy becomes wholly eclipsed by Christianity, for example, due to the inability of the philosophical notion of the 'good life' to provide something sufficiently meaningful, as we move from classical into Hellenistic and Roman culture. Hadot's approach is useful here, but it quickly becomes less secure as we move away from its original Neoplatonist context. Analysing philosophical movements in terms of 'spiritual exercises', he brings them under the rubric of communities with shared values. This something that is characteristic of philosophy in the late Hellenistic period, in the theological nature of the Neoplatonist doctrines that flourished then and the form that adherence to those doctrines took. But it was certainly not typical of philosophy after that period, or even before it, and the danger lies in treating the philosopher in terms of a culturally or socially defined group which has no philosophical identity as such. The distortion that such an approach engenders means that the value of Hadot's work does not lie in trying to think through various philosophical enterprises in terms of 'spiritual exercises'. Its contribution is more modest, though none the less instructive for that. It opens up a window on some of the ways in which extra-philosophical concerns shape what philosophers do, and how they conceive of themselves, and I shall be taking such considerations seriously in what follows.

༄

The third feature of our approach derives from the first two. It concerns periodization. The standard periodization of the history of philosophy, one immediately familiar to every student of the subject, derives from the nineteenth-century neo-Kantian/neo-Hegelian philosopher Kuno Fisher.[10] Fisher identified what he considered to be a change in the concerns of philosophy, from metaphysics to epistemology, in the seventeenth century. On his reading, the metaphysical dichotomy between Platonism and Aristotelianism was replaced by an epistemological one, between advocates of the idea that all knowledge derived from the exercise of reason, the 'rationalists', and advocates of the idea that all knowledge derived from sensation, the 'empiricists'. The distinctions have proved problematic to serious scholars working on seventeenth- and eighteenth-century philosophy. Spinoza, Leibniz, and arguably Berkeley, were as much metaphysicians as any of their predecessors. The founding figure of rationalism, Descartes, was about as empirical a philosopher as one is likely to find in the history of the discipline, devoting large amounts of his time to lens-grinding and to anatomical dissection. Moreover, the idea that there is a continuity of fundamental approach between Descartes, Spinoza, and Leibniz is belied by the rejection by the latter two of what has usually been identified as Descartes's distinctively rationalist procedure, scepticism. The rationalism/empiricism model was devised in the context of the belief that Kant had identified and solved the major problems that rationalism and empiricism encountered, a claim that Kant himself had encouraged, even though he did not formulate it in quite those terms. And indeed philosophy from the middle of the nineteenth century onwards does have a Kantian tenor, including the idea that the form of purely conceptual investigation that it offers provides the only path for philosophical enquiry.

The historiographical schema that I shall be following is not that which identifies as distinct stages Greek, medieval, modern, Kantian, and post-Kantian/contemporary philosophy. Despite its serious defects, I am not advocating a general model to replace this, because I doubt that there is any adequate all-purpose model. Periodization is relative to questions. What I shall be trying to offer is something that grows, organically as it were, out of the developments distinguished as we proceed, mirroring what I identify as the points at which philosophy collapses and is replaced by something else. Three such points are identified. The first comes at the end of the Hellenistic period, and it derives from the failure of classical and Hellenistic philosophy to provide a satisfactory account of the good life, which with the Hellenistic schools becomes tantamount to an undisturbed life. Building on Neoplatonism, Christian theologians offered something that seemed to satisfy what the philosophers had been seeking, and they were then able to incorporate selected elements of earlier philosophies into a wholly theological account, philosophy losing any autonomy in the process.

The second episode comes with the emergence of an autonomous role for philosophy with Aquinas, who envisages a form of metaphysics, subject only to the dictates of reason, as a means of reconciling discordant claims of natural philosophy (science) and Christian teaching. Such a model, as we shall see, is that which dominates much early modern philosophy, above all that of the immensely influential work of Descartes. This idea of metaphysics, now pursued via epistemology, as the epitome of reason, was subsequently discarded on three independent but simultaneous fronts: with Hume, with the replacement of philosophy by medicine in France, and with the rise of a broadly-based form of intellectual enquiry replacing metaphysics in Germany. Here philosophy collapsed for a second time, losing all authority as the highest form of reflection, as something that could stand over and judge all claims to understanding.

The third episode comes with Kant, at the end of the eighteenth century. Hume had set out the limits of metaphysics, and philosophy more generally, showing why it could not possibly achieve what it claimed. Following Hume, Kant argued that the failure of philosophy resulted from a failure to grasp its limits, but he proposed that a philosophical understanding of these limits was possible. Philosophical enquiry could not only be kept within strict limits, but could also provide insight into what lay beyond those limits, for example on matters of morality and religion. Kant offered what was in effect an attempt to provide a theory of everything, in the process defining what a successful philosophy would be like. This was reinforced in the 'all or nothing' approach of Kant's idealist successors, and the problem was that the failure of this programme led to the second option: nothing. In spite of, and in

many respects because of, the efforts of Kant's idealist successors, the idea of philosophy as the theory of everything crum-
pled under its own weight. This paved the way for the third
collapse of philosophy, as its aspirations were taken over by
something that deployed completely different resources from
the second-order conceptual enquiry characteristic of philosophy. Philosophy was replaced by empirical science, with the
claim that if there was anything that could not be grasped scientifically then it could not be known by any discipline, and
was permanently unknowable. Science now became the theory
of everything, not so much because of some internal trajec-
tory within science itself, but because philosophy had built up
expectations about what comprehensive understanding consisted in, and science was the only (non-religious) alternative
when the philosophical theory of everything collapsed.

The Kantian and German idealist 'all or nothing' claims for
philosophy were now transferred to science, and this opened
the door to the fourth episode in our story, the emergence
of new forms of philosophy whose primary aim was accom-
modation to science. Among the forms this took was a series
of attempts to pursue philosophy on the model of science,
to translate its concerns and procedures into as scientific a
form as possible. Here, philosophy loses autonomy in crucial
respects, and has little if anything in common with the historical philosophical projects from which it seeks legitimacy as the
paradigm form of enquiry.

PART I

The Rise and Fall of Philosophy in Antiquity

CHAPTER ONE

The Emergence of Philosophy

PHILOSOPHY IN ANTIQUITY EMERGES AS A NOVEL, distinctive form of enquiry, of unprecedented intellectual power, albeit one that harbours a number of deep-seated problems. The conception of what philosophy is—how it identifies and engages its subject matter—comes down to us from Plato, reinforced and refined by Aristotle. It initially takes shape in Plato's early dialogues, and is revised and built up as he moves from a Socratic concern with morality to a focus in the later dialogues on what subsequently came to be known as metaphysics. In asking what is distinctive about the kind of enquiry that we find in Plato and Aristotle, two forms of characterization, one identifying a gulf between archaic and classical Greek thought, the other identifying continuities, have been pursued. The first sets up a contrast between philosophy and forms of enquiry, or more generally ways of engaging with the world, that are structured in an entirely different way from it. The contrast commonly drawn here has been between myth and reason, and the sticking point is how it was possible to move from the one to the other. If there were to be such a transition, then the boundary must be more porous than the distinction would suggest, but any middle ground has been difficult to discern, and commentators such as Cornford, who have pursued this path, have not in the end been willing to sacrifice the characteristic features of reason in order to secure such middle ground.[1]

The second characterization identifies precursors of the mature philosophical enquiry that we find in Plato and Aristotle. Here, the focus has been on metaphysics and on the matter theory of thinkers from Thales onwards. The category under which these are included, 'Presocratics', dates from the late eighteenth century, and it only takes on significance with Hegel, who offered an evolutionary schema for philosophy in which tracing forebears played a crucial historiographical role. As the term indicates, it is Socrates who marks the turning point, and in spite of the fact that no one in antiquity doubted that Socrates was the key figure, there was disagreement on just what was distinctive about him. It is usual to consider his approach in contrast to the sophists, skilled as they were in forensic debate and oratorical display, but this contrast is somewhat fluid. The sophist Protagoras had notoriously boasted that he could make the weaker argument seem the stronger, but this is just how Aristophanes, in *The Clouds*, portrays Socrates, and writers in the generation after Plato, such as Isocrates and the orator Aeschines, classed him as a sophist.[2]

Plato and Xenophon were clear that what marked out their teacher Socrates was the fact that he abandoned enquiry into nature (*peri phuseōs historia*) for the study of 'human things' (*ta anthrōpina*): the good man and the practice of virtue, as Xenophon put it. Yet when one turns to Plato's pupil Aristotle, Presocratic philosophy is principally associated with those figures identified by Aristotle as holding views on the nature of the world which he criticizes in the course of setting out his own natural philosophy (above all his theory of matter). In other words, 'human things', while treated in an exemplary way by him, are not constitutive of philosophy, and enquiry into nature is not only not disparaged, but comes to the fore of philosophical enquiry. But then, on the other hand, once one asks what establishes the credentials of philosophy in classical antiquity, it is above all the Socratic turn to 'human things'. Cicero, in the Prologue to the fifth book of his *Tusculan Disputations*— a core philosophical work from Roman antiquity, throughout the Renaissance, to the early modern period—writes that philosophy, in large part through its (Platonic) doctrine that virtue is sufficient for happiness, is responsible for the move from barbarism to civilization: the social, cultural, legal, and moral foundations on which the rise of cities was built.

Moreover, although Aristotle himself is clear that it is not Thales but Socrates who is the pivotal figure, he conceives of philosophy in terms of matter theory and an associated cosmology, tracing its origins back to a tradition that starts with Thales, and which Socrates not only makes no contribution towards, but shuns. The difficulty is compounded by the fact that a little probing reveals a gulf between what one and the other was doing. If indeed Thales was pursuing a 'matter theory', it was nothing like Aristotle's metaphysically orientated natural philosophy.

In trying to resolve these questions, we shall be exploring the conception of philosophy in Plato and Aristotle—taking this as constitutive of ancient 'philosophy'—and focusing on two sets of questions. First, are there ways of engaging cognitive issues that are distinct from the epistemological exercises that take over questions of cognition from Plato onwards? Second, what exactly is the relation between ethics, metaphysics, 'dialectic', and natural philosophy as they figure in the classical and Hellenistic conceptions of philosophy, where they are treated as part of a common project? Our initial focus will be on contrast classes, that is, practices among Plato's predecessors and contemporaries that offer something different from philosophy, but overlap with it, and can be seen as being in competition with it. In particular, our interest is not in 'the origins of philosophy', but to understand what marks ancient philosophy out, by distinguishing its characteristics from those of exercises in antiquity that share some of its concerns but pursue them in a different way. In fixing the nature of philosophical enquiry in this way, we can understand how it comes to replace other forms of enquiry in classical antiquity: in what way philosophical forms of enquiry were marked out from, and valued over, non-philosophical ones. Having done this, we can in subsequent chapters begin to explore how Plato and Aristotle and their Hellenistic successors were able to work within this understanding of philosophy.

Coming to Terms with the World

Commenting on the fact that the Greek thinkers of the fourth century were the first to call themselves philosophers, and to define philosophy as a specialized discipline and a unique cultural practice, Andrea Nightingale notes that creating a professional discipline of philosophy 'required an extraordinary effort of self-definition and legitimation. In addition to developing ideas and arguments, these philosophers had to stake out the boundaries of their discipline and articulate the ways that it differed from other modes of wisdom.'[3] One thing that writers in classical antiquity stress, and one thing on which philosophers since have agreed, is the abstract nature of philosophical enquiry. This is something that applies equally to the treatment of the natural and the human realms. Whatever the subject matter, philosophy raises investigation to an abstract level, and this is a qualitative shift, from first- to second-level enquiry. 'Abstraction' is not just a feature of philosophy: it goes to the heart of philosophical investigation. Philosophy is an essentially second-order form of enquiry. Accordingly, we need to clarify just what the abstractness in question is, and what the distinctive features of second-order enquiry are. In the first instance, we can consider second-order enquiry into natural processes, before we turn to the more complex case of second-order enquiry into morality.

In order to be more specific about the nature of the 'abstractness' at issue, we need a contrast case, that is, an example of a way of thinking about natural processes that is not philosophical. There is one feature of an abstract philosophical approach that stands out as potentially an identifying feature. The abstractness of philosophical enquiry comes through standing back from or above phenomena, by contrast with engaging with them directly, such as when attempting to understand them by immersing oneself in them.

Classical Chinese thought offers a striking contrast here. The sinologist François Jullien sets it out in these terms:

> Western thought seeks to adopt a commanding position that provides a theoretical perspective ordering all the material to be organized. This makes abstract thought about it possible, resulting in a vantage point from which one can usually derive some classificatory principle of homogeneity. Chinese reasoning, by contrast, seems to weave along horizontally, from one case to the next, via bridges and bifurcations, each case eventually leading to the next and merging into it. Western logic is panoramic, whereas Chinese logic is like that of a possible journey.[4]

What underlies this conception in Chinese thought is the notion of 'opportunity' or 'propensity' (shi^5), which, dating from the fourth century BCE, took military strategy as a model of understanding, most notably in the idea of using the minimum effort to achieve maximum effect. Can we find something like this in pre-classical Greek thought?

In the most general terms, what we are concerned with is cognitive grasp: coming to terms with the world by means of our intelligence and skills. In classical philosophy, intelligence and skills are separated. The separation is not there from the start, however. The earliest accounts of cognitive enquiry indicate that the classical Greek contrast between *epistēmē* and *technē*—knowledge versus art or skills—arose from an earlier pre-classical unitary conception of cognitive grasp. This earlier conception was centred around the notion of *mētis* ('cunning', or 'ingenuity'), and the model of outwitting opponents was central to the archaic understanding of cognitive grasp.

The idea behind the archaic Greek notion is that, in overcoming an adversary, whether this be in hunting, fishing, racing, working resistant materials such as metals, or overcoming a fast flowing river, there are only two routes open. Either the stronger will win, or, by the power of *mētis*, one reverses the natural course of events through cunning, disguise, quick-wittedness, or some cognate skill: generally speaking, some way of coming to terms with events that involves a form of understanding which enables one to overcome obstacles—including cognitive obstacles—rather than through subsuming these under general principles. An image that we find on a number of occasions is that of changing more swiftly than a rapidly changing nature. One comes to terms with something that is constantly changing by outwitting it—not by standing back from it so that one can fix or resolve it—and nature is a prototypically changing realm.[6] This conception shares with the classical Chinese notion the absence of any idea of immunity to change. The Chinese sage is someone who adapts to change, 'shifting with the ever shifting situation itself', as Geoffrey Lloyd puts it.[7]

The *mētis* model is not confined to what will later be identified as practical pursuits, and has a basis in Greek mythology. In these myths, before Zeus became the sovereign god, there was anarchy amongst the gods and constant battles for supremacy. On overthrowing his father Kronos, Zeus was warned that, like his father before him, he should fear any son. To forestall such an eventuality, he devoured his wife, Metis. In doing so, he not only put an end to the threat, but also gained supremacy over the other gods. In order to understand how he manages to achieve this, we must appreciate the significance of his wife's name. Zeus is not omniscient; his power derives from always being one step ahead. He achieves mastery and absolute order through the power of cunning and deceit, a power that he gains from eating his wife, which renders him the paradigm of *mētis*.

At the terrestrial level, things are different. Divine order and stability are not to be found on earth, and we are constantly faced with unforeseen happenings and ambiguous situations. Earth is a place of becoming and change. In overcoming an adversary, there are only two routes open. Either the stronger will win, or, by the power of *mētis*, one reverses the natural course of events through cunning, disguise, or quick-wittedness: generally speaking, some way of coming to terms with events that involves a form of understanding that enables one to outwit rather than explain, such as building a bridge over a fast flowing, and hence otherwise impassable, river.

Notice the way in which the description of the behaviour of the gods here is completely on a par with the account of natural processes. The traditional opposition in modern commentators between myth and reason—absent in Aristotle, for whom 'he who loves myth is, in a way, a philosopher'[8]— trades largely on the importation of the assumptions of Christianity. Greek religion did not have a basis in dogma or fundamental beliefs, and hence was immune to any conflict between orthodoxy and heterodoxy. Its myths and rituals, which varied radically from city to city, relied on the visibility of cult worship. As Maria Michela Sassi points out, this situation is contradicted only in appearance by what the sources tell us regarding the trials for impiety against Anaxagoras, Protagoras, Diagoras, and Socrates (the only historically documented case). She notes that these trials took place in the aftermath of the Peloponnesian War, a particularly difficult time for independent thinkers, especially those who, like Anaxagoras, had belonged to Pericles's entourage. In the case of Socrates, it is quite clear that 'the prosecution used Socrates's alleged or actual inobservance of cult as a pretext in order to silence an inconvenient critic of the Athenian political class'.[9]

In the light of the nature of myths in the Greek context, consider the transition from 'myth to reason'. In both archaic and classical thought, we find seemingly unobtrusive mention of the gods and elaboration of myths, although the level of integration in the former seems greater, in that in Plato's dialogues, in the *Symposium* for example, discussion in terms of the gods parallels philosophical investigation, whereas in archaic thought it feeds into it more directly. Nevertheless, if we think in terms of a transition from the kind of enquiry centred around ideas such as *mētis* to that centred around the classical notion of knowledge, *epistēmē*, it is wholly misleading to think of it in terms of a move from myth to reason. *Mētis*-based enquiry is as indebted to the use of reason as classical philosophical thought is. There is no *move to* reason, and philosophy does not have a monopoly on reason. *Mētis* has an aim, which in the most general case is that of understanding how to deal with situations subject to constant change, and it uses a reasoned path to achieve that aim. This path is not irrational, or just a question of story-telling. Moreover it is something in which some people are more skilled than others, and the outcome is a sign of this skill: as in the case of the prediction of fluctuations in the olive harvest by Thales, whose skills, as we about to see, were very much within the preserve of *mētis*, not that of *epistēmē*.

The difference between archaic and classical Greek thought lies not in a move to reason, but in the role of disambiguation. This turns on the procedures used to establish a philosophical question. Philosophy is a 'second-order' enquiry, a reflection on questions that abstracts from the subject matter, converting it into appropriate form. There are two essential procedures here: the disambiguation of premises, so that the enquiry works only with statements that are either true or false, and the generation of conclusions via the use of reason or rational argument. Rational argument is independent of disambiguation, as the example of *mētis* shows, and the way in which it is used is transformed when allied with disambiguation. Recognition of this is important for our appreciation of the difference between archaic, non-philosophical forms of argument and philosophical ones. But it is also crucial for our understanding of what is needed for the kind of 'abstraction' that is constitutive of philosophy, especially if we are concerned to understand both the advantages and the drawbacks of second-order enquiry.

A Presocratic Genealogy

It is *mētis*, and the cluster of concepts associated with it, that form the paradigm for the comprehension of nature up to the fifth century. In the fifth century, a radical shift occurs and a new cluster of concepts, centring around the concept of *epistēmē*—science or knowledge—takes over from *mētis*. We can highlight the contrast between forms of understanding centred around *mētis* and those centred around *epistēmē* by noting the two main classical forms of the latter, those of Plato and Aristotle. The basic premise of both (one they share with *mētis* conceptions) is that nature is constantly changing, and the basic aim is to come to terms with this change cognitively. Since *epistēmē* is knowledge of essences, and since sensible nature is undergoing constant change, it cannot be known simpliciter: we cannot know something that is changing, simply because it is changing. To understand it, we must grasp what underlies the change, or, to put the question in metaphysical terms—terms which simply would have had no application as a cognitive goal in the *mētis* conception—we must grasp the unchanging reality underlying the change. In the terminology of classical philosophy, we must subordinate becoming to being. Plato does this by subordinating the sensible world to the transcendent world of unchanging Forms. Because sensible nature changes, we cannot know it as such, but it is related, as a copy is to a model, to the world of Forms, and because Forms are unchanging, we can have knowledge of them.

Aristotle approached the same question in a different way. He followed Plato in the project of subordinating becoming or change to being, but he sought to achieve this by relating change to a naturally occurring realm of unchanging essences. Whereas for Plato unchanging reality lay beyond the sensible changing world, for Aristotle it lay behind this sensible world. Indeed, the subordination of becoming to being is the central aim of the treatment of the 'theoretical'—as opposed to the 'practical' or 'productive'—sciences for Aristotle, and at the beginning of the *Metaphysics* the domains of the theoretical sciences are set out in terms of 'becoming' and 'being' or, as we might rather anachronistically put it, change and existence: 'first philosophy' deals with those things that do not change and have an independent existence, mathematics deals with those things that do not change and have a dependent existence, and physics deals with those things that change and have an independent existence.

In sum, the transition from the archaic conception to the classical notion of cognitive grasp may be described as follows. In both cases the problem is that of how one comes to terms with constantly changing nature. On the classical conception, one does this by subordinating the change to something unchanging, and this subordination gets filled out in terms of construing changing appearances in terms of an unchanging reality. By contrast, the archaic conception should be thought of as an attempt to come to terms with change through ingenuity. How does one catch an animal that can easily outrun one, for example? It depends on the circumstances whether traps, disguise, projectiles, or whatever are appropriate. Ingenuity does not take one form—if it did it would not be ingenuity—but consists rather in the ability to adapt oneself to the circumstances one finds oneself in.

With the contrast between *mētis* and *epistēmē* in mind, consider the case of Thales, identified first by Anaximander and then, following him, by Plato and Aristotle as the first 'philosopher' (not a term that Anaximander uses) in classical antiquity. Aristotle writes that Thales, the 'founder of philosophy'—characterized as a form of enquiry which sets out to identify the unchanging substance whose qualities are changing—, says that the basic principle (*archē*) underlying all other things is water.[10] There is something odd here, perhaps spotted by Nietzsche when he writes that 'Greek philosophy seems to begin with an absurd notion, the proposition that water is the primal origin and the womb of all things. Is it really necessary for us to show respect for this proposition and to take it seriously?'[11]

What grounds does Aristotle have for saying that, on Thales's account, water is a principle, an *archē*? He states that Thales, 'the founder of this type of philosophy', namely one that seeks the fundamental principles of things, says that it is water that is the principle, 'and therefore declared that the earth is on water'. This makes it sound as if something original or novel is being proposed, but Thales's contemporaries generally held the view that water was the source of living and non-living things. The earliest texts of Greek literature, the Homeric epics, identified the sea (*Okeanos*) as 'the origin of the gods' and the 'origin of all things', and water plays a cosmological role in Egyptian and Mesopotamian civilizations. Was Thales just reaffirming a commonplace view, or was there was something special about his treatment of the role of water?

The question hinges on the standing of the *archē* on which this otherwise uncontroversial statement was supposedly based. In Aristotle's sense, an *archē* is a fundamental principle, it is authoritative (*archikē*) over other forms of understanding.[12] Above all, it is an unchanging substratum which underlies the phenomena with which we are familiar through sense perception. The question is whether Thales was claiming that water was an *archē* in Aristotle's sense. This is very unlikely. The term did not denote a 'basic principle' in archaic literature, but rather a command or a temporal beginning (a usage retained in the Latin equivalent: 'in principio erat verbum', *in the beginning* was the word).[13] The most likely meaning is that water is the origin of things. This would fit in with what might broadly be termed a meteorological or cosmographical interest. Note in this connection that Plato reports in the *Theaetetus* that Thales fell into a well while gazing at the stars because he didn't see what was at his feet.[14] Although often taken as an instance of philosophical absent-mindedness, it wasn't philosophical contemplation in which Thales was engaged, but meteorological observation, and Heraclitus refers to him as 'the first to study astronomy'. Aristotle's report in his *Politics* gives us a clue as to what kind of activity Thales was pursuing:

> When they reproached him because of his poverty, as though philosophy were of no use, it is said that, having observed through his study of the heavenly bodies that there would be a large olive crop, he raised a little capital while it was still winter, and paid deposits on all the olive presses in Miletus and Chios, hiring them cheaply because no one bid against him. When the appropriate time came there was a sudden rash of requests for the presses; he then hired them out on his own terms and so made a large profit, thus demonstrating it is easy for philosophers to be rich, if they wish, but that this is not what they are interested in.[15]

This fits well with Herodotus's description of Thales as an eminently practical man who, amongst other things, engineered the diversion of the river Halys in the service of Croesus and his army.[16]

There are two ways in which we can construe what Thales's achievements consisted in. The first is Aristotle's way: Thales, *despite* being a philosopher, shows that he can nevertheless put his mind to practical matters if he wishes. Or should it rather be taken as a paradigm instance of *mētis*? On this latter reading, Thales is not a philosopher in Aristotle's sense, someone who subordinates natural phenomena to a single principle, but rather someone who uses foresight, cunning, opportunity. Aristotle has assimilated Thales to his own conception of cognitive grasp in providing a genealogy for it. Yet although he is adamant in the *Metaphysics* that philosophy has a genealogy going back to Thales, and continues through subsequent Presocratics, he then goes on to dismiss the findings of those he considers to be in the tradition stretching from Thales. Xenophanes and Melissus are dismissed as 'crude', Empedocles 'speaks in baby talk',[17] and he tells us that his forebears, while they each grasped at least one of his four causes (qualifying them as philosophers), did so in a way that was 'vague and unclear'. They were merely 'groping' for the kind of understanding that he himself had set out,[18] like untrained men in battle who 'rush around and often strike fine blows but act completely without understanding'. This kind of assessment is an inevitable consequence of his heavy-handed attempt to show how all earlier natural thought is leading in the direction of his mature system.

Compare this with Heraclitus and Parmenides, who can indeed be taken as engaging in philosophical enquiry. Heraclitus plays on the basic division between the flux of phenomenal appearances and the hidden structure of the world, which is where true understanding lies. Parmenides goes further. 'Being' is unitary, unchanging, and homogeneous. By contrast, the phenomenal world is pluralistic, changing, and heterogeneous: it is the opposite of Being, that is, non-Being, which means it is unreal. One can see how these can be taken to be statements of philosophical positions. Nevertheless, our concern here is not with whether there are any thinkers before Socrates who can be considered philosophers. The negative lesson from Thales is that there are interests which philosophers subsequently took up that were originally meteorological or cosmographical in nature, for example, and were not at all attempts to understand things in terms of 'principles' in the metaphysical or natural-philosophical sense. The positive lesson is that there are various forms of what we might broadly term 'cognitive engagement' which are serious enterprises and yet do not constitute knowledge in the classical philosophical sense.

The Transition to Philosophy

Two features of the shift from *mētis* to *epistēmē* stand out. First, it did not occur without resistance and it seems to have been something that early classical philosophers, especially Socrates and Plato, had to fight for. The early dialogues of Plato, dominated as they are by disputes with sophists, can be read as attempts to reconstrue argument as a means, not of outwitting opponents, but of establishing the truth of the matter. Second, it would be mistaken to characterize this shift as being from a practical to a theoretical comprehension of nature, although it is true that *mētis* has more direct connections with practical manipulation than *epistēmē* has. Rather, what seems to happen as a result of the shift is that a whole variety of topics that had previously been central to cognitive grasp are removed from its purview. This comes out very clearly in Plato's earliest dialogues, where the question of whether virtue (*aretē*) is knowledge (*epistēmē*) or a skill (*technē*) is a dominant one. It should be noted here that a *technē* still has a cognitive dimension, for in the *Gorgias*, Plato, revising normal usage, makes it clear that a *technē* is a skill that involves giving an 'account' of the thing, not a mere practical ability, and he distinguishes between a genuine *technē*, like a medical skill, and one which is not genuine but merely a 'knack' (*empeiria*), such as the ability to cook.[19] This is important because *mētis* was never a mere practical ability either.

At stake in both the archaic notions that we have looked at, the Chinese notion of *shi* and the Greek notion of *mētis*, is the question of whether knowledge or understanding has to be panoramic, by contrast with immersing oneself in phenomena and manipulating them accordingly. The move to a panoramic view is facilitated by the distinction between *epistēmē* and *technē* because the latter can effectively be ignored, as all attention is focused on the former. As Vernant puts it, in discussing Plato, 'None of the psychological aspects of technology appear to him valuable in human terms. He did not consider the concentration demanded by work as a special type of human effort, nor technological thought as playing a formative role in human reasoning. On the contrary, he is at pains to separate and contrast technological intelligence and intelligence proper.'[20] The separation between *epistēmē* and *technē* cuts across the archaic Greek notion of *mētis* and the Chinese notion of *shi*. The upshot of this is the assumption that it is in the nature of knowledge to be panoramic. And this is the core notion of knowledge in Western philosophy. Note, however, that the *epistēmē*/*technē* distinction as Socrates and Plato employed it was not meant to distinguish between cognitive and non-cognitive skills, but between those cognitive skills that can be conveyed in the form of results, or can be learned through imitation, and those that require a form of contemplative understanding. The Socratic point is that virtue is an *epistēmē*, and indeed, Plato notoriously goes as far as to make virtue a form of intellectual understanding. One upshot of this is that, once it has been established that virtue is an *epistēmē*, *technai* effectively drop out of the picture, and the pursuit of cognitive understanding takes the form of a study of *epistēmē*.

We can identify four features of the conception of philosophy with which Plato and Aristotle operate. The first is *the commitment to unambiguous premises*, seen by some commentators as an effect of the move from poesy to prose.[21] Disambiguation sacrifices the wide resources and subtlety of language for statements whose standing as true or false can be assessed, and it had become a sine qua non of philosophical argument. Philosophical argument starts from premises which do not contain ambiguities, vagueness, or anything else that would prevent them being assessed as true or false. Argument discovers their truth or falsity, and for this they need to be the kinds of things that must be either true or false. The process of disambiguation and clarification, so striking in Plato's disputes with the sophists in the early dialogues, can be thought of as getting the raw materials of argument into a philosophical form. For classical philosophy, by contrast with archaic thought, it is a prerequisite of rational argument.

The second feature is *the use of reason*. Philosophy is concerned with inducing conviction. This can be achieved in a number of ways: beliefs can be formed on the basis of authority, on pragmatic grounds, on the grounds of agreement with other beliefs one holds, and so on. The aim of philosophy is to induce conviction through argument. In the ideal cases, if we start from true premises we generate a true conclusion, whereas if we start from false ones we try to demonstrate this falsity by generating a contradiction or an absurdity. These arguments have a probative value: they act as instruments of discovery and refutation. In the most general terms, philosophy induces conviction on the basis of reasoning, and the philosophical tradition construes this reasoning primarily in terms of deductive inference.

The combination of unambiguous premises and the use of reason can be traced to the origins of philosophical enquiry in legal argument, that is to say, as lying in a particular kind of dispute resolution. There were a number of relatively independent developments in the transition from archaic to classical Greece that transformed the discourse by which problems were resolved from what Marcel Detienne has called

'efficacious speech' to dialogue.[22] Efficacious speech had traditionally been the preserve of the poet or orator in praising the
king, and of magic and religion; in both cases the words themselves are often taken to be endowed with causal powers. Detienne has illustrated this in the case of law. In prelegal disputes,
efficacious words and gestures were directed not towards a
judge for the benefit of his assessment, but towards an opponent who had to be overcome. With the emergence of the
Greek polis, however, collective decisions gradually replaced
straightforward commands, and these could only be arrived at
in a satisfactory way through dialogue in which orators sought
to convince through argument. Similarly in the case of law,
use started to be made of witnesses who might produce proof,
and judges were called upon to assess the cases made by both
parties and come to a decision. This is important because, as
Geoffrey Lloyd has pointed out, within the polis, the ability
to argue persuasively gradually conferred status, and this status could be transferred to other areas of intellectual activity,
with the result that we find legal terminology at the root of key
philosophical notions.[23]

From the point of view of our present concerns, the distinctive feature of the use of argument in legal disputes lies
in their starting point: namely, a claim by the opposing party.
One starts the argument from something very specific. What is
at issue is not an enquiry into the nature of the law, or morality, but a particular claim, which can be analysed, perhaps broken down into components, criticized, and refuted. Conflicting
accounts must be freed of ambiguity and resolved into contradictions between purported facts. This approach to argument is developed not only in philosophy, but also in historical
argument, where it first becomes evident in a systematic way
in the histories of Thucydides. Here we find a new probing
search for causes, replacing the traditional narratives, and

requiring an explicit resolution of factual questions. In philosophy, the approach lies at the core of Plato's way of engaging philosophical issues, although it was to be made fully explicit only in Aristotle's syllogistic.[24] Here, not only is the resolution of ambiguities—so prevalent in ordinary discourse, in drama, in poetry, in political speeches—into contradictions a precondition for translation of arguments into logical form, but the idea of contradiction lies at the core of Aristotle's understanding of logic, in the form of the justification of the principle of non-contradiction. This justification is linked closely with the nature of discursive argument, for, as Aristotle points out, anyone engaging in argument in the first place must assume the truth of the principle: if one is prepared to accept contradictions, then anything follows from anything and argument is not possible.

This mode of enquiry and argumentation is not without its problems, however, and Plato for one is highly alert to the limits of following an argument through to where it leads without regard to the consequences. The commitment to pursuing an argument wherever it might lead, which we can consider under the rubric of the Greek term *elenchos*—effectively a form of cross-examination—, is something that its advocates might plausibly have construed as form of intellectual honesty. But, particularly in the context of ethics, it becomes problematic, as Socrates's disputes with the sophists over the nature of virtue show. Where one is establishing the nature of virtue or 'the good life' (*eudaimonia*), it is crucial that one's philosophical arguments are directed towards genuine virtues. Unlike epistemological arguments, for example, where one might simply follow where the argument leads, perhaps toying with sceptical or relativist ideas concerning the reliability of sense perception as a source of knowledge, this is not an option in the case of morality: one does not toy with the idea of dishonour or cowardice as possible virtues. Moral arguments need to be goal-directed in a way that is incompatible with an unquestioning commitment to *elenchos*.

This is where exclusive reliance on the combination of unambiguous premises (i.e., premises with clear truth values) and the use of reason proves problematic. There may be run-of-the-mill cases where these are sufficient, but more is needed with the kinds of intractable questions that arise in ethics, and this is provided by two further features.

The third feature is *the rejection of argument for argument's sake*. There are many ways in which argument can be used—to defeat an opponent, or to display one's skills, for example—but it is crucial for Plato that the ultimate aim of argument in philosophy is to take us to truths, and to reject any argument, no matter how carefully formulated, that does not allow it to do this. This aim can be put in terms of 'intellectual morality'. Thought of in another way, philosophical argument is a way of getting people to believe things that they would not otherwise believe, or providing them with new grounds for things they do believe. The aim is to convince them not just of anything, however, but of something that one believes to be true or right. By contrast, sophists, as presented in Plato's early dialogues, employ arguments, and teach the use of argument, without regard to the truth or otherwise of the conclusions. They are concerned with argument for argument's sake. In this respect it is crucial that Plato's early dialogues are about morality. Morality is the one area where letting an argument take one where it will is highly problematic. Whereas in natural philosophy and metaphysics it is not immediately apparent why we cannot just follow where the argument leads, in moral philosophy it is not so much a question of finding things out as it is of understanding the rationale for, or establishing the legitimacy of, particular ways of behaving.

The fourth feature is *the central role of abstraction*. The rejection of argument for argument's sake concerns the responsible use of argument in ethics. But this raises questions of universality of judgement, by contrast with local prejudices. Universality is a distinctive feature of the transition from archaic to classical Greek culture, and Nightingale has identified a number of developments that promoted a move to universal standards.[25] The first was the spread of an alphabetic system of writing, which not only enabled the articulation of abstract and intricate systems of thought, but thanks to the durability of the written text made it possible for thinkers at different places and times to engage in an ongoing intellectual debate. The second was the development of codes of laws that aimed at impersonal and impartial forms of justice. The third was the development of systems of coinage which established the notion of universal equivalents: a move from personal and private valuations to a universal system of value. Finally, there is the development of panhellenic festivals, which instituted religious and socio-political practices that brought Greeks together into a single space.

Because of the central role of the ideas of morality and the 'good life' in formulating philosophy, the question of the universality of judgement is not something specific to ethics, but becomes constitutive of the philosophical enterprise, as Plato moves from exclusively moral questions to explicitly epistemological and metaphysical ones. The constraint that moral enquiry places on philosophical enquiry more generally takes the form of a commitment to *abstract* argument. The abstractness constraint is achieved by imposing conditions of universality on morality, which require that the arguments take on a level of abstraction in which general norms can be established and articulated. These conditions of universality are not specific to ethics, however, but are general features of the true philosophy and, raised to the requisite level of abstraction, they become the features of metaphysics and natural philosophy. As Plato characterizes it in the *Republic*, philosophizing—a form of contemplation, *theōria*—is a strictly metaphysical activity in which the mind separates itself from the senses and apprehends the Forms. Abstraction becomes distinctive of metaphysical argument, and while this has some precedent in earlier Eleatic thinkers, the route from ethics to metaphysics gives the latter a wholly new standing.

The questions take on a particular importance because, throughout antiquity, philosophy was focused on how to live, on wisdom, happiness, and well-being. As Long notes, right from the very beginning, in sixth- and fifth-century thinkers, the project was salvational as well as rational: the cultivation of true *logos* would lead to a happy life.[26] As we shall see, it is problems in moral philosophy, rather than in matter theory, that motivate the idea that philosophy is above all a form of abstraction, something accommodated by translating it into metaphysics. Here the question of deciding between practical and abstract activities, and the standing of philosophy as a paradigmatic abstract activity, arises in a particularly acute form. A crucial, overlooked, ingredient in the commitment to abstractness comes from considerations about how responsible ethical argument is to be obtained. The route to this is via universality, to be secured by abstract arguments. This then becomes a central ingredient in natural philosophy, and a concern with abstract principles becomes incorporated into natural philosophy, in such a way that it is transformed into an essentially metaphysical activity, by contrast with the practical concerns that had characterized it traditionally.

It is with the origins of philosophical enquiry in a moral context, in Plato's dialogues, that we can begin to explore the benefits and costs of the transformation of enquiry into a philosophical form. But here emerges what is the most profound dilemma of classical philosophy. The move to transfer questions of morality into second-order enquiry, while it is indeed an effective counter to moral diversity, moral relativism, and moral conventionalism, achieves this at a great cost: a failure to capture the diversity and complexity of the circumstances in which moral judgements need to be made. This significantly lessens the value of the moral programme of classical Greek philosophy. Its attempt to establish norms of objectivity and universality in moral judgements involves redescribing and simplifying these to an extent that rids them of relevance to actual moral decision making. Moreover, when we compare Greek philosophical discourse with the work of the contemporary Greek tragedians, for example, not only does a whole dimension of moral complexity come into view, but at the same time, by contrast with philosophy—despite Socrates's commitment to the idea that reason by itself can motivate virtuous behaviour—these dramas offered something that could move one to virtue. And it certainly looks as if this ability was secured by keeping the understanding of morality as part of first-order discourse, something that defeats the object of philosophical enquiry into morality.

Outwitting Opponents vs Intellectual Morality

The two most authoritative accounts of Socrates that we have are Xenophon's *Memorabilia* and Plato's early dialogues. Xenophon emphasizes Socrates's lack of interest in 'the nature of things', and Plato devotes the final part of the *Phaedo* to Socrates's reasons for his dissatisfaction with enquiry into the natural world. Plato's early dialogues in particular are concerned exclusively with the defence of individual moral values against the moral conventionalism of the sophists, which he considers act to the detriment of public morality and the community's well-being. The procedure is to press Socrates's interlocutors to clarify the various values that they are so confident of (piety in the *Euthyphro*, courage in the *Laches*, moderation in the *Charmides*, friendship in the *Lysis*, poetic inspiration in the *Ion*, wisdom in the *Euthydemus*, beauty in the *Greater Hippias*, oratorical skill in the *Gorgias*), by providing a definition of them, in the first instance in terms of a relevant 'skill'. In the *Republic*, after various failed attempts to define justice, Thrasymachus questions whether it is a virtue at all, on the grounds that it is not in anyone's interest to possess virtue: it is simply something of advantage to the powerful, and law and morality are just systems to protect the interests of the powerful. Even though Socrates concludes that, since he does not know what justice is, he cannot know whether it is a virtue or not, nevertheless he argues that the just man will have a better life than an unjust one.[27]

Given the nature of Socrates's condemnation and death, a defence of Socratic values is the focal point of the defence of philosophy for Plato. Socrates is presented in the early dialogues in particular as the adversary of the sophists. The dialogues can proceed because both parties accept the requirements of unambiguous premises and logical argument. The differences between them arise primarily from different conceptions of the point of the exercise. Labelling this exercise 'philosophy' is in fact problematic, because the sophist enterprise fails on the criterion that restricts argument to the uncovering of truths, as opposed to providing a means of showing off one's ingenuity in order to enhance one's reputation ('sophistic' proper in Aristotle's terminology) or seeking simply to win arguments ('eristic' in Aristotle's terminology). It is not just a question of the form of the arguments, but also of the purposes for which they are used. And in this sense, it is questionable whether the sophists are even doing philosophy.

This is not a straightforward matter, however. The sophist can in effect be considered as taking truth to be whatever survives the *elenchos*—critical examination—and then considering what secures truth as impartiality, freedom from prejudices, lack of bias, and lack of partisanship (to put things in modern terms). Indeed, this conception of intellectual morality, wholly at odds with that of Plato, is an attractive one and may well, other things being equal, have greater intuitive appeal than Plato's. But the whole point is that other things are not equal. The notion of truth as whatever survives the *elenchos* might be satisfactory in areas such as geometry, but not in a moral context, where one wants to establish a single, truly worthwhile system of values. For Plato, this is crucial in dealing with the sophists' advocacy of the purely conventional nature of systems of morality. Not just any set of values that emerges unscathed on some particular occasion of argument will be the true system of values, and this matters, because fundamental questions of morality are not the kinds of thing one can disregard, or on which one can suspend judgement. It is important to remember here that Plato draws on the wisdom and virtue of the philosopher in the *Republic* in arguing that the philosopher is the most appropriate ruler: it is particularly important in the context of the doctrine of 'philosopher kings' that philosophers consistently display certain fundamental moral qualities.

Nevertheless, geometry plays an important role as a model of knowledge for Plato. It deals with unchangeable things that are subject to precise definitions, which, once established, lead one to other theorems, exhibiting the kind of unity that he wants for ethics in dialogues such as the *Protagoras*. He can hardly just abandon the rules that work so well in the case of geometry. In fact, he doesn't need to. On closer examination, it becomes evident from the way in which the sophists argue in the dialogues that it is less a question of argument taking one in a particular unwelcome direction, than it is of argument taking one in many different, possibly conflicting, directions. Parmenides had argued that none of these directions is privileged, that no argument can enable us to pass beyond appearances to reality. Gorgias, the most famous and evidently the most formidable of the sophists, saw himself in the tradition of Parmenides, and in the *Encomium of Helen* he argues that natural philosophers each think that they alone have the secret of the universe, whereas in fact all any of them do is pit one opinion against another.[28]

The question for Plato is, then: if argument can take one in many directions, and if only one of these is the right direction, how do we identify and establish this right direction? Examination of the logic of the reasoning process cannot accomplish this; in a cognate case, Aristotle, as we shall see in the next chapter, realized that there were no logical grounds on which to distinguish arguments that yielded explanatory conclusions from arguments that yielded manifestly non-explanatory ones. For Plato, the solution to identifying which argument has taken one in the right direction lies in metaphysics. It is metaphysics that allows one to go beyond the conventional aspects of morality—which the sophists emphasize—to its underlying nature.

The Metaphysics of Morals

The central tenets of Plato's Socratic account of virtue are: that virtue is knowledge; the unity of virtue; the thesis that anyone who grasps virtue will inevitably choose to do what is good and will prefer suffering to injustice; that vice derives from ignorance; and that the correct response to wrongdoing is education. Some of these theses had already been advocated by other thinkers. Democritus, for example, had said that the cause of vice is ignorance, and that it is better to be wronged than to do wrong. But the way in which Plato comes to establish the claims is without precedent. Everything rests on the idea that virtue is knowledge, that is, something that falls within the realm of epistemology. And it turns out that, for Plato, falling under epistemology means falling under metaphysics. Aristotle's assessment of the Socratic project is apposite here. Aristotle notes that 'Socrates busied himself with ethical matters and not with natural ones', but, he goes on to say, Socrates was concerned to seek out the universal in ethics, by focusing on what 'the definitions' of various virtues are,[29] and that this is what lies at the origin of Socrates's (i.e., Plato's) metaphysical concerns.

The basic idea is that, while we can form true beliefs in a number of different ways, knowledge is to be gained only through intellectual insight into an unchanging archetypical realm, that of the Forms. The Forms anchor morality, and provide it with a standard. The postulation of the Forms answers the charge of the conventionality of morals, putting the question in the realm of knowledge rather than opinion, and ruling out the idea that particular moral beliefs could lack an absolute truth value. But establishing the objectivity (as we might put it) or universality of morality does not in itself address the question of how we might establish whether any particular type of behaviour is truly virtuous, because, on Socrates's own admission, we lack any satisfactory definition of the nature of justice, courage, and so on.

Plato develops, and in some respects changes his mind about, his metaphysics between the early dialogues and late ones such as the *Parmenides*, which is very circumspect about the Forms. The freshest and most unqualified account is to be found in two relatively early dialogues, the *Meno* and the *Phaedo*. The former contains an argument designed to show that our knowledge of things does not derive from experience, but pre-exists in our minds in a potential form, waiting to be reawakened. This reawakening typically takes place in the form of learning from experience, but it can be prompted by judicious questioning. In the famous passage on the uneducated slave-boy in the *Meno*, Socrates uses what can only be described as leading questions—although Plato does not describe them in that way of course—eliciting from the boy various fundamental geometrical theorems. The illiterate boy thus seems to have knowledge of these, but where could he have derived it from? The answer, Plato tells us, is that he recollects another 'world', which he must have experienced in an earlier life, but forgotten at birth.[30] Because ethics has been brought under epistemology, the doctrine of recollection applies equally to the ideas of goodness and virtue. The treatment of Forms in terms of recollection is filled out in the discussion of absolutes in the *Phaedo*, where it is noted that we have a perfectly good idea of equality, but that this cannot be derived from experience of any kind, because we only ever experience things that are more or less equal, never absolutely equal. This idea must be prior to our experience of more or less equal things, and Plato argues can it can only have been acquired in a previous existence. Among the absolute qualities that are singled out in this respect are absolute goodness and absolute beauty.[31] They provide templates against which our judgements of goodness and beauty must be measured.

It is not possible to say definitively whether the theory of Forms was devised with the defence of the absolute, universal nature of morality in mind. But it provided an ingenious solution to a specific problem about the nature of virtue and goodness, and it was introduced in dialogues concerned specifically with moral questions. In other words, the first comprehensive metaphysical system, that of Plato, is developed in the context of problems about the nature of morality. In Aristotle, as we shall see in the next chapter, although he has an elaborate account of morality, metaphysics comes very much into its own as a general abstract system which has no special connection to morality, but it does have a close connection with natural philosophy. Indeed, for Aristotle, there is a continuity between the naturalistic concerns of Socrates's predecessors and contemporaries, and a philosophical project in metaphysics that stretches from Socrates, through Plato, to Aristotle himself. Before we turn to developments in metaphysics, however, there is a pressing problem about Plato's metaphysical treatment of morality that we need to address. In what way does the transformation of morality into a second-order form of enquiry, which is part and parcel of its formulation of questions of morality in metaphysical terms, bear on philosophy's ability to come to terms with, on the one hand, the moral dilemmas that were the concern of Greek thought generally, and which dramatists had probed in some depth, and on the other hand, the daily decisions that have to be made by those in various parts of the community who have very different kinds of demand and responsibility placed on them, and who often can only come to decisions on a case-by-case basis?

Moral Complexity

Epistēmē is a second-order cognitive engagement with the world, something that essentially proceeds via abstraction. *Mētis*, by contrast, is an example of first-order cognitive engagement with the world, one that does not proceed via abstractions. Both forms of engagement work on the premise that the world is a place of becoming and change, and both offer strategies to deal with this; the difference is, that the one attempts to engage it directly, whereas the other attempts to subordinate it to something unchanging. But *mētis* does not by any means exclusively capture all forms of first-order engagement. Recognizing and coming to terms with the dangers and difficult judgements that we encounter in the face of unforeseen happenings and ambiguous situations is open to a number of approaches. Greek drama is one such approach, one significantly different from those that we have been considering. It is a first-order approach, but, unlike *mētis*, it does not offer something that is an alternative form of cognitive grasp. It engages the emotions, in a way that Plato's realm of Forms, for example, cannot do. This enables it to offer compelling descriptions of particular kinds of moral complexity: situations of ambiguity, unforeseeable circumstances, acting under duress or at least under constraints that restrict one's moral choices, acting in circumstances where the consequences cannot be assessed.

Many of the elements in a good life—successful citizenship, love and friendship, activities in which courage and justice can be displayed—take place in the context of events beyond our control. As Martha Nussbaum notes, good people can do bad things which are otherwise repugnant to their ethical character and commitments, because of circumstances whose origin does not lie with them.[32] Simply to abstract these from a person's moral behaviour as if they were extraneous circumstances abandons any sense of the conditions under which ethical judgements are required in the first place. Thinking of ethics in these contexts, which are those explored in Greek drama, presents a picture of moral judgement wholly at odds with that in which such judgement is a matter of identifying and acting in accordance with an abstract, archetypical ideal of goodness.

The tragic poets treated powerful emotions, especially pity and fear, as sources of insight into the good human life. They lay at the heart of moral responsibility. Plato, by contrast, denied the role of these emotions, confining moral judgement to the intellect, and separating it as far as possible from the disturbing effects of sense and emotion. As he tells Euthyphro in the dialogue of that name, competing moral claims are simply repugnant to reason, and if we accepted them 'the pious and the impious would be one and the same'.[33]

Philosophy as such could not do what the Greek tragedies could do, nor could the Greek tragedies do what Greek philosophy could do. Proper appreciation of the former is particularly apposite, because Greek philosophy had vast ambitions. It offered a programme in which it seemed that almost anything could be translated into second-order philosophical terms: morality, politics, natural philosophy, sense perception, the nature of the mind, and so on. But this translation assumed that the raw material on which it worked was something that could be rationalized, put in terms of unambiguous premises, and subjected to a regime of deductive reasoning. The treatment in philosophy was completely contrary to the treatment of the moral issues in terms of the emotions in Greek drama, the success of which depended on its sure grasp of the emotions: philosophy simply taking over the insights of drama would not be viable. Nevertheless, given the richness of the material in the dramas, some awareness of this in philosophy is rather important. The philosophical tradition after Plato moved in this direction. Aristotle, and particularly the Stoics, thought carefully about affective states, but the problem remained as to how it was possible to accommodate an account of the good life that depends on sensibility and the emotions to a philosophical programme that works in second-order terms.

Moral complexity is equally evident in a second, less dramatic and (in a classical context) relatively unexplored source of problems deriving from an abstract account of morality, although it can be detected as early the discussion of the duties of the shepherd in Book 1 of the *Republic*. This is the existence of what can be described as a separate realm of responsibility, including moral responsibility, which we might term the morality of office (a term that comes into use with Cicero). Here, morality is in large part a function of whether one satisfies the responsibilities of one's occupation, rank, office, or standing. The soldier, the ruler, the mother, the advocate, the teacher, the priest, the head of the household, the hero: each had very different sets of responsibilities, and very different expectations were placed upon them. What is needed here is not an account centred on the moral responsibilities derived from an abstract account of goodness or justice, but instead one that focuses on how various different kinds of moral and political responsibility are generated, especially given that one and the same person may fall under several of the categories, and that what was due in one capacity might conflict with what was due in another. The problem here is not conventionalism, or the relativism raised by culturally alien moral practices that the Pyrrhonists will adduce, but something that lies at the heart of the basic daily responsibilities and expectations to which members of different social groups are subject. The challenge for the Platonic picture is to reconcile the idea of values as universal with the highly differentiated sets of values that exist in societies. It is one thing for Socrates to show Thrasymachus how justice must be universal; it is quite another to give us some idea of how this universal justice is to be manifested in the very different social and personal roles that bring with them their own specific responsibilities and expectations, especially when overlapping roles bring with them conflicting responsibilities. And unless this can be done, one cannot begin to face up to the issues. A particularly pressing problem here is that decision making in carrying out an office is of necessity casuistic, the opposite of any reliance on top-down guidance.

In short, there are a number of sources of difficulty, not just for the specific kind of programme in moral philosophy that Plato envisages, but more generally for any approach whose modus operandi is to engage the problems by raising them to a second-order form of enquiry. What is at issue is a question inherent in the nature of philosophical enquiry, particularly evident in the first stages of development of Greek philosophy, in Plato's dialogues. In Plato's case, this procedure enables him to address some basic problems, not least whether morality is merely conventional; but the means he deploys restrict the subject matter so severely that the richness and complexity of moral judgements, due in large part to the particular contingent circumstances in which such judgements are made, are lost. A more fruitful investigation of the moral issues that arise in these contingent circumstances would require reference to the emotions as well as reason, something revealed in Greek drama, and to casuistry, in order to be alert to those features of moral expectations peculiar to particular cases, as revealed in the everyday mundane—but occasionally consequential—decisions with which people are faced. At the same time, we must not lose sight of the problem of establishing a functional moral consensus. It is far from clear that philosophical considerations can secure this. Plato's programmes, in the *Republic* and the *Laws*, for education just do not look appropriate. Rather, the use of role models, explicitly deployed in Roman literary culture,[34] but there in Greek culture as well (for example in the person of Socrates), and developed into an art form in Christianity with its creation of exemplary lives of the saints, was part of moral understanding right from the beginning, even if only implicitly, and had immediate effects on behaviour that moral philosophy did not.

The philosophical exercise becomes one in abstraction, effectively preventing it, as it stood, from being translated into any plausible or realistic form of practical action. The criticism of philosophy that will hound it throughout much of its history will be that it is a useless discipline, and the paradigm example of its uselessness will be its reflections on moral questions. Two much later proposed 'solutions', those of Kant and the utilitarians, will offer accounts of moral reasoning which not only remove questions of morality from those of rank or office, but eschew sensibility and treat moral behaviour as exclusively a matter of reasoning. We will consider these later. But we must bear in mind a more obvious alternative right from the start: namely, that what we are witnessing here are intrinsic limits to what philosophical enquiry can achieve.

CHAPTER TWO

Metaphysics as a Form
of Understanding

WE HAVE SEEN how a particular commitment to abstraction arises in Plato's moral philosophy, and I have indicated that such a notion of abstraction shapes the development of natural philosophy and metaphysics. But the idea of metaphysical understanding, one of the defining features of classical thought, quickly comes to take on a life of its own. Morality had been approached in both non-abstract and abstract ways, the latter becoming constitutive of the philosophical approach. The same is true of the study of natural phenomena. But metaphysics was never available in a non-abstract form. It is an intrinsically abstract type of enquiry, and in this sense it can act as the paradigm of philosophy. There is no non-philosophical form of metaphysics. Philosophy *was* metaphysics: to pursue philosophy was to pursue metaphysics. In this chapter, we consider the way in which metaphysics controls other forms of understanding, before turning in the next chapter to the costs of this approach.

In Greek moral philosophy, it was not so much a question of finding things out as it was of understanding the rationale for, or establishing the legitimacy of, particular ways of behaving. But we must not overdraw the contrast with natural philosophy. In Aristotle's natural philosophy, for example, the two approaches—discovery and demonstration—typically work in tandem as a form of probative enquiry. The means for this are supplied by logic and by metaphysics, and between them they establish philosophy as an essentially second-order form of investigation. Simplifying somewhat, metaphysics establishes the fundamental principles of understanding, while logic, guided in its aims by metaphysics, regulates the connections that can be established between these fundamental principles and natural phenomena. One thing that I want to bring out is the way in which metaphysical considerations shape the aims of the whole of philosophical enquiry, including logic, for establishing validity is just the first stage in logic in antiquity. It is ultimately directed at explanation, and explanation is shaped by one's metaphysics, evident in the difference between Aristotle and the Stoics.

In general, Aristotle's approach relies on an elaborate classification of subject matters ('first philosophy', natural philosophy, mathematics, natural history, the 'mixed mathematical' disciplines, rhetoric, syllogistic, and morals and politics), and a no less elaborate philosophical preparation of the material in order to make it susceptible to enquiry. The subject matter to which Aristotle applies metaphysics and logic, however, is primarily natural philosophy, not ethics. By contrast with Plato's account, natural philosophy is an autonomous discipline, not something to be subsumed under a supernatural realm of Forms. The basic universal principles underlying the change that characterizes the sensible world are to be found in things themselves, in their essential natures. Indeed, it is in his account of explanation of natural phenomena that Aristotle's philosophy comes into its own, and presents a powerful picture of the world that was to lead the way, less in antiquity—where it quickly became overshadowed by the Hellenistic philosophies—than in the revival of philosophical thinking from the thirteenth century onwards.

Aristotle identified three 'scientific' disciplines: 'first philosophy', mathematics, and natural philosophy. The first deals with pure forms (i.e., separate from matter) and there is no great gulf here between Plato's conception and that of Aristotle. But for Plato this is effectively a master discipline, and the other two are strictly subordinate to it: mathematics because mathematical objects are also pure forms on his account, and natural philosophy because it is only in transcending changing physical things and moving to the realm of the unchanging that we can properly explain them. For Aristotle, by contrast, mathematical objects are not pure forms—their forms are imposed on 'intelligible' or 'noetic' matter[1]—and are not something that exists in a realm that is independent of us, but on the contrary are our constructs. The natural realm is to be explained by referring it to a realm of essences, but these essences inhere within things, and not in some separate realm. Given the definitions of natural philosophy as concerning those things that change and have an independent existence, and the definition of mathematics as concerning those things that do not change and have no independent existence, and given that the task of explanation is to account for physical and mathematical questions in terms of the essential properties of the physical and mathematical domains respectively, there can be no role for mathematics in physical explanation.[2] Natural philosophy is an autonomous discipline, reliant only on its own principles.

Aristotle was not alone in questioning the Platonic doctrine of Forms. Plato himself, in later dialogues such as the *Sophist,* the *Statesman*, and the *Parmenides*, had raised probing questions about the doctrine, on two issues. The first concerned how sensible things 'participate' in the Forms, which appeared to involve a regress which Aristotle named the 'Third Man' argument: large things derive their largeness from participating in the Form of the Large, but since these large things together with the Form of the Large also come under the category of the large, the combination of the two must derive its largeness from some third entity, and so on *ad infinitum*. The second concerned the relation between the Forms themselves: whether there are, for example, Forms of the non-beautiful as well as Forms of the beautiful, which leads Plato to conclude that there are Forms of non-Being as well as Forms of Being. The arguments are presented as inconclusive, not in the sense that the search for definitions in the early Socratic dialogues is inconclusive, but because the theory of Forms presents genuine paradoxes which Plato struggles to find the resources to resolve. It is instructive that his long-time students Aristotle and Xenocrates, when speaking of their master, show great doubt as to the meaning of his later metaphysical doctrines.[3]

Explanation by Essential Properties

Philosophy in antiquity faced two interconnected tasks: translating problems into a philosophical form, and building up the resources needed to offer a comprehensive understanding of this newly constructed subject matter. Aristotle was the formative figure in this respect, and it is his account of natural philosophy that provides the best illustration of the depth and complexity of the problems that this raises.

What might seem the most basic and unproblematic aspect of the idea of natural philosophy—*phusikē*—is that of 'nature', *phusis*; but in fact this presents significant difficulties. The idea of a 'natural realm' is absent in Aristotle, for example, and indeed only really emerges in the twelfth and thirteenth centuries with the separation of the supernatural and natural realms, and the subsequent division of responsibilities for investigating each. When Aristotle turns his attention to *phusis*, it is not to anything resembling what we might consider 'the natural realm', but rather to the 'natures' of things. For Empedocles, who was the first to think in terms of *phusis*, and to whom Aristotle's genealogy for his own natural philosophy owes a great deal, it was the process by which a thing developed into its fully fledged form: its growth from birth to maturity. By contrast, Aristotle thinks of *phusis* as the end product of such a developmental process, the true nature or form of the fully developed thing. In both cases, the model is clearly living things, and it is notable that when Aristotle gives examples of such notions as substance (*ousia*) it is always in terms of higher animals, never inanimate things, even though the concept is designed to apply equally to both. The aim of explanation is to identify the essential features of things and deduce their behaviour from this, and identifying the natural behaviour of a cow or a sheep, for example, in terms of its essential features is an intuitive and well-entrenched activity. There is nothing philosophical as such about it. The move to natural philosophy comes when this is made into a general principle, and this is what the novelty, and power, of Aristotle's conception consists in.

Indeed, this move defines what it is to be philosophical. Like Plato, Aristotle distinguishes the sophistical from the genuinely philosophical argument in terms of going beyond what emerges from the *elenchos*. But whereas Plato introduces something external to philosophical discourse—appeal to the Forms—, Aristotle advocates procedures internal to it. Distinguishing sophistical knowledge from genuine knowledge he writes,

We suppose ourselves to have unqualified demonstrative knowledge of something, as opposed to knowing it in the accidental way in which the sophist knows it, when we think we know the explanation/cause on which it depends, as the explanation/cause of that thing and of no other, and, further, that the thing could not be other than it is.[4]

Knowing the explanation or cause identifies those truths that spring from the nature of something,[5] and these are the object of philosophy, by contrast with things which just happen to be true, which sophists don't distinguish from accidental knowledge. The task of natural-philosophical demonstration is the understanding of phenomena in terms of their causes.

The general principle that explanation is demonstration from essential natures is in fact required by the natural-philosophical resources that Aristotle deploys to separate out natural from unnatural behaviour. Aristotelian natural philosophy can only explain behaviour that is a result of the essential properties of things. There are many physical phenomena that are not the result of essential properties, from stones thrown upwards and bodies raised from the ground by pulleys, to monstrosities and unnatural births. These are purely accidental, in the sense of not following from the natures of things, and as such have no explanation. In this respect, the way in which Aristotle translates issues into philosophical terms is different from competing programmes, whether those of Plato or the atomists. Plato subordinates everything to the Forms, and accordingly the subject matter of philosophy contains neither a distinct 'natural realm' nor a division between those things or events that have essential natures and those which do not (assuming there are any of the latter in the Platonic universe). It includes everything, effectively without distinction. Similarly with the diametrically opposed atomist programme. Like Plato's account, it encompasses the totality of things. There is no 'natural realm' separated out because, in Epicurean atomism, explicitly promoted as a form of natural philosophy, everything is reduced to the activity of atoms alone: inanimate things, animate ones, souls, and the gods. One way we might put this is to say that in Plato everything is ultimately supernatural, whereas in the Epicureans everything is ultimately natural. Both bring everything under a single regulatory principle. In Aristotle, by contrast, there are many forms of behaviour that, in explanatory terms, cannot be counted natural or supernatural. They are accidental. Accidents do not figure in Plato, and they are denied by Epicureans and Stoics. It is true that Epicurus introduced a 'swerve' (*parenklisis*) into his account, but this was a desperate post hoc attempt to mitigate the problem of how atoms, whose natural motion is in a straight line, all with the same unvarying speed, could interact to form worlds, and it is at odds with the basic principles of Epicurean atomist natural philosophy, which take no account of it once an initial interaction of atoms has been established.

Accidents are a crucial ingredient in the idea of explanation in terms of essential properties, and there is a gulf between Aristotle and the Hellenistic schools, who rejected the idea of accidental events. Whereas for the Stoics, for example, every state of affairs was a necessary consequence of a chain of preceding causes, on Aristotle's account it is not a question of chains of cause and effect interwoven in a nexus extending to infinity. Accordingly, he can assert that there are fresh beginnings (*archai*), not confined to human agency, without supposing that there is a deterministic causal nexus occasionally interrupted by undetermined events; for he simply does not see the question in these terms.[6] The possibility of uncaused events is a basic point of contention between the Aristotelian and the Stoic views. Aristotle is clear that there are events that result from chance rather than necessity, where chance events are those 'unnatural' events which natural philosophy is not called upon to explain. By contrast, all natural processes are associated with necessity, because they are the result of the activity of intrinsic causes.

A good deal here hinges on the relation between causation and explanation. The Stoics didn't accept that there are such things as accidental, coincidental, or chance events. The fact that we cannot explain all events simply means that we cannot find the requisite cause: lack of explanation does not necessarily mean lack of cause. But Aristotle tends to treat causes as simply what explanations identify as the relevant factors. This makes causes context-relative: what will count as a cause will be determined by the kind of explanation one is seeking. On such a view, to say that a coincidence lacks an explanation is indeed to say that it lacks a cause. Aristotle gives the example of a man who goes to the market and chances to meet his debtor.[7] To provide the cause of the man's being at the market at a particular time and to provide the cause of the debtor's being at the market at the same time is not to provide the cause of their being at the market simultaneously. We want to be able to make the distinction between intentional outcomes and accidental outcomes, between the case where the man went to the market so that he might meet his debtor, and the case where it was a purely chance encounter. In the first case, the cause of the man's being at the market at a particular time plus the cause of the debtor's also being at the market at that particular time will add up to a cause of their both being at the market at the same time, for the causal chains are genuinely connected. But in the case where the meeting is accidental, there is simply no cause for their being at the market at the same time.

On the Stoic and Epicurean accounts, the relation between explanation and causation is straightforward.[8] We assume that, at some level of description, everything in the universe is causally connected with everything else: as a consequence, there are no events for which there are no connecting causal chains, provided we are prepared to search back far enough through causal ancestors. Explanations are simply statements of cause, and causes always necessitate their effects. On the Aristotelian account, by contrast, causes are what figure in explanations, and these are richer than the kinds of thing that the Stoics considered. What are usually identified as the four 'causes' in Aristotle are therefore best considered relative to the explanations in which they figure, which in turn are best thought of as four types of explanation. These are: material explanations, in which we account for the behaviour of the thing in terms of the material that constitutes it; formal explanations, in which we identify a state of something or a change in the state of something, such as its shape or the arrangement of parts that it takes on, by reference to a form (*eidos*) or archetype (*paradeigma*); efficient explanations, which either identify something separate from the object which, by interacting with it, changes its state, for example its state of motion in collision, or some internal factor that has this effect; and teleological explanations, which account for a thing or an event in terms of its purpose or end.[9]

In sum, natural philosophy is identified as dealing with those things that change and are independent of us (i.e., not objects of thought like numbers and geometrical figures), and this is a unique characterization which picks out what is distinctive about them. These natural phenomena are then translated into a philosophically tractable form, which builds on a notion of understanding the behaviour of animals in terms of their different essential natures, and Aristotle develops this into a general account of change. But an account in terms of essential natures requires that a sharp distinction be made between behaviour that results from the essential features of the animal or object, and that which does not. The latter is characterized as accidental, and Aristotle offers an elaborate understanding of explanation and causation that allows him to specify the various possible forms of legitimate explanation. Accidental occurrences—those that do not follow from the nature of the thing—cannot be brought under these, and so fall outside natural philosophy proper (as well as any notion of a 'natural realm').

Logic as a Route to Understanding

Once the theoretical connection between essential principles underlying things and their observed effects has been established, there remains the task of connecting these in a way that generates explanations, or, more generally, understanding. Here questions of argument, reasoning, and inference come into play. Argument is a means of convincing someone to believe something that they might not otherwise believe, or of confirming something that they believe, or of getting someone to behave in a way that they wouldn't otherwise have behaved, and so on. In the case of knowledge, it is a means of demonstration of things that one didn't know. Argument might work through authority, threats, faith, or something else. The philosophical tradition is concerned with those cases where it works by inference: inference is what takes one from premises that one agrees on or believes to be true or knows, to a conclusion that follows from those premises. In his syllogistic, Aristotle provided a formal account of inference, and he writes that he is the first to have considered the nature of deductive inference, something that has caused him much trouble.[10] Syllogistic marshals arguments into a particular form, based on the relation between the subject and the predicate of a statement, and then sets out to identify all and only those forms of inference that legitimately take one from premises to conclusion: in the paradigm case, those that are guaranteed to take one from true premises to a true conclusion. Such forms of inference are valid purely in virtue of the form of inference.

In short, the aim is to identify those arguments in which truth is preserved between premises and conclusion. But what is the point of this for Aristotle? Much later in the history of logic, effectively starting in the nineteenth century with Boole's attempts to connect syllogistic with developments in algebra, capturing formal validity took on a new importance. But no one before Leibniz explored a connection between logic and mathematics, and that was certainly not Aristotle's motivation. In his earlier writings, such as the *Topics*, Aristotle had elaborated procedures for the 'discovery of knowledge'. These procedures were designed to guide one in uncovering the appropriate evidence, discovering the most fruitful questions to ask, and so on, and they did this by providing devices or strategies for classifying or characterizing problems so that they could be posed and solved using set techniques. In his later works such as the *Prior* and *Posterior Analytics*, by contrast, there is a marked change of emphasis. Aristotle now pursues the question of the presentation of results, as his interests shift to the validity of the reasoning used to establish conclusions on the basis of accepted premises: syllogistic. But it would be a mistake to see this as a simple shift from an interest in discovery to a concern with demonstration, for discovery plays a role in demonstration. In some ways it motivates it, and this was to be a highly problematic and contentious issue.

There are two important moves that Aristotle makes in thinking through what we can expect of syllogistic reasoning. The first is a test for validity, the second a test for informativeness. Both of these bear directly on the standing of logic, whether in Aristotle's version (syllogistic) or in that of the alternative propositional logic of the Stoics. What informativeness consisted in was something regulated by metaphysics, and because Aristotle's metaphysics of individual natures and Stoic holistic metaphysics differed, they had different conceptions of what one was seeking from logic. In both cases, logic is not an end in itself, but a means of attaining forms of understanding dictated by metaphysics.

As regards the establishment of validity, there is significant overlap in what is at issue with modern logic. But preserving truth between premises and conclusion was not the only thing that either Aristotle or the Stoics were seeking from their logics. Setting out to distinguish formally valid arguments from those that were not formally valid was only the first step. In contrast with modern logic, the ultimate aim was to distinguish informative valid arguments (those which reach an explanatory conclusion) from uninformative valid ones (those which reach a merely factual conclusion). And it was here that both Aristotle and the Stoics hit an insuperable obstacle, for even in the case of instantly recognizable uninformative but valid arguments, there was no logical means of characterizing the difference. Aristotle resorted to positing a form of intellectual insight (*nous*) by which we recognize informative inferences, but he was unable to provide any details. There is no doubt that this was a serious setback for Aristotle's project (the Stoics had similar problems), and it raises a question as to the contribution that syllogistic makes to scientific understanding. Aristotle's successors, particularly in the early modern period, were deeply worried about this question, but what motivated these worries was less how we grasp informative inferences, than whether syllogistic was capable of ever being informative in the first place. Early modern critics of Aristotle argued in particular that syllogistic could not possibly be part of a method of discovery, and that many of the problems in Aristotle's account of a whole range of natural-philosophical matters could be traced to his having attempted to employ this useless method.[11]

Epistemology and Morality

The single greatest difference between Aristotle and Plato was that Plato believed that the essences of things, by reference to which we were to understand and explain those things, lay outside them, whereas for Aristotle they lay within them. This difference led to two radically different accounts of the sources of knowledge. The theory of knowledge had been a central ingredient in classical philosophy since Plato who, in Book 7 of the *Republic*, introduced the famous Analogy of the Cave to illustrate his theory that all knowledge is knowledge of the Forms and not of sensible things.[12] He imagines a group of men who have been chained to the wall of a cave all their lives: all they ever see are shadows projected from a fire behind them onto a wall. They take these shadows to be reality, but one day they are freed from their chains, and moving around the cave they discover a passage leading outside, where they see the sun for the first time, and realize that the shadows they have perceived to this point are mere illusions. So it is with ordinary sense perception, Plato has Socrates argue: the philosopher is like the occupants of the cave, believing that their sense impressions show them that everything there reflects reality. When they encounter the Forms, although at first blinded by them as the cave-dwellers were by the sun, their eyes slowly adjust to the light and are able presently to gaze on things in the metaphysical realm, including the Form of the Good. They are enlightened by their experience, ascending to the supreme form of wisdom, *theōria*, and accordingly must return to educate others about the nature of ultimate reality. The cave analogy plays on the traditional meaning of *theōria*, as a journey or pilgrimage made by ambassadors or observers (*theōroi*) who were sent to witness the preparations for panhellenic games or festivals, or envoys to consult oracles, returning home with an eyewitness account. Plato retains the metaphor of a journey, making the journey now a private one in which the realm investigated by the traveller is one of contemplation, the cultivation of which provides the basis for the good or fulfilling life.[13]

An alternative route to enlightenment, described in the *Meno*, is through recollection of an earlier life. This depends on the incorporeal nature of the soul, which was disembodied prior to the person's birth, and accordingly able to grasp the Forms in a way that an embodied soul cannot, although, as we have seen, some degree of recollection is possible. The argument is a basic one about the distinction between appearance and reality, namely that appearances are not the guide to reality that we take them to be. This is particularly marked in the case of ethics, but it is a general epistemological doctrine.

For Aristotle, by contrast, sense perception, properly considered, is the only guide to reality. There is no question of transcending appearances. Accordingly, the task Aristotle faces is how to determine under what conditions sense perception is a genuine guide to reality, and how to establish that this is what it actually delivers. Sense perception had been marginal in Plato's account of epistemology: after all, once it had been established as unreliable, there was little further need for consideration of its nature. Aristotle, on the other hand, has an elaborate account of what veridical perception consists in. The core doctrine in this account is the incorrigibility of sensation of something to which the sense organ is naturally fitted,[14] such as the sensation of colour by the eyes, assuming the conditions of sensation (lighting, etc.) are normal. The idea is that each sense is fitted to receive one specific kind of sensible quality so that the natural function of the sense is activated when it is actually perceiving that sensible quality. When each organ functions properly, it fulfils its purpose properly, since otherwise nature would have made an imperfection in a fully developed organ. In the case of vision, this means that our perception of colours is accurate under normal circumstances, that is, in circumstances that are natural to, and therefore appropriate to, the functioning of the sense organ. Such perception cannot be mistaken, because it provides the standard by which we judge incorrigibility. Vision under normal circumstances is the only means we have by which to judge what colour something is, so it is not so much veridical as constitutive of the very notion of veridicality.

This is supported by Aristotle's account of what happens in vision, which is premised on his metaphysics of substance. Substance is composed of matter, which is a substratum having no properties in its own right, but which can become something definite when endowed with form; and of form, which is the bearer of properties and needs a substratum in which to inhere. What happens in the transmission of light is that the colours overlying the surfaces of visible bodies produce disturbances in the intervening medium, which in turn acts upon the sense organ.[15] As a result, the sense organ becomes assimilated to the object by becoming physically qualified in the same way as the object. It actually takes on the form of the object perceived: and the 'nature' (*phusis*) of the object now resides in the perceiver's intellect.

Although it is based on a very different understanding of natural philosophy, it is striking that in one of the main competitors to Aristotle's account of sense perception, that of the Epicureans, an analogous process guarantees veridicality. Everything is ultimately to be accounted for in terms of motion, weight, collision, and dislocation, these being what both knowledge and feeling, which are ultimately the same thing, consist in. Truth is in the senses, and there is nothing that we can appeal to beyond the senses to guarantee their veridicality. They are our sole source of knowledge, and what they tell us is that the universe is comprised of material bodies governed by the laws of physics. Accordingly, Epicurean epistemology held that the clarity of our sensations is the sole criterion of truth, and that the affective states that follow upon each of them—the way we are affected by them—are the sole criterion of what is good.

The Stoic account of epistemology mirrors this strongly naturalistic strain in Epicureanism. Like the Epicureans, the Stoics held that we acquire all our knowledge by means of the senses. The way things appear to us makes a kind of 'imprint' on us, and this results in a sensory image, or *phantasia*, in the mind. Once the *phantasia* has been deposited in the mind, it must be evaluated by the perceiver: some kind of acceptance by the person's mind of the propositional content of the appearance. The weakest form of this is 'assent' (*sunkatathesis*) and the next weakest 'belief' (*doxa*). The next stages, are 'apprehension' (*katalēpsis*) and 'knowledge' (*epistēmē*). With apprehension comes the shift from a mere belief to something about which you cannot be wrong. And it is apprehensive appearances that provide the Stoics with their 'criterion of truth', which gives us a guarantee that things are one way rather than another. If the appearance I assent to is apprehensive, then things are the way they appear to me to be; for I couldn't be wrong. The rationale for this is basically the same as that of Aristotle's account of veridicality: perception under normal or optimal circumstances is veridical because there is simply no other standard to be met. Apprehension is not the end of the matter in Stoic epistemology, however. The Stoics distinguished between apprehension and knowledge, and this is a distinctive feature of their account. Apprehension is the stage at which one could not be wrong: unlike belief, this kind of assent is guaranteed to get things right. If knowledge were simply a grasp of facts that excludes error, then we would have knowledge at this stage. But knowledge proper is actually a further stage, and this is not achieved until the particular facts are grasped in systematic interconnection, one that supports explanations. Apprehension, requiring less, can be done by anyone. Knowledge, for the Stoics, is very much the result of building up beliefs: the nearer you get to knowledge the more coherent, cohesive, and mutually supporting are your beliefs. The idea of a knowledge beyond mere apprehension is part of Stoic holism: ultimately knowledge is not knowledge of the bits, but of the whole, and only the latter is true or ultimate knowledge, because only it results in true understanding.

The Stoic account of epistemology mirrors Aristotle's account of the demonstration in crucial respects. Just as the Stoics argue that knowledge in itself cannot be the ultimate aim of the exercise, that one needs to proceed to systematic connections, so too Aristotle insists that establishment of clear validity of arguments cannot in itself be the ultimate aim of the exercise; that one cannot stop at what the syllogism provides, but must go on to distinguish conclusions that 'spring from the nature of things'. The point of ancient epistemology is different from that of modern epistemology, in that it has a constraint absent in the latter: it must result in understanding, and mere knowing whether or not something is the case is not understanding. The ultimate aim in Aristotle is to grasp not just truths, but also how these truths arise: to supply something with genuine explanatory power. The Stoic programme makes even stronger demands: the explanation must capture and reflect the interconnected holistic nature of the cosmos. Genuine understanding must ultimately mirror the structure of the cosmos.

There is a moral dimension to understanding the cosmos and one's place in it, and it is metaphysics that leads one to the ethically motivated constraints on philosophical enquiry. The moral dimension of Hellenistic epistemology is manifest even in the Pyrrhonists, who denied that nature provides us with a guarantee of veridicality, and argued that we cannot reliably form beliefs about the world. Accordingly, they advocated suspension of judgement, but suspension of judgement is a means to an end for the Pyrrhonists, not an end in itself. The ultimate point of the exercise is what is termed *ataraxia* or *apatheia*—'freedom from disturbance', 'tranquillity'—and it is achieved by an intellectual journey. The journey begins when one investigates some question or field of enquiry and finds that opinions conflict as to where the truth lies. The usual hope of the investigation—for Epicureans and Stoics, for example—is that *ataraxia* will be attained only if we can discover the rights and wrongs of the matter and give our assent to the truth. The difficulty is that, in any matter, things will appear differently to different people according to one or another of a variety of circumstances. Conflicting appearances cannot be equally true, so one needs a criterion of truth. But, the Pyrrhonist argues, no such criterion is available, with the result that we are left with conflicting appearances and the conflicting opinions based on them, unable to find any reason for preferring one to another, and therefore bound to treat all of equal strength and equally worthy (or unworthy) of acceptance. But we cannot accept them all, because they conflict, or make a choice between them, for lack of a criterion, so we cannot accept any: we are forced to admit the equal strength of opposed assertions. So far as truth is concerned, we must suspend judgement. And it is only when the Pyrrhonist suspends judgement that the possibility of *ataraxia* arises. It is ultimately directed towards a state in which, by suspending all one's beliefs-cum-opinions-cum-judgements, one is finally completely at peace with the world. This understanding of one's place in the world as constitutive of morality offers an integrated conception of morality, as the end point of understanding, as an account of what we aim for in life. Such an integrated conception of morality, which in various forms is characteristic of ancient philosophy, stands in stark contrast to what Anscombe identified as 'modern moral philosophy',[16] in which what is at issue are duties, obligations, rules, and laws. Rather, metaphysical, epistemological, and moral ends come to be interrelated and coordinated, in ancient conceptions of the good life.

For each of the four forms of philosophical enquiry that we have considered in this chapter—those of Aristotle, the Stoics, the Epicureans, and the Pyrrhonists—what is ultimately at stake is understanding our place in the world, and this has cognitive, affective, and moral dimensions. Whether one is pursuing epistemology, metaphysics, natural philosophy, or ethics, self-understanding is a central part of the exercise, variously conceived under the rubric of *eudaimonia*, *apatheia*, or *ataraxia*, all of which can be considered a general search for wisdom.

The attraction of philosophy had depended crucially on its ability to supply a general picture of a range of questions, from our place in the cosmos to self-understanding. It is on this that the value and legitimacy of ancient philosophy rested. And it was philosophy's success in this respect that came into question at the end of the Hellenistic period, as a wholly different kind of discourse offered conceptions of self-understanding and one's place in the order of things that turned out to have far greater appeal.

CHAPTER THREE

Philosophy's Loss
of Autonomy

WE HAVE JUST SEEN THAT questions about how to live one's life are not confined to ethics in Hellenistic philosophy. In fact, from Plato onwards, no classical or Hellenistic philosopher treats morality as an autonomous realm of enquiry, separating moral from natural-philosophical or metaphysical questions: these are always considered interlocking parts of the whole. But the centre of gravity does vary. Whereas for Aristotle, for example, *eudaimonia*—'the good life' or 'human flourishing'—has 'excellence' or virtue (*aretē*) at its centre, and while for the Stoics *aretē* is in effect constitutive of *eudaimonia*, for the Epicureans and Pyrrhonists the questions do not centre on *aretē*. In Epicurus, the key to *eudaimonia* lies in his psychological theory, one of the principal aims of which was to deny the survival of the personality after death, showing that beliefs in a system of rewards and punishments as recompense for life on earth are mere mythology. This is very different from virtue, as understood in Aristotle or the Stoics. The Pyrrhonists also see the goal in terms of achieving a particular state of mind, tranquillity, which has little connection with virtue as such. Moreover, both the Epicureans and the Pyrrhonists embed *eudaimonia* within a naturalistic context. For the Epicureans, everything is composed simply of atoms, and sensations and morality are thought through in these terms. For the Pyrrhonists, we are so integrated with the world that it is impossible to transcend the particularity of the world.

More generally, we can trace a move towards more naturalistic understandings of the good life from Plato onwards. But as well as this increase in naturalistic understanding, there is another clearly discernable movement. In the *Nicomachean Ethics*, Aristotle notes that while there is very general agreement that *eudaimonia* is the highest good, there is no agreement on what it consists in.[1] As we move into the Hellenistic era, there is a shift that goes beyond simple disagreement. The Greek terms—*ataraxia* (tranquillity) and *apatheia* (serenity)—that come to be employed to describe the good life are negative terms, bearing the alpha-privative prefix. The term *ataraxia* designates that one is *un*troubled by external things, while *apatheia* designates an *un*disturbed mind. The good life is 'peace of mind', freedom from various things, not something positive as it is in Aristotle, for whom *eudaimonia* is living and doing well. Literally, *eudaimonia*—good or well (*eu*) spirit or god (*daimōn*)—means being in the state of a benevolent deity. *Ataraxia* and *apatheia*, by contrast, have a decided air of resignation about them. What is at issue here is not a question of Aristotle and the Hellenistic philosophers having a philosophical disagreement about the nature of *eudaimonia*. In the wake of the collapse of Athens and the dispersal of its maritime allies at the end of the fourth century, the challenges facing the population change significantly: the economy was in serious decline and wars (now fought almost exclusively by professional mercenaries) became endemic. In the wake of

Alexander's conquests, the self-contained polis was replaced by the *oikoumenē*, 'the world'. The Hellenistic philosophers are redefining the good life in the light of a major cultural shift, one that is going to prove problematic for the standing of philosophy in the ancient world.

The Good Life

The Greek term *ēthikē* meant, as John Cooper notes, 'the philosophical study of human moral character, good and bad, and of the determinative function in structuring a person's life that their character was assumed to have—character being their particular, psychologically fixed and effective, outlook on human life, and on the differing weight and worth in a life of the enormously varied sorts of valuable things that the natural and the human worlds make available to us'.[2] Socrates's discussion of *aretē*, as presented in Plato's early dialogues, ties it directly to *eudaimonia*. The claim is that it is necessary and sufficient for *eudaimonia*. At the same time, he associates it with knowledge, so that there is in effect a tripartite connection between *aretē*, *eudaimonia*, and *epistēmē*. The association of the first two is not as surprising as it might seem, for while the meaning of the Greek term *aretē* covers 'virtue' in the modern English moral sense, it is not confined to it, more generally designating any 'excellence', including physical qualities. It is when it is combined with *epistēmē* that it takes the form of a distinctive doctrine, for this focuses its meaning. The combination evolves from Socrates's forensic probing of his interlocutors' views on the nature of such qualities as justice and self-control, showing that morality in general is not only deeper seated, but typically more poorly understood, than these interlocutors suppose. In the process he brings to the surface some of the confusions that he believes plague it, and opens up questions of moral responsibility. Pursuing honour or riches, he argues, cannot lead to the *eudaimonia* that we all seek. Instead, we need to grasp what is good, and understand why it is good. This is why *aretē* is a form of knowledge. Such knowledge is crucial to care for one's soul, it provides guidance as to what is and is not valuable, and it provides motivation to follow such guidance. This makes philosophy central to *eudaimonia*. It enables us to uncover the reality beneath the appearances, so that we do not find ourselves acting simply on the latter, and this is a universal desideratum, for everyone acts in accord with what they hold to be best. As Socrates puts it in the *Protagoras*, philosophical understanding shows us the truth, and as a consequence provides us with peace of mind firmly rooted in truth.[3]

In the early 'Socratic' dialogues, the search for virtue and *eudaimonia* is to be found in human affairs. When Plato subsequently comes to elaborate on this Socratic thesis, he fills out the argument that selfish and calculating notions of justice— for example, that of Callicles in the *Gorgias*, or Thrasymachus in the *Republic*—cannot lead to *eudaimonia*, and that virtue is necessary for a happy or contented life. But a new element appears in the middle dialogues. The Form of the Good comes to the fore, and ultimate moral values are sought in the Forms, which are independent of the sensory world, and accordingly that of human affairs. A further change is evident in the later dialogues, as an association between the realm of Forms and the sensory realm is suggested. Here Plato identifies the characteristics of the virtuous mind that mark it out as eudaimonic in terms of fostering an inner harmony and unity: it makes one whole. In fact, as early as the *Republic*, justice had been put forward as the unifying quality of the soul,[4] but the theme of harmony comes into its own in the later dialogues, particularly in the *Timaeus*, where Plato tells us that we must exercise 'the highest part of the soul' in such a way that it achieves harmony with the universe, and that in this way it is assimilated to a form of divinity.[5]

For Aristotle, as for Plato, the key to *eudaimonia* lies in *theōria*. Plato maintains that *theōria* informs useful and necessary action in the practical world, and the *Republic* makes it clear that the philosopher who has grasped the Form of the Good must return to educate the political class. This rests on a fundamental misunderstanding in Aristotle's view, namely the assumption that the Forms, such as the Form of the Good, could be useful for practical action. Practice, he points out in the *Nicomachean Ethics*, deals with particulars, with the complex shifting world of human affairs, for which the Forms could not possibly be of any use.[6] For Aristotle, *theōria* must be a disinterested form of activity, and he explicitly privileges useless knowledge: it actualizes *nous*, our divine part, and it comprises purely noetic activity, of the kind that the gods engage in. Its value lies in its being an end in itself, self-sufficient, a completely independent form of activity. This enables it to be noble and ennobling, closely associated with the idea of an aristocratic value. The route to the conception of *theōria* as self-sufficient gives this some plausibility. Aristotle's discussion in the *Nicomachean Ethics* starts with goods on which all would agree: friendship, pleasure, health, honour, courage, and so on. The question of which of these is the highest good is not straightforward, however, and he supplies three criteria by which we might recognize the highest good: it must be desirable in its own right; it must not be desirable for the sake of anything else; and any other good must be desirable for the sake of this highest good alone. It is *theōria* alone that meets these criteria.

The problem is that severing the link between *theōria* and the practices of daily life has the consequence that the contemplative theorist need not be an ethically good person, or, if they are, this cannot be due to *theōria* per se for, as Nightingale points out, *theōria* operates in a sphere that has no connection to ethical and political life.[7] The separation means that we must distinguish between theoretical and practical reasoning. In the *Nicomachean Ethics*, theoretical wisdom (*sophia*) is knowledge (*epistēmē*), combined with a more intuitive form of intellection (*nous*), of those things that are highest by nature; and possession of it is, we are told, rare, marvellous, difficult, and divine, but also useless for any practical concerns. By contrast, practical wisdom (*phronēsis*) 'is concerned with human affairs and matters about which it is possible to deliberate. For we say that the ability to deliberate well is the characteristic of the practical man, but nobody deliberates about things that cannot vary, or have no practical goal'.[8]

Nevertheless, Aristotle wants to keep theoretical and practical reasoning as closely connected as possible, and he suggests that practical reasoning is concerned with a 'kind of truth':

> What affirming and negating are in thinking, pursuing and avoiding are in desire. Because moral virtue is a state that is expressed through its purposes, and purpose is a deliberative desire, then the reasoning must be true and the desire must be good if the purpose is to be good, and the desire must pursue what the thought affirms. This is the kind of reasoning and the kind of truth in which the practical consists. As regards the intellect, which is contemplative and not practical or productive, the good and the bad are truth and falsity respectively (for this is what is done by whatever is intellectual). As regards the part which is practical and intellectual, the good state is truth in agreement with right desire.[9]

The difficulties in connecting the theoretical and the practical realms are exacerbated due to the close relation between ethics and politics, which are jointly indispensable for our well-being. The *Nicomachean Ethics*, as its final section indicates, is in effect the first half of a work whose second half is the *Politics*, where the explicitly practical knowledge that comprises political understanding is set out. There can be no doubt that Aristotle deals with these questions in a particularly thoughtful and considered fashion, but there remains a gap between his account and his explicitly philosophical treatment of the good life. What this shows is that, with intellectual sophistication, ethical and political questions can be dealt with in a thought-provoking and plausible way. The problem is that one can do this without philosophy. But the whole point of the exercise was surely to show how philosophical enquiry leads to a way of life that is superior to any other. The lack of connectivity means that it is difficult to understand what contribution Aristotle's philosophical conception of *eudaimonia* could make.

Alternatively, we must consider the possibility that we are reading Aristotle's account in too Platonic a top-down way. The discussion at the beginning of the *Nicomachean Ethics* suggests that we can look at the question differently. There, Aristotle argues that no one can take part in the philosophical study of ethics and politics without first having acquired good and virtuous habits of feeling.[10] The suggestion is that meeting this condition allows one to seek a rationale for moral behaviour that one is already engaging in. In other words, it may be possible to establish a connection between moral behaviour and the philosophical notion of the good life by starting from the former. Someone whose behaviour displays the commonly recognized social and moral virtues, but who has only an intuitive grasp of morality (*epieikēs*), needs to use the philosophical notion to provide a broader and deeper understanding of, and justification for, this behaviour, to become an *agathos*. But the problem remains, that not only does there not seem to be anything distinctively moral about the philosophical understanding of *eudaimonia*, but it is difficult to understand in what way the conception it offers bears on morality. Such worries increased after Aristotle, particularly among the Roman Stoics, and Seneca, as Cooper notes, 'often ignores or downplays philosophical argument in favor of other ways of encouraging his readers to embrace a Stoic way of life'.[11] This reflects a deep problem about the efficacy of philosophical argument in understanding the good life.

What is happening in the move from a Platonic conception of morality and the good life to an Aristotelian one can be summed up as follows. Plato, in an attempt to counter moral conventionalism, had ended up making it subject to a purely contemplative realm. Aristotle believes that such contemplative reasoning fails to capture the nature of morality. And he is surely correct in this for, as we have seen, much—perhaps all—moral reasoning is crucially tied up with the emotions and/or subject to casuistic decision making that is a function of particular circumstances. I have taken the discussion of behaviour in Greek drama as indicative of the former, and day-to-day reasoning relative to one's 'office' as indicative of the latter. But it is unclear to what extent these two are subject to philosophical—second-order—reasoning, reasoning that establishes unchanging universal principles. Accordingly, what Aristotle sets out to do is to join the two realms by establishing how the forms of reasoning appropriate to each are intimately connected. He makes no attempt to show how the content of the one can be subsumed under the other: he does not reduce moral decision making to a set of purely intellectual considerations derived from reflection on the nature of morality. Plato's attempts had shown the futility of going in this direction. But Aristotle's approach does generate a serious problem. To make the relation one of patterns of reasoning does not allow the gap between contemplative reasoning and moral behaviour to be closed up in such a way that the paradigm bearer of theoretical knowledge is ipso facto moral. For that, one would need to assimilate the content of the two realms, and that is precisely what he realizes he cannot do.

This division is reflected in Aristotle's conception of god, or gods—Aristotle is not consistent about the number of gods, and it is clearly not something he considers very important. The subject of his 'first philosophy' is something that is independent of us and unchanging. In the *Physics*, this entity is identified as an 'unmoved mover', ultimately responsible for changes of position or state. In chapter 9 of *Metaphysics* Λ Aristotle explores the nature of this god's activity. God is pure form—the only pure form that Aristotle allows; so its activity is thinking, and the object of its thought must be constant, otherwise it would be changing; and the highest and most appropriate object of thought is itself. The relation between the theoretical and the practical, problematic in Aristotle's moral theory, becomes unbridgeable in his theology.

How could one respond to Aristotle's dilemma? One solution would be to make morality a matter of casuistry and forget about seeking universal principles. Another, perhaps complementary, solution would be to make moral decision making depend on sensibility and affect, and forget the idea of morality being regulated by rationality. But, certainly for classical philosophers, and to a great extent for subsequent philosophers, this would effectively be to remove morality from the realm of philosophy. On the other hand, it is hard to see how there could be a successful assimilation of casuistry and sensibility to an abstract, universal account of the nature of morality, that is, to a *philosophical* account of morality, as understood in antiquity. The business of explanation cannot be handed over, even in part, to non-philosophical forms of understanding, because then the precepts of morality would cease to be abstract and universal: we would no longer be in the realm of philosophy, but in that of drama or common sense. This prompts the question of what is to be gained from translating ethical questions into a second-order discourse.

The Undisturbed Life

As we move from the philosophies forged in the democratic Greek city state to those developed in the monarchies of the increasingly cosmopolitan, but violent and unpredictable, Hellenistic and then Roman imperial worlds, philosophical thought shifts gear. Above all, what is expected from *eudaimonia* changes radically. Yet there are some underlying continuities, even if they take on a new dimension. In Plato, as we have seen, the idea of *eudaimonia* as a form of harmony gradually comes to the fore. The conception of harmony as a regulative principle, displacing single principles such as water, air, or fire first comes with Anaximander, whose cosmos, in which 'opposites' struggle for power, is ruled by a system of justice. By contrast, the idea of an *inner* harmony comes to the fore in Hellenistic conceptions of *eudaimonia*, and a great deal of attention is paid to obstacles to inner harmony: including a full-scale assault on the emotions in the case of the Stoics, who consider them distorted or false value judgements. It is helpful to think of *eudaimonia* less as something well defined, that takes different contents at different times, than as a series of differing responses to perceived new threats to well-being. Indeed, in the case of Roman philosophy these were deadly threats, with its two greatest representatives, Cicero and

Seneca, respectively being beheaded and forced to commit suicide. Political and other issues were mixed up here, but we do know of at least one Stoic philosopher, Musonius Rufus, who was explicitly sent into exile for his philosophical views alone. *Eudaimonia* is anchored in natural philosophy for Epicurus. The soul (*anima*) is a material body, but since soul atoms are unusually fine and round, they do not cling together. They need to be held in place by the larger and more tightly assembled atoms of the body. At death, when the soul atoms are scattered, the body loses all feeling. One of the consequences of Epicurus's psychological theory, which denied the survival of the personality after death, was the rejection of beliefs in a system of rewards and punishments as recompense for life on earth. Such beliefs were a source of anxiety for those who held them, and the principal aim of Epicurean atomism was the removal of anxiety. As he argued, and as Lucretius would elaborate at much greater length, most fear death because they believe it to be the end of all sensation. Lucretius uses an argument to remove such fear, which simply asserts that this is a true belief and therefore no grounds for anxiety: for why, he asks, would anyone fear something they could not perceive? Events that took place before we were born do not disturb us, for we weren't aware of them, so why should we have any worries about what happens after we die? Nothing can disturb us when we cease to be conscious of it.

What about when we are alive? The Platonic and Aristotelian conception of the necessity of public life is rejected by Epicurus. Justice, one of the virtues most associated with public life, is correspondingly subordinated to pleasure (*hēdonē*): its aim is to establish the maximum of security and untroubledness. In fact the virtues generally are wholly subordinated to pleasure—the life of pleasure and the trouble-free life are the same thing—and as a consequence there is nothing that we could call moral obligation or moral evil in the Epicurean system. Our senses feel pleasures and pains, and these pleasures and pains indicate what is appropriate and inappropriate to our human natures. Pleasure is a guide to a certain aspect of reality, and pain indicates what is hostile to our existence as human beings. Consequently, Epicurus argues, we direct our lives in accordance with these criteria, and it is right that we should so direct them.

What is distinctive of the Epicurean position here is that, whereas Plato and Aristotle had considered *eudaimonia* within the context of the polis, the Epicurean notion of the good life depended on an exclusively personal ethics, not something specific to the polis, or any other form of social organization. This is reflected in Epicurus's account of the gods which, compared with that of Aristotle, highlights a shift in how *eudaimonia* is conceived. The 'sublime happiness' of the gods is incompatible with any involvement in our affairs. This is close to Aristotle's understanding, but Epicurus's reason for arguing in this way is analogous to his reason for rejecting public life in the case of human beings: happiness, whether human or divine, requires for its full realization a life of uninterrupted tranquillity or freedom from pain. Aristotle had considered that a life free from certain kinds of cares, something that takes a paradigmatically aristocratic form, was necessary for *eudaimonia*, but for Aristotle these are the preconditions of *eudaimonia*, whereas for Epicurus they are constitutive of it.

As with Epicurus, the connection between ethics and natural philosophy in Stoicism turns on the question of naturalism, albeit a very different form of naturalism from that of the Epicureans. Although Aristotle defined the soul, *nous*, in terms of its functioning in a natural relationship with the body, he still considered it immortal and separable from the body.

There were consistency problems here. Aristotle's followers realized this, as did the Stoics. Despite the fact that he had relocated the Platonic forms within material beings, they were still forms, principles of structure. His ambivalence between the Platonic formal and structural way of looking at being and an account that works in terms of an internal dynamic principle is reflected in his fluctuating between the notion of a form—*eidos*—which is static and imposed on matter, and that of activity or actualization—*energeia*—which is internal, to describe what goes on in substances. By contrast, the founder of the Stoic school, Zeno of Citium, purged the cosmos of its last traces of Aristotelian transcendentalism. He saw both being in general and the universe of individual beings as an immense physical organism, and so was led by the analogy with living beings to an internal principle that had already been discussed in fifth-century medical circles: the *pneuma*, or vital spirit.

Zeno promoted the *pneuma* to a prominent position as the vital fluid or breath that flows throughout organic being, and *logos* became a principle that extended throughout the system, from the person to the entire cosmic organism. *Pneuma* was part of the vital continuum that ran through the organism of the universe, in its upper regions as the pure fire of the sun and the planets, and elsewhere in a progressively grosser corporeal form. Everywhere, above and below, it represents reason, *logos*, as well as a divine creative and providential force. The idea of the unity of philosophy plays a crucial role for the Stoics here, for it belongs to the very essence of metaphysical reflection, corresponding as it does to the organic coherence of the cosmos. All parts of the universe are interdependent, and the cosmos is a living organism, animated and permeated by creative spirit or reason. The cosmos and all within it are in the grip of an inexorable and purposeful chain of causality, the soul of each individual being a particle of the divine substance that penetrates everywhere. Because of this divine animation, no part of the universe can be affected without having some impact on the whole. In particular, celestial bodies and their movements can affect terrestrial events, since they both belong to the same organic unity. Human life, because it is included in an organic whole and develops in the course of time, is constantly influenced by the totality to which it belongs. Every aspect of our lives forms part of a coherent whole, a whole ultimately regulated by considerations of the good life.

The Vagaries of Platonism

Both Plato and Aristotle founded schools: the Academy and the Lyceum respectively. The Lyceum initially covered the full range of Aristotle's interests, but later there was a divergence between those members of the Lyceum, such as Ariston of Ceos, whose main concern was with ethical questions, and those interested almost exclusively in physical questions, most notably Strato, who shaped Aristotelianism in the Hellenistic era. However, while it is true that there were extensive commentaries on Aristotle's works, by Aristotelian philosophers such as Alexander of Aphrodisias, and by Platonist philosophers such as Simplicius and Philoponus, these were works written for a very select few, and Aristotle's ethical works in particular were almost completely ignored.

By contrast, the Platonist tradition experienced something of a revival towards the end of the Hellenistic period, and 'Platonic' philosophy took two very different directions: one following Socratic forms of questioning, distinctive of Plato's early dialogues, the other, the 'Neoplatonists', developing Plato's metaphysics, distinctive of his later dialogues, in a theological direction. The first was a feature of the Academy from 265BCE, when Arcesilaus took over as its head. Rather than any specific Platonic doctrine, Arcesilaus promoted a form of Socratic *elenchos*. The procedure, one of cross-examination, was exclusively critical: it was to examine a position and show how it led to a self-contradiction. There was no belief or claim that could not be shown to be unreliable. But there is a stark contrast with Pyrrhonism here. In Arcesilaus, it is a matter of criticism, and there is no trace of what, for Pyrrho, was the point of the exercise. This is also true of a later figure in the Academy, Carneades, who focused on undermining the knowledge claims of the Stoics. Academic scepticism led nowhere.

The Academics and the Neoplatonists, despite their shared connection with Plato, could not have been more different. Although it had predecessors in the 'Middle Platonists' of the first century BCE and the first two centuries CE, Neoplatonism effectively began with Plotinus.[12] Both Middle Platonism and Neoplatonism are characterized by a high degree of syncretism, concerned to blend seemingly disparate philosophies into a single doctrine, although Neoplatonism does have a particularly distinctive element: its embrace of the doctrine that the realm of Forms is ontologically prior to the sensible world, and that the world is ontologically tiered, with a highest Form that is the single principle (*archē*), which is creative and divine. Here ontology comes into its own right. Not only does everything depend on the 'degree of reality' that a thing has, but everything ultimately derives from the highest Form—'the One', also referred to as 'the Good', because Plotinus identifies it with the Form of the good in Plato's *Republic*—in that the next lowest ontological level consists of 'emanations' from the highest level; but it is this next lowest level that gives rise to the next ontological level down through emanation. In other words, although everything can be traced back to 'the One', it does not actually create the rest of the cosmos in its own right: this is a sequential process. At the same time, nothing exists at a lower ontological level which is not prefigured at a higher level.

The first emanation of 'the One' is intellect or consciousness (*nous*), which is described as a *hupostasis*, the fundamental reality that supports everything else. It is a 'second' *hupostasis*, and its activity consists in turning back on its origin, understanding the precondition of its own existence. In this respect it is not unlike Aristotle's god, except that instead of engaging in a purely intellectual contemplation of itself it engages in a purely intellectual contemplation of its cause. This approach is reflected in Plotinus's account of the virtues. The 'civic virtues'—such as justice, moderation, and courage— are the desires of appetite, resulting from 'habits and exercises', and play no role in human self-fulfilment. The purificatory or purifying virtues, by contrast, are those that enhance one's capacity for thought about the Forms, and are our route to a more divine, less embodied state. They are those virtues that draw us away from attention to the body and its experiences (note the way in which these are defined negatively). There is no sense at all in Plotinus of *eudaimonia* as the good life of an embodied human being: 'living well' comprises intellectual activity directed at the Forms.

The Hellenistic schools of philosophy, particularly Epicureanism and Stoicism, had between them an appeal across a range of sectors of society, but Neoplatonism had an exceptionally wide influence, to such an extent that it looks in certain respects like a different kind of enterprise. It acted as a unifying programme to which virtually anyone—with the exception of advocates of atomism—could subscribe, from Christian zealots to cultivated pagan intelligentsia, from marginalized groups to political leaders. The major Western religions—Christianity, Islam, Judaism—each came to make use of Neoplatonism to provide a philosophical formulation of theological doctrines, but it also held an appeal for secular thinkers. Why was this? Neoplatonism was committed to disengaging oneself from the material world entirely and moving to a purely intellectual realm, and one can perhaps see some attraction in this for those living in the violent and unpredictable world of the early centuries of the common era. But beyond this, the level of abstraction at which Neoplatonism works makes it difficult to understand what connection it could have with other philosophical doctrines. It is really a metaphilosophy of philosophy, encompassing other schools within itself in its totalizing syncretism, taking the idea of philosophy as an essentially second-order form of enquiry to a new third-order level.

But what form does this third-level enquiry take? There are some arguments in thinkers like Plotinus, on the nature of sense perception, for example, that are philosophically distinctive, and unlike other Neoplatonists, Plotinus's syncretism does not lead him simply to assimilate Plato and Aristotle.[13] But in general, engagement with the issues is what might be described as contemplative, rather than investigatory. Of the precepts that we identified earlier the focus is very much on the last two, the rejection of argument for argument's sake and the central role of abstraction, rather than on the first two, the disambiguation of premises and the use of reason. Indeed, in such an all-encompassing holist project, it is hard to imagine how disambiguation could not be sacrificed. 'The One' is effectively construed as ineffable, yet it is treated as the ultimate source of all else. What we can say about it is that it is completely abstract, not 'one something' but simply unity, and that it provides unity for the multiple nature of everything else.

This is important, because degree of unity mirrors ontological stratum: the visible world, for example, in virtue of being spatial and temporal, lacks the degree of unity of the realm of Forms, and is therefore ontologically dependent on them. The Forms themselves are treated, following Plato's account in the *Timaeus*,[14] as the objects of thought of a divine intellect.

As well as the Intellect (*nous*), there is another *hupostatis*, 'Soul' (*psuchē*), and Plotinus divides the world into these two: they cover the intelligible and the sensible respectively, and the Soul is responsible for connecting the intelligible and sensible realms. Two of three ways in which priority and dependence in the hierarchy are exercised are familiar from Plato: the lower stratum 'participates' in the higher one, and the higher one generates the lower as an imperfect image of itself. The third is the distinctive Neoplatonic doctrine of 'emanation', and Plotinus uses the analogy of the sun radiating light, which has diminishing power the further it is radiated from the source. The lowest level, that is, the furthest from the source, is matter, conceived as a propertyless receptacle or substratum, and just above this is matter endowed with qualities, with form, a reflection of the higher-level Platonic Forms. Note, however, that the lower levels are different kinds of instantiation of the higher ones, and are not distinct in their own right: there are no individual souls, for example, simply many instantiations of the highest 'Soul'.

Abstraction is a necessary feature of philosophy in antiquity, as we have seen, but Neoplatonism is more like an abstract reflection on philosophies than a philosophy in its own right. It brings together selected elements of classical philosophy, particularly Plato, but also Aristotle, and Hellenistic philosophy, above all Stoicism. The Hellenistic search for a harmony of understanding now becomes a search for a unity of understanding. It promotes a synthesis of these philosophical ingredients under what can only be described as a second level of abstraction (i.e., a third level of enquiry), by contrast with Plato's Forms, for example, which are part of philosophical understanding, not something that stands above it. This second level of abstraction is something completely transcendent, in that there is nothing that we can say about it, and no way in which we can comprehend it. It does not look at all like a level of *philosophical* abstraction, and it is entirely contentless from a philosophical perspective. But what if it could be given content, in such a way that it could stand over philosophical abstraction and subordinate it to extra-philosophical criteria? This is what the Christianization of Neoplatonism does, subordinating philosophy to a theological programme, robbing it of autonomy, and replacing philosophy as the vehicle for understanding the world and our place in it. Philosophy, as it was understood in Plato and his successors, is now considered to have failed in its tasks, and is replaced by theology, which draws on the philosophical tradition simply as one resource among others. It rewrites the history of philosophy as simply a pale version of Christianity, one in which, according to the late second-century Church Father Clement of Alexandria for example,[15] the Greeks had stolen their wisdom from the Hebrews, but distorted it, so that the task was now to recover the original, genuine religious content.

Perhaps the best way to capture how Neoplatonism helps effect the transition from philosophy to theology is to consider the different ways in which Plato's Analogy of the Cave can be read. The distinctive feature of genuine philosophical enquiry for Plato is that it seeks the reality underlying the appearances. By engaging the world of appearances appropriately we can see through them to the world of Forms, the realm of reality. His image of the cave, whereby there is a completely different world from that of the shadows which are all we have had access to up to this point, might suggest parallel worlds of appearance and reality. But in classical and Hellenistic philosophy the aim is not to renounce appearances, but to use them as a guide to reality. We see the world differently as a result of philosophical enlightenment only in a metaphorical sense, not literally. For the Neoplatonists, by contrast, the aim is to transcend appearances completely and grasp reality directly. The problem derives from Plato, for despite his insistence on the idea that the path to reality is via reason, Plato's cave suggests the idea of a separate realm of truth existing independently of our ordinary cognitive life, in which case it is unclear why reason should provide the route to this reality. Nor is Christianity the only religion to see an opening here. The Neoplatonism of the late fourth-/early fifth-century philosopher Iamblichus was a pagan mirror of the developing Christian view of philosophy. Believing that the soul was damaged in its metaphysical descent into the material world, and that, *contra* Plotinus, reascent was impossible by purely intellectual means, he argued that (pagan) forms of ritual were needed.

The Neoplatonist movement had a commitment to reason, but it was a reason that one ultimately transcended once one had reached reality. Indeed, it is striking that those who take up the Platonist option, both in late antiquity and in the Renaissance, see their project in terms of an interpretation of nature, something which uncovers hidden truths, and which is more like interpretation of a sacred text, in which one seeks to uncover a hidden and unique truth, than something to be pursued in terms of philosophical or empirical investigation. And it is no less striking that it is such a notion that pervades Christian theology and Augustinian metaphysics, where we cannot reach a transcendent reality through rational means, but also require the sacraments.

The Christian Assimilation of Philosophy

Christianity was originally in open competition with Neoplatonism, and with philosophy more generally. 'What can there
be in common between Athens and Jerusalem, between the
Academy and the Church, between heretics and Christians?'
asks Tertullian, the founder of Latin theology, in Book 7 of
his *De præscriptionibus hæreticorum*. 'We have no need for
curiosity since Jesus Christ', he tells us, 'nor for enquiry since
the Evangelist.' Tertullian's hostility to philosophical learning derives from what he identifies as the use to which it had
been put by heretics, and his aim is to establish a single source
of authority, a single route to truth, namely Christian teaching, at a time when there were moves in the eastern parts
of the Roman Empire towards forms of religious pluralism,
and when there was an upsurge in theological speculation.[16]
When Tertullian tells us that 'secular wisdom rashly under-
takes to explain the nature and dispensation of God' and that
'heretics and philosophers deal with the same material, and
their arguments are largely the same', he identifies a problem
that is going to hound Christian thought. Christianity was
offering doctrines on questions on which there had been a
great deal of philosophical thought, and in writers like Tertullian it is offering these doctrines not initially on the basis
of engagement and criticism of earlier views (in the way that
Aristotle set out to refute and replace Plato's doctrines, for
example) but on the basis of a theologically motivated system of belief that runs along a completely different trajec-
tory. Yet many early Christians, Tertullian included, had been
converted from Neoplatonism. That is, they had moved from
a philosophical system to a theological one. They had abandoned a philosophical search for the truth for a theological
one. If these two routes conflicted then there were a number

of possible options open, along a spectrum running from abandonment to assimilation.

By the fourth century it was assimilation that was proving the more attractive path for those seeking to covert pagans and others to Christianity. In the Patristic period, we witness the gradual 'Christianization' of philosophy, begun by the early Latin Fathers and brought to completion by Augustine in the late fourth and early fifth centuries. In its early stages, the project is that of nurturing what is worthwhile in pagan thought in the nourishing atmosphere of Christian teaching, with Tertullian's Latin contemporary Clement of Alexandria, for example, presenting himself as Christ's gardener, cutting twigs from the rank, dried-back, and brittle bushes of pagan literature, and grafting them onto the stock of Christ's truth. In its later development, especially in the writings of Augustine, the project amounts to nothing short of a total translation of all philosophy into Christian terms. Christianity is conceived of as the final form of philosophy. Using the language of the classical philosophers to formulate his theology, Augustine attempts to show that Christianity is able to answer all the questions of classical metaphysics. In general terms, not only does Christianity supplement classical philosophy here, but it appropriates the teachings of this philosophy, denying that they were ever the property of the ancients in the first place. It not only construes every philosophical question in terms of Christian teaching, but initiates a widespread rejection of the moral and other qualities that marked out the ancient philosopher as the embodiment of wisdom and virtue.[17]

This appropriation of earlier thought made it possible for Christianity to present itself as the final answer to what earlier philosophers were striving for, and we should not underestimate just how successful it was in this respect. The main schools of Hellenistic philosophy had each sought to present a philosophy that transcended the flux and disorder of life and achieved peace of mind (*ataraxia* or *apatheia*). The Christian version of the search for peace of mind and tranquillity associates it with a state not fully achievable in this life, but which is a reward for what one does in this life, and which relies as much upon sacramental as upon intellectual enlightenment. It translates it from a philosophical project into something that meshes philosophical and religious concerns together into a synthesis whose phenomenal success indicates that it offered far more than any of the available religious or philosophical systems taken in their own right.

Clement had claimed that philosophy served the same function for the Greeks as the Torah did for the Jews, foreshadowing the coming of Christ; but the key figure in the gradual project of Christianization is Augustine. Drawing on a long tradition of thinking about the prehistory of Christianity, he sets out the basis for a reconciliation between Christian and classical thought. 'What is now called Christian religion', he writes, 'has existed among the ancients, and was not absent from the beginning of the human race until Christ came in the flesh; from which time true religion, which existed already, began to be called Christian'.[18] In other words, Christianity had, in some way, always existed, even before the incarnation. In fact, for Augustine, both the true religion and the true philosophy existed from the beginning of the time. In his discussion of Plato in Books 8 to 10 of the *De civitate dei*, a work written in the aftermath of Alaric's sack of Rome and very much with pagan refugees from Rome in mind, he speculates as to whether Plato could have had some knowledge of the Hebrew scriptures, and he suggests that the God of the 'Platonists' (i.e., Neoplatonists) is the same as that of Christianity, and even that they speak, albeit in a confused way, of the Trinity. Yet, he tells us, these same Neoplatonists cannot know God. They mistakenly believe that they can reach him by purely intellectual means, whereas in fact he can only be reached through the sacraments, which were instituted with the incarnation of Christ. For Augustine, the superiority of Christianity over ancient philosophies and over the contemporary rivals of Christianity lay in the institution of the sacraments. Augustine's claim is not that Christianity is ancient philosophy plus the sacraments; it is that ancient philosophy is Christianity minus the sacraments. Christianity is the culmination of all previous philosophical reflection and religious belief, something that can be glimpsed by the appropriate allegorical readings of the ancient philosophers and sages just as much as it can by the allegorical reading of the Old Testament.

The real challenge for theologians like Augustine was not paganism, however, but rival movements within Christianity: his aim is to establish Nicene orthodoxy. The idea of the presence of Christianity in the pre-Christian era has a doctrinal cutting edge, and the claim that Christianity is not something new is crucial to the version of Christianity that Augustine managed to establish. The issue on which everything turned was the vexed one of the relation between Christianity and its religious forebear, pre-Christian Judaism. In the early centuries of Christianity, there was for a while a close contest between those who, like Tertullian, saw Christianity as the true development of the religious precepts contained in the 'Old' Testament—as Christians came to designate it—and those who saw the two as completely opposed. The Manichaeans and Gnostics had held that the Old Testament had been abrogated by the coming of Christ, and that as a consequence it should be discarded. The second-century Gnostic Marcion, in his *Antitheus*, had set out the moral and theological discrepancies between the Old Testament and the Gospels, and argued that the former was the record of the Jewish God of Hate, something which was now superseded by the message of the God of Love in the Gospels. Christianity, for Marcion, began with the incarnation.[19] The God of the Old Testament was still accepted as divine, however, with the result that two independent realms of evil and good were postulated, with independent Gods ruling over these.

Augustine had himself been a Manichaean in his early twenties, but later became one of their fiercest critics. There was one feature of Manicheanism that he continued to accept, however: the idea that the natural world was alien to us, that we did not belong in it, and were not at home in it. This belief would continue throughout the Christian tradition, and indeed would underpin its authority, for it alone claimed to identify the source of this alienation.

The most pressing problem that Augustine faced in abandoning Manicheanism was to account for the source of evil. This was very much a theological issue, but his solution to it generated a long-standing philosophical problem. The difficulty lay in the range of solutions open to Christian theologians, which were constrained by the idea of God's omnipotence, a crucial feature of the Christian God, one that marked it out from the Greek and Roman gods. The conception of evil as simply a lack of goodness was at odds with a strong Christian sense of evil as a power, typified by the serpent in the Garden of Eden, that needed to be combated. The question then arose of the source of evil, so construed. God, who was a paradigm of benevolence, could not be responsible. The Manichaean separation of the vengeful God of the Old Testament from the God of love of the New Testament was not acceptable. This left human beings, but how could human beings be held responsible? The answer, for Augustine, lay in positing a new faculty in human beings: free will.[20]

The Stoics had devoted some attention to the will, and considered that possession of a will was what marked out humans from animals, who relied exclusively on instinct to guide their behaviour. Moreover, acting in accord with reason and contrary to our emotions was not something that reason alone could secure: it clearly involved an act of will. The conflict between the two is the subject of discussions of *akrasia*, which is the behaviour that results from a failure to follow what reason dictates, acting rather on motives that are contrary to it. Augustine's account of the will offers a contrast to accounts of ethical motivation couched in terms either of reason or sensibility. The ethical consideration of the passions now comes to be formulated in terms of the action of the will. The affections, which he treats as the soul's motions, cannot simply be referred to a criterion of rationality, as the Stoics had urged, but must be assessed in terms of the act of will from which they arise. For Augustine, if the will is wrongly directed the emotions will be wrong, whereas if the will is right, the emotions will be not only blameless but praiseworthy.[21] So, for example, a virtuous form of sadness or despair is ruled out on the Stoic view, but quite possible on Augustine's conception. The fundamental character of the will, which guides its inclinations, is love, and virtuous affections are to be distinguished from vicious ones in terms of the moral quality of the love that rules in the will.

Augustine's account can be considered as a response to a philosophical account, that of the Stoics, and as a response to what begins as a theological problem—the existence of evil in a world created by a perfectly good God—but then becomes a philosophical problem: that of whether the postulation of a 'free will' clarifies the question of responsibility for action. On the Stoic account of the cosmos, everything is governed by fate, identified with a sequence of causes. Nothing could happen otherwise than it does, and in any given set of circumstances one and only one result can follow; otherwise an uncaused event would occur. Fate is also identified with providence and with god, and thus with the *pneuma*, the instrument of the divine will, which penetrates the entire universe, bringing about and governing all processes within it and giving each thing its character. Chrysippus, however, sought to reconcile this with human responsibility (*eph'hēmin*) and with the ideas of praise, blame, punishment, and reward. He argued that we are responsible for those actions which, even though they are predetermined, depend chiefly on ourselves rather than on external factors, using the analogy of a cylinder and a cone. Just as the fact that these roll in different ways when pushed on a slope depends primarily not on the person who pushes them, who is only an auxiliary or initiating cause, but on their shape in each case, so the way in which different people react to the same stimulus depends primarily on their own characters. This raises the question of responsibility for character, which for the Stoics is a question of one's initial endowment and its development.

The reconciliation between the two—compatibilism—is certainly problematic, and it might seem that the postulation of 'free will' frees us from the necessity for such a problematic reconciliation, because it breaks the grip of determinism. But it does not, and in fact Christian theology found itself faced with much the same philosophical problem as Stoicism, offering much the same solution. The difficulties arose in the most direct form from the doctrine of God's omniscience. God knows about everything, including future contingent events. In other words he knows how we will behave in the future. But this surely means that our future behaviour cannot be within our power, but is predetermined. One solution, that of the sixteenth-century Jesuit Luis de Molina, was to argue that we

have free will, but because God foresees how we will exercise
that free will, he knows how we will behave. But rather than
resolving things, this complicates the philosophical problem
immeasurably. In particular, replacing the notion of 'free will'
with that of Stoic 'character' would change nothing: we could
reconcile God's foreknowledge with our own responsibility
for our actions by arguing that God has foreknowledge of our
actions because he has knowledge of our character, and knowledge of our character leads to knowledge of our behaviour.

Augustine's proposed solution to the theological problem
of the origin of evil is to translate the traditional philosophical concern with *akrasia* into an issue of the freedom of the
will. He argues that God has given us free will so that we can
decide whether to follow his precepts or reject them, and in
rejecting them we give rise to evil. Acting in a moral context on the basis of one's free will is supposed to secure two
things: to clarify how human beings are responsible for their
actions; and to identify a feature of moral reasoning that gives
it its distinctive character. But can it actually achieve either of
these? Consider an Aristotelian-type account of practical reasoning. On such an account, at least in ideal circumstances,
we reflect on the considerations relevant to a course of action
and, on the basis of this, we draw a conclusion and act on it.
The considerations may be poorly or ill thought out, and the
judgement may be a good or a bad one, but it is this process
that secures our responsibility for what we do. Nothing else is
required. The free will account effectively denies that we have
established responsibility in this way, and adds an extra stage
to secure responsibility, in which we judge whether or not to
act on the conclusion. In the extra stage of decision making,
we are not bound by rational argument or anything else, so are
'free' to act for or against the conclusion we have come to. Our
moral responsibility arises not in the process of the practical

reasoning by which we come to a decision as to how we should behave, but rather in the act of assenting to or dissenting from this decision.

But on what grounds does the will override a conclusion that we have come to about how the behave? It seems that the 'free' act, if it is to be free, must be unconstrained. We decide on the right course of action, but then, in order to make ourselves morally responsible for our behaviour, we show ourselves free to accept or reject it. Far from securing moral responsibility, this effectively insulates morality from practical reasoning and makes it the outcome of a random decision-making process. Indeed, can we even talk about the will being free? As Locke was to point out, the notion of freedom applies not to the will, but to our ability to act, and it is this that makes such acts voluntary. 'Free will' does not solve a philosophical problem about what it is in decision making that makes us responsible for our actions. What I want to draw attention to here is the way in which the notion of free will, and the will more generally, illustrates the use of philosophical arguments to establish a given theological position. There is nothing exploratory about such arguments: they provide a rationale, they are wholly justificatory. Philosophy is not only being put to use in a way that rids it of autonomy, but core ethical questions in classical and Hellenistic philosophy, such as the nature of friendship, drop out of consideration, as one's relations to others are refracted through the divine.

But what happened was due, at the most fundamental level, also to a failure of philosophy. Not a failure of particular schools of philosophy, but a failure of philosophy as a way of investigating fundamental questions about how to live. It was replaced by Christianity because Christianity found a non-philosophical way of dealing with the questions, one that had an immediate appeal. It secured the harmony that the

Hellenistic schools had sought by offering an uncompromis-
ing understanding of the unity of thought, and directing the
search for understanding away from an unsuccessful probative
form of enquiry into a successful form of contemplation.

Classical, Hellenistic, and Roman philosophers had considered the ultimate aims of knowledge to be wisdom, happiness,
and well-being. But Christianity transferred such aims into a
purely spiritual realm, such that they could only be attained in
a union with God, which was not realizable until after death.
The view of Christian theologians was that they had accom-
plished something that philosophers had been seeking in vain,
and they began to set out where philosophy had gone wrong.
In the early centuries of the Christian era, it began to be argued
that philosophy was intrinsically incomplete, unable to resolve
the fundamental questions it raised by relying wholly on its
own resources. But incorporated into Christian teaching, philosophy, as a set of tools subordinated to theological doctrine,
finally realized its true standing. This did not mean that the
reconciliation of various philosophical systems—or more usually selected ingredients from various philosophical systems—
with revelation and Christian dogma was not contested during
the Patristic era. But it did mean that philosophy was evaluated with respect to the contribution it made to the whole, a
whole that was ultimately governed by revealed religion: there
was one truth, one reality, that of Christianity. Philosophy simply dropped off the map in the Christian West, any tasks it had
set itself now sidelined or taken over by theology.

PART II

Philosophy Re-Purposed as the Ultimate Arbiter

CHAPTER FOUR

The Creation of an Autonomous Role for Philosophy

IN THE THIRTEENTH CENTURY a new and unprecedented role was forged for philosophy as a tool of reconciliation of different forms of understanding. This brought with it a degree of autonomy, reinstituting philosophy as an independent form of enquiry. This was not a straightforward or unproblematic development, and we need to understand how the notion of reconciliation came into the picture. As we have seen, Augustine had incorporated various philosophical systems into Christianity, making them parts, in themselves incomplete, of a Christian understanding of the world and thereby stripping them of any independent role. What the Church Fathers generally, and Augustine in particular, produced was a synthesis to which the notion of reconciliation was not only unnecessary but alien. Accordingly, we need to understand how the idea of reconciliation subsequently arose, and why the tool of reconciliation that emerged took

the form not only of philosophy, but a philosophy antitheti-
cal to the Neoplatonism that had provided the philosophical
terms in which Christian orthodoxy had largely been formulated. The need for reconciliation and the form it took are
separate questions, but in neither case was the motivation
philosophical: in the former it was politico-religious, in the
latter theological.

Philosophy as a Tool of Theology

In the course of the eleventh century, a new political and religious order began to be established in Europe. The forced
abdication of Pope Benedict IX by the Holy Roman Emperor
Henry III at the Synod of Rome in 1046 was followed by a
seventy-year dispute over the powers of popes and monarchs,
the Investiture Controversy. Gregory VII, who ascended to the
papacy in 1073, objected to the appointment of clergy by monarchs and nobles, and his first target was the removal of the
monarch's power to appoint popes. Asserting papal supremacy
over the entire Western church, he declared its independence
from secular control. The resolution of the Controversy in 1122
was the formative event that in effect made possible the re-
emergence of a philosophical culture in Europe. The Church
achieved a legal identity independent of emperors, kings, and
feudal lords, and what resulted was a separation of the ecclesiastical and secular realms. This was a formative development,
for the division into *ecclesia* and *mundus* gradually covered
every aspect of political and intellectual life. Its first manifestation was the legal division into autonomous ecclesiastical
and secular legal systems. In the wake of this, the emperor
Gratian codified canon law around 1140, harmonizing the
various legal traditions and providing new foundations for the
law. These developments created a new 'science' (*scientia*) of

law, establishing a principle of authority and legitimacy over discordant parties.

The procedures introduced to reconcile legal systems provided a model for the reconciliation of a range of other potentially conflicting systems, not least in the realm of theoretical understanding. The theology of the Church at this time was the integrated conception of the world which had received its canonical statement in Augustine. On this integrated conception, philosophy was a tool of theology, and there was no division into autonomous secular and ecclesiastical realms. With the subsequent division of the two, the potential for questions of reconciliation arises.

Around the same time as the Investiture Controversy arose, the intellectual standing of the Christian synthesis began to be tested with the expansion of Europe into the territories surrounding the Mediterranean basin, and there were concerted moves to convert various non-Christian groups. Islam posed a particular problem, for it had built up a body of sophisticated philosophical and theological doctrine. The response required a rethinking of the role of natural theology. Since the authority of revealed theology was primary for the Church Fathers and Augustine, natural theology traditionally occupied only an auxiliary role, one of elucidating and supporting the deliverances of scripture. But revealed theology was irrelevant for those who did not share the same sacred texts, and it is therefore at this juncture that we witness the beginnings of attempts to develop a natural theology, one in which basic Christian beliefs can be established independently of revelation.

Here arises something probably unique in the history of philosophy: a genuine need for philosophy. Consider two cases. The first is the dispute between Berengar and Lanfranc in the middle of the eleventh century, on the sacrament of the eucharist. Berengar had argued that accidents cannot subsist without a substance in which to inhere, so if in the eucharist the accidents of bread remain after the consecration, then its substance must remain, in which case a new substance must be added to that of the bread. In opposition to this view, Lanfranc argued that the substance of the bread is transformed into the 'true body' of Christ. His case depended crucially on the Aristotelian vocabulary of substance and accident, which he had learned from Boethius's translations of Aristotle's logical writings, but it was clear that without considerable refinement of the philosophical resources, little progress could be made on these contentious issues.

Fifty years later, the problems were exacerbated, as complex questions of the trinity and the incarnation were debated between Anselm and Roscelin. The issues raised the philosophical question of universals, and in the case of the question of the nature of the trinity, turned on the problem of whether species and genera have a reality of their own.[1] Anselm, taking a traditional Platonist view, assumes that they do, but Roscelin, following Aristotle's doctrine in the *Categories*, maintains that only individuals exist. Roscelin makes a move that is indicative of the direction the debate will take. In commenting on Aristotle's logical works, Boethius had contrasted two positions one might take on logical or semantic grounds: one is to assert the analytical priority of abstract ideas or universals, the other is to assert their analytical posteriority. Roscelin applies the distinction to metaphysics, arguing that individual things and the concepts signifying them are more real than the universal things. He then draws theological consequences from this metaphysical position. The Father, the Son, and the Holy Spirit are indeed true deities, and their names are meaningful. The term 'God', by contrast, which signifies the divine nature possessed by all three persons of the trinity, is a meaningless abstraction. Roscelin was charged with tritheism at the

Council of Soissons in 1092, one of his principal accusers being Anselm. Anselm's own position had been that just as when we say of someone that he is 'white', 'just', and 'literate', we do not thereby mean he is three separate entities, so when we use the terms 'Father', 'Son', and 'Spirit' of God we do not mean he is three entities. Roscelin subsequently replied that Anselm's view committed him to collapsing the three persons of the trinity into one. Anselm's response is to point to his limited intentions in making the distinction in the first place. The aim was simply to use an analogy to illustrate how the terms 'God', 'Son', and 'Spirit' could be predicated of God without generating three Gods, not to suggest the identity of the Father and the Son. But far from resolving the issues, the upshot of this dispute was to make it clear that far more work on the question of universals was needed before any philosophical defence of the orthodoxy could be mounted.

In the twelfth century, Abelard set out to refine the philosophical discussion of substances and their properties or accidents, and he introduces a significant tightening up of philosophical resources. He starts by arguing that questions of whether universals are prior or posterior are logical questions, and not questions about the degree of reality or being of things that are designated by universal concepts. Quite the contrary: both ideas of particulars and ideas of universals are, he insists, less real than what they refer to, for a concept derives from what it refers to, which is independent of the concept in the sense that it can exist without anyone having a concept of it. But some concepts are more derivative than others. We acquire ideas of individual things first, forming concepts of these things and giving each a name which we can use in the absence of the thing itself; and Abelard insists that logicians deal only with these names, not with the essence or existence of the things named. The concept that we form of a thing by acquaintance with that thing is a concept that has a concrete significance. We can also proceed to abstract common traits from our concepts of similar things, and in this way form a concept that has an abstract significance. Abelard's move from knowledge of individual things, to knowledge of their concepts, to knowledge of abstract concepts, is in sharp contrast to the Platonist tradition, where knowledge of the most general and abstract forms the starting point for all knowledge, whether such knowledge be seen in terms of pure intellectual reflection on essences or in terms of divine illumination.

Abelard's attempt to move from his understanding of the nature of universals and how we come by knowledge of them to theological questions was not a success, if the defence and vindication of orthodoxy was the aim. In particular, his application of the semantic theory that nouns and verbs have a univocal signification to the persons of the trinity leads him to the highly heterodox conclusion that the terms 'power', 'wisdom', and 'goodness' are attributable pre-eminently to the Father, Son, and Holy Spirit respectively as proper names; but this suggests, amongst other things, that the Father does not intrinsically—that is, by his very nature—possess wisdom and goodness, that the Son does not intrinsically possess power and goodness, and that the Holy Spirit does not intrinsically possess power and wisdom. Yet despite his problematic incursions into theology, having rethought the role of logic, Abelard is able to engage the question of universals in a far more methodical way than other thinkers who had tried to establish a systematic theology on a philosophical basis. The basic dichotomy that emerges from his account is that between knowledge via abstraction and knowledge via descent from abstract universals, and despite the heterodoxy of some of his conclusions, the former, abstractive knowledge, seemed to provide something whose logical and epistemological credentials were both more thorough and more coherent than those of the Platonist alternatives. The question was, whether an abstractive epistemology could be adjusted to give an orthodox account of fundamental theological questions.

The rediscovery of the Aristotelian corpus, with its elaborate defence of abstractive knowledge, provided what seemed, to an increasing number of theologians in the course of the thirteenth century, to provide exactly the right resources with which to develop a fundamental philosophical vindication of those key theological issues—such as the trinity, the incarnation, and transubstantiation—which required a particularly sophisticated account of substance and its properties, and the relation between particulars and universals. In this way, Aristotelianism seemed to hold the key to a set of fundamental theological questions, and this, above all, is what was to secure its philosophical primacy over traditional Neoplatonism.

If this were all that was at stake, we might expect a relatively smooth transition from the pre-Aristotelian scholasticism of Abelard and his contemporaries to the thirteenth-century Aristotelian scholasticism of Albertus Magnus, Thomas Aquinas, and their successors. But what actually happened was quite different. Aristotelian scholasticism was introduced in the face of massive resistance and condemnation from theologians. A crucial determining factor here is the role of natural philosophy. The doctrinal differences between Platonist and Aristotelian systems have very significant consequences for how philosophy is pursued, and the distinctive thing about following the Aristotelian route in abstractive epistemology is that you must start from sense perception, which in terms of the Aristotelian division of areas of philosophical enquiry means you must start from natural philosophy. This transforms the nature of philosophical enquiry in a number of ways, not least in that it makes the entry into the philosophical foundations of systematic theology something which is largely independent of the kinds of area in which theologians, and the clergy generally, had taken an interest.

To understand why the introduction of Aristotelianism was so bitterly opposed and condemned in the thirteenth century, we must appreciate that the issues go beyond any straightforward doctrinal question. They go right to the heart of the Church's authority. The new Arts Faculties of the universities were staffed by a new kind of clerical *magister*, who now not only immersed himself in secular learning, particularly the liberal arts, but saw this very much as part of his identity, by contrast with the monk, for example, for whom such learning was very marginal to how he conceived his role. While these Arts Faculties gained some administrative autonomy, at Paris for example, what resulted from the setting out of the Church's responsibilities and powers was a focus on questions of metaphysics and natural theology to a degree previously unknown, as the Church took responsibility for its newly defined domain with a heightened vigilance. Aristotle's texts on metaphysics and natural philosophy were introduced at just the time that this new focus was consolidated, so that they were subjected to a scrutiny of a wholly new intensity, by a clergy who had a new sense of their rights and authority in such matters.

The conflict between what the Church regarded as its areas of authority, and the sensibilities of those teaching this material, came to a head quickly. With the introduction of Aristotle's natural philosophy texts and their Arab commentaries, something became evident that had for all intents and purposes remained hidden since the Patristic era, namely the realization that there may be more than one legitimate way of dealing with certain basic questions—such as whether the soul could persist after the death and corruption of the body, and whether the world had existed forever—and that different ways of arriving at a conclusion on a question might generate different conclusions. One of the Arab commentators, Averroes, had maintained that theology and Aristotelian natural philosophy were each wholly autonomous disciplines which could generate conflicting and irreconcilable doctrines. Averroism undermined the separation of powers that gave the Church its legitimacy, by raising the possibility that, in the intellectual realm, these powers might overlap or compete.

For the thirteenth-century opponents of Averroism, what was at issue was the doctrine of 'two truths', that is, the doctrine that theology and Aristotelian natural philosophy were each a wholly autonomous source of truth which could each generate conflicting truths. But the Paris Faculty of Arts masters who envisaged philosophy as an autonomous discipline did not conceive theology and philosophy to be doing the same kind of thing.[2] They saw themselves as different from theologians, and their model was Aristotle, whom they treated as a kind of latter-day Socrates, subservient to no authority and free of dogmatism. Theology was conceived to be an unveiling of the truth concealed in the words of sacred texts, and so was essentially a form of interpretation. Philosophy, by contrast, was not conceived as the uncovering of the truth that lay hidden in a unique authority: there was no hidden truth in a philosophy text, but rather it was one source among many, which may contain errors that should be exposed. Such a mode of reading does not require texts to be reconciled with theology, because it is not engaged in uncovering truths which can then be opposed to different truths which have been uncovered by different means. Philosophy worked in the realm of opinions (by contrast with dogma), and judged these opinions by assessing their strengths and weaknesses and contrasting them with other opinions. The method is most strikingly exemplified in the work of Nicholas of Autrecourt, whose treatise *Exigit ordo executionis*, composed around 1340, advocated atomism, the existence of a void, and the eternity of all things, as well as offering corpuscularian accounts of both transubstantiation and the resurrection of the body.[3] Nicholas's claim is not that these are true doctrines, only that they are more probable than alternative opinions. He clearly sees himself as working in a domain of enquiry quite distinct from that of theology, where questions that could never even be raised in a theological context can be pursued in some detail in a purely hypothetical way.

It might seem that this is a weaker claim than the doctrine of 'double truth', but in some respects it is more radical, for it is postulating the existence of two completely different kinds of enterprise, which engage some of the same questions, but in completely different ways. It is not potentially conflicting results that matter, so much as how one goes about thinking through complex fundamental questions in the first place. The threat lies not in conflicting discourses, but rather in the emergence of parallel discourses, with different aims and concerns: it lies in the issue of the range of ways in which one can engage particular questions, as much as in the conclusions one comes to.

The Revival of Aristotle

The first in a series of crucial moves establishing the centrality of reconciliation of doctrines came with Aquinas's mentor, Albertus Magnus, who offered the idea of natural philosophy as a discipline that explored something different from theology: natural philosophy was concerned with natural truths, and theology with supernatural ones. He defends the idea of natural philosophy as something which, within theologically determined limits, can be pursued for its own sake. It is with

Albertus's separation of the natural from the supernatural as distinct realms of study that the idea of nature as a 'natural realm' appears, for, as we have seen, this was absent from philosophers of classical and Hellenistic antiquity. The next move comes with Aquinas's revision of the Aristotelian conception of metaphysics to enable it to play a mediating role between what had become the two independent sources of knowledge, natural philosophy on the one hand, and revelation and Christian teaching on the other. Metaphysics is able to play this role because it is conceived as dependent purely on truths of reason, and its reconciliatory function is so important because of the radical significance of the introduction of Aristotelian natural philosophy into our understanding of the world. Because Aristotelianism made sense perception the sole source of knowledge of the natural world, an understanding of the natural world that deployed purely natural resources was created, and this was a fundamental concession. It was necessitated by the realization that Aristotelianism provided far more powerful systematic philosophical resources than anything else available for resolving fundamental theological dilemmas such as the nature of transubstantiation and the trinity. As a consequence, it was now metaphysics, not theology, that tempered claims about the natural world.

The adoption of Aristotelianism came at a price, and met much resistance, but it had become the pre-eminent means for understanding natural philosophy and metaphysics by the end of the thirteenth century. In contrast to the Platonism that had dominated theological and philosophical thought up to the thirteenth century, the core of the new understanding of the world and one's place in it lay in natural philosophy. Here, for the first time, there emerges a culture in which scientific values take centre stage, in this case those of Aristotelian natural philosophy. This required a major rethinking of the resources on which the understanding of the world could draw, and as part of an attempt to bolster these resources, metaphysics becomes de-theologized in the hands of Aquinas. In contrast to earlier conceptions, on which metaphysics is a science of 'being-qua-being', that is, something that covers both the philosophical and the theological realms, Aquinas construed metaphysics as a neutral discourse which, governed solely by reason, can decide conflicts between natural philosophy, reliant on sense perception, and theology, reliant on revelation. The latter was considered to have a degree of certainty lacking in natural philosophy, which gave it a more secure standing; nevertheless, it was metaphysics that was called upon to resolve contradictions between the two: on the question of the immortality of the soul, for example, and on the eternity of matter.

In short, theological resources were no longer deployed in our understanding of the natural world, which had now became exclusively tied to natural philosophy. This was a theologically motivated move, not a philosophically motivated one. The adoption of Aristotelian metaphysics provided resources for dealing with pressing theological issues in a far more satisfactory way than the alternatives. But Aristotelian metaphysics came as part of a package in which natural philosophy provided exclusive access to the natural world. In adopting it, Christianity took on a unique feature: a fundamental engagement with science, which set it apart from all other religions, transforming it radically and giving it a distinctive identity. Islam was the only other religion which had had a full-scale engagement with science, and Aristotelianism had also provided the route for this engagement: indeed the scholars of thirteenth-century Paris were deeply indebted to the Arabic Aristotle tradition, without always realizing it. But the commitment to theocracy in medieval Islamic culture resulted in the Arab engagement coming to an end just as the Christian one was beginning. Theocracy was something that the division of responsibilities that emerged in the wake of the Investiture Controversy had effectively made impossible in Christian Europe. The upshot was that it was developments in Christianity, from the thirteenth century onwards, that secured for science an integral role in the understanding of the world.

The Role of Metaphysics

Following Albertus Magnus, Aquinas conceived of natural philosophy and theology as autonomous disciplines, employing legitimately different procedures of enquiry, the first being premised on the reliability of sense perception, the second on the reliability of revelation. Natural philosophy was basically Aristotelian, revelation was Christian revelation, and the combination of the two yielded a Christianized Aristotelianism. However, there were discrepancies between Aristotelian natural philosophy and revelation on a number of fundamental questions, such as whether the world had been created, and whether the soul could enjoy personal immortality after the death and corruption of the body. Theology could not simply override natural philosophy on this conception, for that would be to deny the latter autonomy and legitimacy in its own domain. What had to be provided was some way of bridging the two disciplines in order that corrections could be made, and for this some third discipline that was neutral with respect to theology and natural philosophy was needed, that is, something which was dependent neither on revelation nor sense perception, but rather on reason alone. On Aquinas's conception, it was metaphysics that was fitted to this role, just as it was the very neutrality of metaphysics, as Aquinas conceived of it, that enabled it to provide defences of the Christian understanding of God that met the demands of those (pagans,

Muslims, Jews) who did not recognize the sacred texts of Christianity.

Aquinas's conception of metaphysics as a bridging discipline was a radical departure from the traditional conception, and it did not have the field to itself by any means. The competitors each offered fundamentally different understandings of the relation between metaphysics and natural philosophy, and two stand out: another scholastic conception, that of Duns Scotus and his followers; and a non-scholastic revival of Neoplatonism. On the Scotist understanding of metaphysics, it was not a neutral discourse, but rather one which could be intimately connected with theology. It had the advantage that it was closer to Aristotle's own conception in some respects. Aristotle had conceived of metaphysics as a general science of being, and Duns Scotus had offered this as an alternative to the Thomist conception, on the grounds that there must be some unified notion of being, provided by metaphysics. It was a discipline whose subject matter was 'being-qua-being', and consequently our understanding of infinite being—theology— and our understanding of finite being—natural philosophy— were grounded in a discipline which was not neutral with respect to them, but unified the two as part of a general cognitive enterprise. On the Scotist conception, metaphysics was integrally bound in with Christian theology. With the revival of Scotist notions, in the scholastic textbook tradition that emerged in the second half of the sixteenth century, there is an overriding concern with questions of systematic derivation from general principles. These textbooks had as their explicit aim the systematic reconstruction of Aristotle's metaphysics and natural philosophy from first principles, rearranging material in Aristotle as necessary. They recast the whole Aristotelian tradition with two main aims: to show how the truths of a Christianized Aristotelianism could be derived from first principles, and to show how this was a single, coherent, comprehensive system.

The revived Neoplatonist metaphysics was very different from both Thomism and Scotism. As represented by the work of Ficino in the fifteenth century, and in that of Patrizi in the late sixteenth century, it was driven by a theological metaphysics, conceived as a wholly comprehensive system, in which natural philosophy was really little more than a materialization of basic metaphysical principles. Its content was dictated by these principles, and it had no autonomy. Ficino's treatise *De sole et lumine* (1493), for example, proposes a light cosmogony deriving from the doctrine of emanation, where light is construed as the 'first corporeal form', with the material universe itself evolving from a primordial point of light. On this conception, the study of 'physical' light is a prerequisite to the understanding of the origins and structure of the material universe. In the Neoplatonic view, all causation in the material universe operates on the analogy of the radiation of light, and to study light was to study the emanations of God. The revived Italian Neoplatonism turned out to be heterodox, however. New sets of problems had arisen since the eleventh century, and collapsing theology and natural philosophy into metaphysics did not provide a route back to the orthodox Augustinian synthesis. Quite the contrary: as Spinoza was to show a century later, the pursuit of basic questions via metaphysics alone could be utterly destructive of the whole Judeo-Christian tradition. But Neoplatonic metaphysics did have one claim to orthodoxy. Whatever the superiority of scholastic Aristotelianism on the core doctrines of the trinity, transubstantiation, and the incarnation, it floundered when it came to that of giving a defence of the doctrine of the personal immortality of the soul. Neoplatonism had never had any difficulty with personal immortality, at least

once Plato's complementary doctrine of the pre-existence of
the soul had been abandoned.

Losing Control: Renaissance Naturalism

It was on the question of personal immortality that the Neoplatonist revival promoted itself, and it did indeed touch a sore
point. The Fifth Lateran Council of 1512–17, while confirming
a commitment to Thomism, asked philosophers to defend the
doctrine of personal immortality, effectively acknowledging
that the Thomist account—the doctrine that the soul is the
form of the body and that it enjoys personal immortality—was
in need of support on this question. The problem was that
the threats to the doctrine derived from Aristotelian sources.
Aristotle had offered a naturalistic account of the 'soul' in the
first two books of *De anima*, and one more (but not wholly)
consonant with Christian teaching in the *Metaphysics* and the
third book of *De anima*, and there was dispute among Aris-
totelians as to what the philosophically defensible and consistent position was on what happens to the soul upon the
death and corruption of the body. One view, associated with
Alexander of Aphrodisias, was that since the soul is defined by
Aristotle functionally, as the organizing principle of the body,
without the body there can be no soul, so the soul cannot enjoy
immortality. Another was the view associated with Averroes,
that the soul is not subject to corruption, so cannot perish, but
it cannot be individuated in separation from the body—it no
longer has the sensations, memories, affective states, and so
on that make it *my* soul—so that, in a disembodied state, we
can only talk of one soul or one mind, and this is identical
with God, insofar as we conceive God to be a purely spiritual
entity. In other words, we have immortality, but not personal
immortality.

In the late fifteenth and early sixteenth centuries there was a revival of interest in Averroes in the northern Italian universities, accompanied by a spate of translations of his Aristotle commentaries. The term 'Averroism' is generally used to pick out two distinct doctrines held by Averroes. One ('double truth') concerns the autonomy of natural philosophy. The other is a distinctive natural-philosophical doctrine about the fate of the soul when it leaves the body at death, namely the doctrine of 'the unity of the intellect'. The unity of the intellect—the doctrine that disembodied souls are indistinguishable from one another—is clearly contrary to orthodox Christian teaching, and hence was held to be untrue, yet because it is a natural-philosophical doctrine, and not a theological one, its natural-philosophical credentials were not necessarily undermined by this. Its natural-philosophical inadequacy could be demonstrated only in natural-philosophical terms, and the real dilemmas arise when no natural-philosophical inadequacy can be shown. These problems come to a head in the work of Pietro Pomponazzi, whose stated aim was to uncover Aristotle's doctrines, compare them with Church teaching, and to try to draw conclusions as to what it was reasonable to hold. In his *Tractatus acutissimi utillimi et mere peripatetici* (1518), he defended his philosophical conclusions on the grounds that it was his duty to interpret Aristotle and therefore not to deviate from what Aristotle thought. This conservative gloss on his project should not mask the radicalness of what he is proposing: what Pomponazzi does is to open up the whole question of whether Aristotelian natural philosophy—accepted, in its Christianized version, as orthodoxy in the scholastic tradition—can in fact serve the role of a philosophical foundation for a systematic theology. If, as Aristotelian natural philosophy required, the soul was the substantial form of the body, how could it survive the death and corruption of the body?

Aquinas had dealt with a number of issues, including Averroist conceptions of the disembodied soul as one in number, but there was little doubt that this was one area in which the original Platonist conception of the soul as an intermediary between sense perception and the realm of Forms, and having no essential relation to the body, fitted rather more easily with Christian teaching.

What has now happened is that Pomponazzi has undone a little of the careful work done by Aquinas, and in the course of opposing both Neoplatonist and Averroist accounts of the soul he treats them purely in philosophical terms, only to find that, in purely philosophical terms, the conclusion drawn is at variance with Aquinas's Aristotelian defence of Christian teaching on the issue. Aquinas had separated lower functions of the soul, such as growth and sense perception, which he considered do indeed end with the death and corruption of the body, from higher cognitive and intellective functions, which do not. But it is crucial on his Aristotelian account that, for human beings, the activities characteristic of the higher functions, in particular the grasp of universals, must start from sense perception, that is, from something intrinsically corporeal. In particular, all knowledge works from sensory images. In advocating this doctrine, however, Aquinas distinguishes between the kind of intuitive grasp of truth characteristic of the intellect, and the reasoning processes which underlie and accompany sensation. All knowledge starts from sensation, but once the intellect is engaged and has done the work of abstraction, sensory images are no longer needed. This is where Pomponazzi's difficulties with the Thomist account begin, for the idea of a form of cognition that does not involve a representation of the object cognized is, he argues, just not cognition; and the representation can hardly be pure form, for no Aristotelian account of cognition could countenance pure forms. Consequently, the mind cannot act in cognition without corporeal representations, that is, without the body. Philosophically, Pomponazzi advocates the view that the soul is the 'highest form'—and it is interesting how even he has to resort to Neoplatonic notions at this point—but philosophy cannot establish its immortality.

The implications of the failure of Aristotelian natural philosophy to supply the appropriate philosophical support for a core doctrine go beyond the issue of personal immortality. At the most fundamental level, what is at stake is the failure of Aristotelian natural philosophy to provide a philosophical basis for a systematic theology. By the early to middle decades of the sixteenth century, such a failure had become deeply problematic, because the need for a reliable philosophical foundation was greater than ever, and the need for it to take the form of Aristotelian natural philosophy was also greater than ever.

Regaining Control: The Abandonment of Aristotle

The problems attendant on the attempt to re-purpose philosophy as a natural foundation for Christian theology by tying its fortunes to those of Aristotelianism can be summed up by considering the case of Descartes's contemporary and correspondent Marin Mersenne. Mersenne was the most influential critic of naturalism in the seventeenth century. In a series of writings attacking atheists, deists, and free-thinkers, beginning with his *L'Impiete des Deistes* (1624), he identifies the core error of naturalism as being its blurring of the distinction between the natural and the supernatural. This can result either in a tendency to deny the very existence of the supernatural, as in naturalism proper, or to mistake the natural for the supernatural, as in theories of natural magic. In both cases, the root problem derives from a tendency to see nature as being full of all kinds of power, and in both cases it results in the truly supernatural being effectively left out of the picture. Naturalism, broadly defined, is the doctrine that the truly supernatural (God alone) does not need to be invoked to explain a whole range of events in which it was traditionally thought to be required. Whether the explanations offered in place of traditional ones are naturalistic or quasi-supernatural is not the key issue for Mersenne. The key issue is the exclusion of the (genuinely) supernatural. This is the characteristic feature of naturalism for him, and it is this that makes it a threat to established religion, and hence something to be opposed as strongly as possible.

Mersenne saw that a return to the Aristotelian conception of nature that had served medieval theologians and natural philosophers so well was not going to be successful in countering these forms of naturalism.[4] He did not reject scholastic Aristotelianism as such, and was committed to a number of its central tenets, especially the clear separation between the natural and the supernatural, the personal immortality of the soul, and the rejection of determinism. All of these had been challenged in various ways by Renaissance thinkers. The trouble with Aristotelianism was that it had simply not been able to offer an effective answer to these challenges, and the problem lay largely in the fact that many of them were in fact defensible on Aristotelian grounds. The two deepest derived from the idea that nature, or, more strictly speaking, matter, was in some way essentially active. This had consequences for how nature was to be understood, and for how the human being was to be understood. On the first question, naturalism had undermined the sharp line that medieval philosophy and theology had tried to draw between the natural and the supernatural. Aristotle had thought of natural things and processes on a biological model, construing change teleologically, for example, and this gave natural processes an organic feel. This had encouraged Renaissance naturalists to offer a picture of nature as an essentially active realm, containing many hidden or 'occult' powers which, while they were by definition not manifest, could nevertheless be tapped and exploited, if only one could discover them. Such powers often acted at a distance—magnetic attraction was a favourite example—rather than through contact, and what one was usually dealing with were powers that brought to light connections and affinities that were not explicable in a traditional way, Aristotelian or otherwise.

The other side of the coin was a conception of God as part of nature, as infused in nature, and not as something separate from his creation: something like a pagan 'mother nature'. This encouraged highly unorthodox doctrines that tended in the direction of pantheism, the modelling of divine powers on natural ones, and so on. Worst of all, it opened up the very delicate question of whether apparently supernatural phenomena, such as miracles, or phenomena that offered communion with God, such as the sacraments and prayer, could perhaps be explained purely naturalistically—in psychological terms, for example. The problems were exacerbated by a correlative naturalistic thesis about the nature of human beings, whereby the soul is not a separate substance, but simply the 'organizing principle' of the body; that is, something wholly immanent in the matter of the body. It did not matter much whether mortalism was advocated in its Averroistic or its Alexandrian version: in either case, personal immortality is denied, and its source in both versions is Aristotle himself.

Mersenne saw the source of both naturalism and mortalism as lying in the construal of matter as being in some way active, and his solution was to offer a metaphysical version of mechanism, the core doctrine of which is that matter is completely inert. The threat to established religion posed by naturalism was a radical one which had countless ramifications, and Mersenne's solution is to cut them off at the root, by depriving them of the conception of matter on which they thrive. If there is no activity in matter, then the supernatural will have to be invoked to explain any activity. In criticizing the various forms of naturalism, Mersenne points to the credulity of many forms of Renaissance thought, and he extols the virtues of a purely mechanical conception of the natural realm for a quantitative understanding of nature. But what is fundamentally at issue is not the triumph of quantitative science over credulity, but the defence of the supernatural against appropriation by the natural. This defence is undertaken by making the natural realm completely inactive, stripping it not merely of the various sympathies and occult connections postulated by naturalists, but also of the Aristotelian forms and qualities that provided the original inspiration for these.

The Persona of the New Natural Philosopher

In considering the idea of philosophy in antiquity, we saw that each of the philosophical movements was associated with a 'way of life', particularly the Hellenistic schools. Particular personal qualities were expected of the philosophical adherents of the different schools, qualities that helped shape the distinctive identity of the Stoic, the Epicurean, or the Pyrrhonist. Philosophy was not just an intellectual pursuit: it was directed towards investigating the nature of, and living, the good life, where morality played a crucial role in the terms in which this was conceived. The idea of a 'way of life' is not something peculiar to the philosophy of antiquity. Cicero's remark that Cato had applied himself to philosophy, not that he might dispute like a philosopher but that he might live like one, was quoted several times in the early modern era, most notably by Bacon. It is true that there were no philosophical movements offering a way of life comparable to those of late antiquity in the early modern era: such activity, especially in post-Reformation Europe, had become the preserve of religion. And it is true that, to the extent to which moral dictates had been shifted to religion, the proof of the worth of philosophy, for philosophers, no longer resides in its contribution to the moral reform of behaviour. I say 'for philosophers' because this is precisely what many early modern critics of philosophy thought to be a failing of philosophy. The criticism that philosophers prefer useless learning to virtue goes back to Petrarch, and was a mainstay of Renaissance humanism. The poet Philip Sidney, Bacon's contemporary, defended poetry on the grounds that it not only instils a love of virtue in its audience, but does so by moving their will, making them want to be virtuous. Philosophy, he complains, fails to move the soul to action, and so fails in the ultimate goal of knowledge.

Various seventeenth- and eighteenth-century philosophers were indeed concerned with how to move the soul to action. The problem is not just whether there were any philosophical resources that could be deployed in this respect, but whether philosophers themselves, in thinking about morality, in fact draw on a range of non-philosophical resources. Descartes's correspondence with Princess Elisabeth of Bohemia raises a number of moral issues, not least, for example, on the question of preparing oneself psychologically for moral agency. What is at issue in the specific case of Elisabeth is overcoming melancholia, something that prevents one from taking full moral responsibility for oneself. A kind of training is recommended, and this is a theme that bears some resemblance to the kinds of training that the Hellenistic schools offered, but it is psychological rather than philosophical.

If there is indeed a concern with something that can be called a 'way of life' in the philosophical cultures of the early modern period, it is less a concern with the morality than with the standing of the philosopher. The focus is on the natural philosopher, who is pitted against the scholastic, and who accordingly takes on some traditional qualities of the sophist. A crucial part of Bacon's project for the reform of natural philosophy, for example, was a reform of its practitioners. One ingredient in this was the elaboration of a new image of the natural philosopher, an image that conveyed the fact that the natural philosopher is no longer an individual seeker after the arcane mysteries of the natural world, employing an esoteric language and protecting his discoveries from others, but a public figure in the service of the public good, that is, the Crown.[5]

Renaissance humanists raised the question of the responsibilities appropriate to the humanist, in particular whether the life of activity in affairs of state (*negotium*) should be preferred to that of detachment and contemplation (*otium*). What Bacon effectively does is to transform philosophy into something that comes within the realm of *negotium*, as something good and useful, and thus as intrinsic to the active life. This is completely at odds with the conceptions of philosophy of classical antiquity and the Christian Middle Ages. With Bacon, natural philosophy starts to become a paradigmatic form of *negotium*. One crucial factor in this transformation is the self-fashioning of the natural philosopher, through mastery of his passions: something particularly evident in Bacon's account of his scientific utopia, *New Atlantis*, where self-respect, self-control, and internalized moral authority are central. This is a model inappropriate to the artisan, and it gives the new natural philosopher a dignity and standing that the collective nature of his work would not otherwise suggest. The new natural philosopher manifests his worth through his persona, the aim being not merely to discover truths, even informative ones, but to produce new works for the public good. For Bacon, the natural philosopher is not simply someone with a particular expertise, but someone with a particular kind of standing, a quasi-moral standing, which results from the replacement of the idea of the sage as a moral philosopher by the idea of the sage as a natural philosopher. We expect the moral philosopher to act in a particular way, like a sage, and this is an indication of the worth of his moral philosophy. The shift from moral philosopher to natural philosopher as the paradigmatic sage means that the natural philosopher now takes on this quality. The worth of a natural philosophy is reflected in its practitioners, just as the worth of a moral philosophy is reflected in its practitioners—or, perhaps one should say, embodied in its practitioners.

How does one become such a sage in the Baconian sense? In the most general terms, at least one ingredient in the answer is a very traditional one: the purging of the emotions. But Bacon puts a distinctive gloss on this. The sage, for Bacon, must purge not just affective states, but cognitive ones as well. This is the core of his doctrine of the 'idols' of the mind, set out in the *Novum Organum*, where we are offered an account of the systematic forms of error to which the mind is subject. Here the question is raised of what psychological or cognitive state we must be in to be able to pursue natural philosophy in the first place. Bacon believes an understanding of nature of a kind that had never been achieved since the Fall is possible in his own time, because the distinctive obstacles that have held up all previous attempts have been identified, in what is in many respects a novel theory of what might traditionally have been treated under a theory of the passions, one directed specifically at natural-philosophical practice.

Bacon argues that there are identifiable obstacles to cognition, arising from innate tendencies of the mind (idols of the tribe), from inherited or idiosyncratic features of individual minds (idols of the cave), from the nature of the language that we must use to communicate results (idols of the marketplace), or from the education and upbringing we receive (idols of the theatre). Because of these, we pursue natural philosophy with seriously deficient natural faculties, we operate with a severely inadequate means of communication, and we rely on a hopelessly corrupt philosophical culture. In many respects, these are a result of the Fall and are beyond remedy. The practitioners of natural philosophy certainly need to reform their behaviour, overcome their natural inclinations and passions, and so on, but not so that, in doing this, they might aspire to a natural, prelapsarian state in which they might know things as they are with an unmediated knowledge. This they will never achieve. Rather, the reform of behaviour is a discipline to which they must subject themselves if they are to be able to follow a procedure which is in many respects quite contrary to their natural inclinations. In short, the reform of one's persona is needed because of the Fall: after the Fall, it is lacking in crucial ways. Whereas earlier philosophers had assumed that a certain kind of philosophical training would shape the requisite kind of character, Bacon argues that we need to start further back, as it were, with a radical purging of our natural characters, in order to shape something wholly new.

Bacon's understanding of the intellectual virtues of the natural philosopher centred around the notion of freedom from prejudice. The theme also occurs in Descartes, despite the fact that he is working in a very different context. Descartes attacks Gassendi, for example, for raising objections to his *Meditations* which are not those that a philosopher would raise. Amongst other things, he charges Gassendi with using debating skills rather than philosophical argument; with being concerned with matters of the flesh rather than those of the mind; and with failing to recognize the importance of clearing the mind of preconceived ideas. The dispute pits Descartes the advocate of a complete purging of the mind against Gassendi the defender of traditional learning. But in fact matters are not quite so simple, and if we distinguish the project for purging of the mind described in works designed to legitimate his natural philosophy such the *Meditations* and the *Principles of Philosophy* from the discussion of the qualities required in the natural philosopher in *The Search for Truth*, we see that, in the latter, Descartes's concern is with the requisite state of mind and character of the natural philosopher, a concern that invokes psychological and moral considerations as much as epistemological ones. There, the thrust of Descartes's discussion is that the *honnête homme* has not been corrupted by book-learning, and so is trainable as the kind of natural philosopher that Descartes seeks. The *honnête homme* alone is identified as the kind of person who uses his natural faculty of forming clear and distinct ideas to the highest degree; or, at least, it is he who, when called upon, uses it to the highest degree. This does not mean that the *honnête homme* alone is able to put himself through the rigours of hyperbolic doubt and discover the true foundations of knowledge: in theory everyone is able to do that, scholastics included. But if the aim is to develop and refine natural-philosophical skills as one progresses, then we require something different, as we must recognize that some are more fitted than others to follow the path of instruction in natural philosophy. In *The Search for Truth*, Descartes realizes, practically, that people come to natural philosophy not with a tabula rasa, but with different sets of highly developed beliefs which are motivated in different ways and developed to different degrees. These rest upon various things, and this is what leads him to construct an image of the *honnête homme* as a model in which the moral sage and the natural philosopher meet. Full responsibility for what one is advocating, by contrast with simply subscribing to a philosophical system which has been passed down, is now the cornerstone of intellectual morality, and questions of intellectual morality pervade early modern philosophy no less than they did ancient philosophy, even though this intellectual morality is the inverse of that of classical antiquity.

CHAPTER FIVE

From Natural Philosophy to Epistemology

IT IS USUAL, in histories of philosophy, to treat Augustine and Aquinas together under the rubric of medieval philosophy, marking this period out from antiquity on the one side and early modern philosophy on the other. But this chronology is that of socio-political history, and there is no reason intrinsic to the development of philosophical thought which justifies its deployment. Quite the contrary: the distance between Augustine and Aquinas is vast, as I hope will now be clear. At the same time, the latter's conception of metaphysics standing over, connecting, and mediating natural philosophy and Christian teaching can be seen as a model for much early modern philosophy, a model that will come into question only in the middle of the eighteenth century.

Perhaps the most significant difference between Augustine and Aquinas lies in the role of natural philosophy, something absent in Augustine but our sole route to knowledge of the natural world in Aquinas. This role is reinforced in early modern natural philosophy, and in this chapter we shall be looking at the way in which it has a profound influence on epistemology. To all intents and purposes, epistemology becomes a new kind of subject, as novel developments in natural philosophy provide an impetus for the reform of thinking about knowledge. The formative figure is Descartes. In an effort to defend his heliocentric cosmology, he raises fundamental questions about what kinds of thing we can know, making how one responds to a general form of scepticism about knowledge a central problem of epistemology, and directing it towards the provision of foundations for knowledge. The impact of this depended significantly on a second development, however. This was his application of the optics of the telescope to vision, which makes the objects of perception representations of things in the world, rather than the things themselves. This means that one of epistemology's key problems is now how we can go beyond representations of the world to the world itself. At the same time, it becomes a premise of epistemology that there is a gulf between the knowing subject and the world. In this way, scepticism/foundationalism and representationalism together go to make up 'the problem of knowledge' that will quickly become constitutive of epistemology. Both are stimulated by developments in natural philosophy, and although they are of quite different kinds, it is nevertheless the case that natural philosophy is setting the agenda.

In both cases, philosophy is called upon to deal with an issue generated by developments in science. The first case looks like a straightforward application of the Thomist procedure of using metaphysics to reconcile conflicting natural-philosophical and theological accounts, but philosophy is now taken in a wholly new direction as a result, as the exercise becomes one in the foundations of knowledge. In the second case, the fact that representationalism is seemingly grounded in a scientific discovery imposes severe constraints on its resolution, and Locke's subsequent attempt to provide a philosophical response is instructive for the way in which he attempts to devise a purely philosophical solution, showing that sense perception is not replaceable by natural philosophy, as Cartesians argued. As we shall see in subsequent chapters, the threat of the replacement of philosophy by science generates a crisis for philosophy from the second half of the eighteenth century onwards. It is therefore significant that Locke's establishment of the legitimacy of sense perception as a form of access to the natural world can at the same time be thought of in terms of being a defence of the limits of scientific reasoning.

Reconfiguring Knowledge

The origins of Descartes's reworking of epistemology lie in his response to challenges to his natural philosophy. His chief aim in his treatise *The World* was to use his theory of the properties of matter to establish the Copernican theory that the Earth revolves around the sun.[1] One problem that defenders of Copernicanism had was that of explaining how the planets remained in stable orbits around the sun, and how planetary satellites—moons—remained in stable orbit around the planets. On Descartes's account, the sun rotates, and like any rotating body there is, he believes, a centrifugal force acting outwards from the centre. The rapid rotation of the sun in the centre of our solar system also causes the sea of liquid matter which surrounds it to swirl around it, just as a whirlpool in the sea causes the water to swirl around it. And just as the swirling water will carry objects such as boats along with it, so too the swirling of the fluid matter carries the large objects made of the bulkiest configurations of matter, the planets, around it. The further from the centre, the thicker the sea of celestial matter in which the planets float, while the nearer the centre the thinner it is, because the centrifugal force acting from the centre will throw heavier clumps of matter further out. The planets, depending on their size, will be arranged in stable orbits around the central swirl, an effect of centrifugal forces pushing them outwards and heavier matter pushing them inwards. And each planet in turn will act as a mini–solar system, since each planet rotates and hence carries a smaller amount of celestial matter around with it, so that satellites of planets, or moons, will rotate in stable orbits around their planet. In this way, *The World* offers an explanation of how the orbits of planets are formed, given a central rotating sun. And it does this without invoking mysterious forces which act at a distance through empty space. But just as he had completed his defence of Copernicanism, Descartes learned of the Roman Inquisition's condemnation of Galileo. Galileo's principal weapons in the establishment of Copernicanism had been the theory of the tides, the movement of sunspots, and a doctrine of inertia which explains why motions in which one shares (such as the Earth's orbital and diurnal motions) were undetectable. These natural-philosophical arguments were rejected by the 1633 condemnation not on the grounds that they were false, but because they were thought to be inappropriately hypothetical: mere natural philosophy could not be used to establish Copernicanism when there was an overt conflict with scripture. The argument was that such matters could not be decided definitively by natural-philosophical means alone: they could only be established as possibilities, whereas Galileo was claiming to offer something that went beyond the realm of possibility.

The outcome of this crisis is a new direction in Descartes's work. He had primarily pursued natural philosophy up to this point, and he now rises to the challenge of the condemnation of Copernicanism in a rather startling way. His overriding concern with natural philosophy comes to an end, and a creative period in legitimatory metaphysics begins. He does not abandon interest in natural philosophy, and to the end of his life continues to think it has been his most important contribution, but his interest in it is now confined largely to polemics and systematization, as he begins to follow up the question of the legitimation of knowledge in a new and radical way.

Since purely scientific arguments for Copernicanism were unacceptable to the Church, Descartes set out to provide an irrefutable *philosophical* argument for mechanism, the doctrine that the natural world consists of micro-corpuscles of inert matter of differing sizes and speeds, whose behaviour can be described in terms of mechanics. Since mechanism leads inexorably to Copernicanism on Descartes's account in *The World*, then in establishing mechanism, he has effectively established Copernicanism. What is surprising about the exercise is that mechanism is an empirical natural-philosophical doctrine about the nature of the physical world, and Descartes now proceeds to demonstrate it in a way that makes no reference whatsoever to empirical or natural-philosophical questions. He establishes it metaphysically, by subjecting knowledge to radical doubt and then building it up on new foundations designed to show that it is the only possible way to proceed in asking about the nature of the physical world.

Descartes's procedure here goes beyond the reconciliatory function of metaphysics. Nevertheless, in order to perform this reconciliatory function, metaphysics, in the re-purposed version devised by Aquinas, had to be able to stand over the disciplines that it was reconciling, providing a vantage point. This vantage point now takes on a life of its own, as in many respects the empirical and observational disciplines that contribute to our understanding of the motion of the Earth become translated into manifestations of an overriding metaphysics. As in antiquity, albeit for different reasons, and with different consequences, the abstractness and second-order nature of metaphysics enables it to become constitutive of understanding per se.

Doubt plays a crucial role in the exercise, but the doubt that Descartes engages in—hyperbolic doubt—is quite different from that advocated in antiquity. Hyperbolic doubt is that form of doubt that questions things about which you can be (and may remain) absolutely certain. For example, hyperbolic doubt about whether the external world exists is something you can take seriously at a philosophical level without actually ever believing that there is in fact no external world. The challenge is to justify your belief in something that you can be absolutely certain about. It is a form of epistemological doubt, questioning whether our beliefs constitute knowledge, by contrast with the epistemic doubt of antiquity, which questions our beliefs. It is driven by a discrepancy between the stringent requirements that Descartes places on knowledge, and the kind of support that our knowledge claims can receive. The idea is not that we might in fact be wrong about the existence of the physical world after all, but that if we have trouble justifying this, we will have trouble justifying any beliefs. Such scepticism does not affect our behaviour or our mode of life: in this respect it is the opposite of the relativist/sceptical arguments in antiquity. Hyperbolic doubt leads one to question whether one's beliefs amount to knowledge, but it does not necessarily lead us to abandon those beliefs. Accordingly, hyperbolic scepticism is usually idle. But the use that Descartes puts it to transforms its standing, using it to wipe out traditional sources of knowledge as unsatisfactory, and substituting for them something of his own devising.

Modern philosophers have reconstructed the history of scepticism by reading back from Descartes, finding less radical forms of epistemological doubt in earlier times. But Descartes is not simply taking a traditional epistemological problem, radicalizing it, and providing a new solution. He is posing a new epistemological problem, quite different from anything that had gone before, one whose original motivation arises in a context that is more metaphysical than epistemological. This is evident as we turn to the relations between the three substances introduced in the *Meditations*—God, mind, and matter. The relation between God and corporeal nature, and that of the relation between mind and corporeal nature, are explored in straightforwardly metaphysical terms. But the third relation, between mind and God, is more problematic. Yet it is here, and not in the relation between mind and nature, that the epistemological questions arise. Indeed, in Meditation 6 our cognitive relation to the world turns out to be something ultimately subordinate to our cognitive relation to God, Descartes writing that 'if nature is considered in its general aspect, then I understand by the term either God himself, or the ordered system of created things established by God'[2].

The problem of our relation to God is that of what relation we can stand in to a completely transcendent God, a problem that had been raised in stark terms in letters to Mersenne of 1630, in which the question of the standing of eternal truths was discussed. The thrust of the doctrine is that a transcendent God is cognitively omnipotent: he creates truths and accordingly can make anything true. God is not constrained by what we can conceive to be the case, and he could have created very different mathematical truths, for example, from those we are familiar with, even though we cannot even conceive what their truth would consist in. The doctrine of eternal truths doesn't appear again after the early 1630s in Descartes's writings, not because he has abandoned it, but because it is a metaphysical doctrine which has now been reformulated epistemologically, in terms of hyperbolic doubt. In its metaphysical version it is insoluble, for all one can do is point to the chasm dividing divine understanding from human understanding: the doctrine of the divine creation of eternal truths is a dead end. The epistemological reformulation of the problem does yield a solution, however, and far from being a dead end it turns out to be the key to the defence of Cartesian natural philosophy. Descartes has translated a metaphysical problem into an epistemological one, but it is still ultimately subordinated to metaphysical ends, namely the provision of metaphysical foundations for his natural philosophy, foundations required because of the onslaught against Copernicanism which forced him to abandon *The World*. Descartes uses scepticism, as Montaigne had done before him, not as something problematic which needs to be answered, but as something that directs us inexorably towards the metaphysical question of how we bridge the gap between a transcendent God and human cognition.

The discussion of hyperbolic doubt of Meditation 1 contains two traces of the earlier doctrine of eternal truths. The first is the evil demon, who has the powers of a deceitful transcendent God. Here we have a direct attempt to translate the problem into epistemological terms. We are asked to imagine the evil demon deceiving us into thinking that the corporeal world exists, when in fact it does not. Note that the evil demon here has the powers of a transcendent God, for ex hypothesi we have neither the perceptual nor intellectual faculties to detect the deception. And lacking those faculties, we also lack the ability to understand in what the deception consisted in the first place. Descartes had raised an analogous problem in the *Rules for the Direction of the Mind*, telling us that 'if someone is blind from birth, we should not expect to be able by force of argument to get him to have true ideas of colours just like the ones we have', and that, by the same token, 'if there is in the magnet some kind of nature which our intellect has never before perceived, it is pointless to hope that we will ever get to it by reasoning; for that, we should need to be endowed with a new sense, or with a divine mind'.[3] By analogy, we might argue that if the evil demon has access to a reality which our intellect has never before perceived it is pointless to hope that we will ever get to it by reasoning; for that, we should need to be endowed with a new sense, or with a divine mind. But Descartes's point is not that there is something intrinsically unintelligible about hyperbolic doubt—such an admission would clearly undermine his whole project—, but rather that we cannot meet hyperbolic doubt by relying wholly on our own resources. We need a divine guarantee that what we perceive clearly and distinctly is true.

The second trace of the origins of hyperbolic doubt in the metaphysical question of our relation to God lies in the fact that mathematical truths are included. A useful and common epistemological way of thinking of hyperbolic doubt is as something that goes beyond doubt which deals with states of affairs that are empirically possible, and envisages those which are merely logically possible, that is, involve no logical contradiction. But in Meditation 1 Descartes allows that mathematical truths such as $2 + 3 = 5$ can be subjected to hyperbolic doubt, and here, because all other mathematical truths remain as they are, there may well be a logical contradiction. Completely epistemological versions of hyperbolic doubt tend to focus on the case of the existence of the external world, leaving the mathematical case to one side as unintelligible, but it is in fact no more nor less intelligible than hyperbolic doubt about the existence of the external world. Indeed, the mathematical case more clearly reveals the metaphysical origins of Descartes's account. Descartes raised this question in his metaphysical discussion of eternal truths in letters to Mersenne well before any mention of hyperbolic doubt. It is hard to explain why it subsequently reappears in the context of hyperbolic doubt if this is not construed as being motivated metaphysically, for it makes no epistemological sense: how could the world be exactly as it is and yet $2 + 3$ not equal 5? It is simply incomprehensible to us, and Descartes himself never claimed otherwise. What he did claim was that what is comprehensible to us does not constrain God.

If Descartes's aim in introducing hyperbolic doubt was to show that we cannot legitimate our knowledge claims by relying wholly on our own resources, what role does the *cogito* play? It cannot act as a foundation for knowledge, and Descartes nowhere suggests that it does. But it does serve two crucial functions: it blocks off the regress of doubt, and it acts as a paradigm application of the criterion of clear and distinct ideas. Once the *cogito* has blocked the regress of doubt, the key question becomes that of determining whether there is anything extramental that corresponds to my ideas. In the case of God, Descartes sets out to demonstrate that God's existence is the only thing that could cause me to have the idea of him. God's existence and the nature of the mind are, he argues, two things that we know clearly and distinctly when we reflect on them. What role does the *cogito* have in this? Descartes tells us that it is 'the first principle of the philosophy I was seeking', but this cannot mean that it is the first principle in the sense of being a foundation, for in summarizing Part IV of the *Discourse on Method*, he tells us explicitly that the nature of the human soul and the existence of God are the foundations of his metaphysics. Moreover, the clarity and distinctness that we experience when we reflect on the *cogito* itself requires grounding in God if it is to deliver the truth, and 'once the knowledge of God and the soul has made us certain of this rule, it is easy to recognize that the things we imagine in dreams should in no way make us doubt the truth of the thoughts we have when awake'.[4] The *cogito* presents us with a paradigmatic case of clarity and distinctness of the kind that Descartes is seeking, but it does not legitimate the use of clarity and distinctness as a criterion. That task rests ultimately with God, whose existence we can deduce from the idea that we have of him. God then acts as the foundation for knowledge, by guaranteeing all those ideas of which we have a clear and distinct grasp. But how do we move from the conception that we have of something to its extramental existence?

Descartes's reconstruction of the corporeal world starts from our ideas, and seeking to discover whether there is any extramental reality that corresponds to them. But we can only start from those ideas that are clear and distinct, and in the case of the corporeal world Descartes wants to restrict our ideas to those that are mathematical. Although our sensory ideas may be confused, and so not represent corporeal things as they really are, these things 'at least . . . possess all the properties that I clearly and distinctly understand, that is, generally speaking, all those which come within the subject matter of pure mathematics'.[5] 'Pure mathematics' here turns out, of course, to be geometry, for what Descartes means is that we have a clear and distinct grasp of corporeal bodies insofar as we grasp them under the category of extension. The strategy is, then, to start from ideas, to decide which of these are clear and distinct, and then to investigate the correspondence between these and reality. Since Descartes is effectively only prepared to allow that mathematical conceptions of corporeal reality are clear and distinct, he is able to establish (metaphysically) the unique legitimacy of a particular way of pursuing natural philosophy, without raising a single natural-philosophical question.

The sceptical doubt and foundationalism of the *Discourse* and the *Meditations* are, then, means to an end for Descartes. As he insists to Frans Burman in 1649, one should not waste too much time on metaphysical questions, especially his *Meditations*, as these are just preparations for the main questions, which 'concern physical and observable things'.[6] And it is striking that philosophers after Descartes, such as Spinoza, Leibniz, and Locke, dismiss the idea of pursuing questions of epistemology and metaphysics through hyperbolic doubt, although the standing of metaphysics, which has been established in this way, remains wholly secure. At the same time, natural philosophers developing Cartesian natural philosophy, such as Henricus Regius, abandoned the legitimatory apparatus and proceeded straight to the matter theory and kinematics of motion.

Why, then, has a sceptically driven epistemology continued to fascinate many philosophers since? One reason is the development of a complementary doctrine in Descartes, representationalism. This has typically been taken just to be part of the more general sceptical programme which questions whether we can have any knowledge of the external world. But in fact, it emerges wholly independently of any sceptical arguments, from natural-philosophical considerations that are absolutely crucial to the legitimacy of the doctrine.

Optics and Representationalism

One of the most recalcitrant problems in Cartesian epistemology has been the role of representations in vision. Major advances were made in the understanding of vision and optical instruments in the early decades of the seventeenth century, and Descartes did much to further this understanding. Among the most influential developments in early modern epistemology was the discovery that vision acts like a camera obscura: radiated light entering the eye is refracted and brought to a focus, forming a reversed and inverted image on the retina. This work was based, in the formative writings of Kepler and Descartes, on the study of optical instruments, which were taken as a model for visual cognition. But the epistemological use of the optical instrument model gave rise to a problem about the role of representation. Specifically, it gave rise to the conclusion that what we are aware of in vision are proxies—not things in the world, but representations of things in the world—and as a result it trumped even mind/body dualism in creating a notion of separate 'inner' and 'outer' worlds.

What became the dominant form of Cartesian epistemology, that of Nicolas Malebranche, took the optics of vision to have established conclusively that the mind is aware of representations of things, not the things themselves, and he set out to develop an epistemology that embraced the idea that we do not see things in the world.[7] Hardly anyone followed his idiosyncratic conclusion that, ultimately, we see things not in our minds but in God. But the reading of a representationalist epistemology through a representationalist optics became standard fare for many philosophers from Malebranche up to the sense data theorists of the early twentieth century.

One voice of protest against this reading was Antoine Arnauld, who offered, in his *On True and False Ideas* (1683),[8] a series of arguments against representationalism. These were cogent and in many respects compelling arguments, but in the end they were ineffective. In exploring why they were ineffective, we need to trace the difficulties back to a particular optical instrument model of the eye, for as long as this was accepted, as it was by Arnauld, it was virtually impossible to dislodge the idea that what we perceive in vision are representations.

The problems derive from the extrapolation of an account of the production of images in the telescope to vision, on the assumption that the eye acts like a telescope. What is especially interesting about this development is that it is the first significant case of the use of a well-established scientific theory to sideline further philosophical enquiry, and it results in one of the most disastrous developments in modern philosophy. The problem was not that the scientific theory was wrong, for it wasn't, but rather that a scientific guarantee was sought for a philosophical theory, representationalism, which was manifestly inadequate on a number of grounds, not least in its radical divergence from the phenomenology of perception.

With Kepler's demonstration, in his *Paralipomena* (1604), that the eye functions like a camera obscura, the treatment of visual perception began to hinge on optics, in particular the formation of the retinal image. Earlier accounts, which go back to antiquity, took a different approach to vision. Extramission theories held that the eye emitted a ray of its own, a visual ray, and that this visual ray came into direct contact with an object. Intromission theories, by contrast, held that rays carrying information about external objects were transmitted from the object into the eye. Vision consisted in some form of response to these rays, which in the most fully developed version of the theory, that of Aristotle, consisted of the form of the object seen being imposed on the 'watery substance' of the eye. Although accounts of the nature of light played a part in some of these accounts, optics had no significant role. But one thing was clear in the wake of Kepler: one could not provide an adequate account of vision unless one got the optics right. None of the traditional visual ray theories could be revised to take account of optics. In particular, none of them could accommodate the central role of refraction, and without the ability to bring light rays to a single focus through refraction, vision (as opposed to mere sensitivity to illumination) was not possible.

It was Descartes who first proposed to set out the philosophical consequences of the optics of vision in a decisive way. Kepler had described the optics of the process in the camera obscura whereby light from a distant object enters an aperture so that an image is formed on the side facing the aperture. Similarly with the eye. Light rays from different objects, in the form of light cones, enter the eye, cross over, intersecting at the pupil and, after being refracted in various ways on passing through the aqueous and crystalline humours, converge as points on the retina, producing a reversed and inverted image. Once one substitutes light rays for visual rays, the traditional accounts no longer work. Descartes was particularly concerned to press this point and, translating the optics into epistemology, took as his target the fact that on the Aristotelian account what we see must resemble the object perceived, whereas this was not possible on the new understanding of vision: rather, the relationship had to be one of representation, not resemblance.

It was Malebranche who pushed the representationalist programme in the direction that was subsequently identified with Cartesianism, in effect treating the optics of the formation of the retinal image as the skeleton on which an account of visual cognition was constructed, so that, with the optics of retinal image formation in place, all that was needed was a fleshing out. He and his critic Arnauld agreed on the question of the function of sense perception: our sense organs are designed to help us preserve our bodies, not to enable us to know what the world is like.[9] This was a basic assumption of Cartesianism. The point of Descartes's sceptically driven epistemology was to show that traditional modes of understanding the natural world were at best inadequate, and at worst misleading. If we want to understand the nature of the world, the answer lies in Cartesian natural philosophy, which is the work of reason aided by tightly controlled sense perception which has no degree of autonomy.

Where Descartes's successors disagreed was on the question of representation. Malebranche presented detailed arguments to the effect that what we are aware of in vision are not things in the world, but visual representations of things in the world. Light rays registering on our retinas produce proxies which our mind and/or visual system work on to produce visual images. When we analyse the visual process into its distinct components, he argued, it emerges that what we are actually aware of are these visual images, not what they are the images of. Visual perception is a tripartite relation between the object in the physical world, a representation of the object, and the perceiver.

In his criticisms of Malebranche's theory of perception, Arnauld denied that what we are aware of in perception is a proxy that stands between the observer and the object that gives rise to the proxy: Malebranche simply conflates having a visual representation of an object and seeing a visual representation of that object. Optics teaches us that we see by means of visual representations of the world; it does not teach us that we see visual representations of the world. Because Malebranche falls victim to this conflation, he is mistakenly led to ontologize representations, to make them discrete entities intervening between the perceived object and the mind of the perceiver. For Arnauld, by contrast, to say we have a visual representation of a tree is just another way of saying that we see a tree. We can describe seeing a tree in mental/psychological terms, or we can describe it in terms of optics and physiology, which is where talk of representation comes in. What is at issue are different but complementary descriptions of the same thing. This kind of approach finds some support in Descartes, if one reads his use of the term 'ideas' in this context as equivalent to 'perceptions', and reads the description of ideas 'being present in the mind' to mean simply that such ideas are understood. John Yolton has offered an elaborate defence of such readings in Descartes and his contemporaries. What emerges from this kind of approach is an account in which which thinking, perceiving, and knowing are integrated, by contrast with the Malebranchean approach, whereby they are quite separate forms of activity, occupying different stages in the perceptual process.[10]

This is the direction in which Arnauld was moving, but he was unable to proceed very far. The problem he faced is a profound one. It is fine to say that we need to separate the vocabulary by which we describe the optics and physiology of visual perception, which works in terms of representations, from that which we use to capture the phenomenology of visual perception, which doesn't, or at least shouldn't. The problem is that the optics determines that what is involved is a two-stage process. We register a retinal image, which is very impoverished in comparison to what we actually see. The extra content—the move from a two-dimensional image to a perception of the world in three dimensions for example, and the interpretation of optical stimulation in terms of colours—must come after the formation of the retinal image, and the process by which this is achieved starts from that image. The phenomenology of perception has got to connect with the optical/physiological processes that we have discovered are involved in vision. If it can't, then one is entitled to question whether this phenomenology might simply rest on mistaken beliefs, formed on the basis of an understanding of perception which is outdated and has been completely replaced by developments in the understanding of optics.

The specific problem for Arnauld here is that representations are not just a way of talking, appropriate in one context but inappropriate in another. Arnauld's realism was difficult, if not impossible, to reconcile with the account of the mechanism of vision that was universally accepted by this time, and which he himself has no hesitation in accepting. Specifically, he accepts that the formation of visual representations is a real process, and that the representations are subsequently subjected to various forms of interpretation. The problem is that, compelling as many of Arnauld's arguments are, while thinking about vision was centred on the formation of the retinal image it was difficult to avoid the idea that what we are aware of are representations. And it is a short step from this to the idea that what we are directly aware of are proxies, not the world itself. How then can we rescue the idea that we do not see representations of the world? In particular, is there a way of thinking about what happens in visual cognition that matches the phenomenology of vision? The core question is whether purely epistemological arguments are able to settle this issue, or whether we need to re-examine the nature of vision. That is to say, do the problems begin with the philosophical gloss on the optics—with the idea that the eye functions like an optical instrument?

We need to begin by noting that there is a feature of the early development of representational accounts, in Kepler and Descartes, the significance of which has gone largely unnoticed. In both cases, their interest in optics was stimulated by concerns with optical devices designed to yield clear images of astronomical objects. Kepler's account of the eye formed one chapter of *Ad vitellionem*, which was above all a defence of astronomy. Tycho Brahe had originally assigned to Kepler the task of defending astronomy against the Aristotelian attacks by Ursus, who had claimed that the heavens were too distant to be observed properly. Kepler's response was to argue that what we are concerned with in vision is light, no matter how distant the object seen, and light does not decay in being transmitted from a distant celestial object: rather it is dispersed, and this is something which geometrical optics can deal with in a precise way. What light produces is an image. This does not need to be an image in the eye, and he describes his 'ecliptic' device, an angled wooden frame, for projecting an image of the moon onto a sheet of paper, so that it can be examined in detail. The aim is to produce a clear image of luminous radiation coming from a distant object, with the aim of producing as distinct an image of the object as possible.

In Descartes's case, in the 1620s he was concerned with calculating the shape of the anaclastic: that shape which a lenses must have to bring parallel rays incident upon it to a single clear focus. Spherical lenses were unable to do this, producing multiple blurred images. He was able to show that the ellipse was an anaclastic, but grinding aspherical lenses was a difficult matter, a problem to which he devoted elaborate experiments over several years. Telescope lenses needed to yield a single clear image if they were to be a viable astronomical tool. Again, the aim was to produce as clear an image as possible of a distant object.

Here we have the model deployed for vision. But does this model capture what vision does? Is the task of vision properly subsumed under the optics of producing clear images of distant objects? Constructing an account of vision on the basis of an adequate understanding of optics and ocular anatomy (and later sensory physiology) was a basis of modern theories of vision. But does this actually tell us as much about vision as we need to know, or does it rather confine our attention to one particular function of vision, at the cost of others that reveal much more about why we have vision in the first place?

Since the middle of the twentieth century, the case has been building up that the answer to this question must be in the negative. In his investigations of visual perception, J. J. Gibson abandoned the idea that the role of the retinal image in visual cognition is to represent objects as point images as clearly as possible. Accounts of vision up to this time had taken as their starting point a static observer who does not interact with the world, but Gibson gradually began to realize that this was also where the problems started, for it is not a matter of receiving information and subsequently analysing it, but of actively exploring one's visual environment. The fact that the senses have evolved as exploratory mechanisms plays a central role in his account. Interaction with the immediate environment is the evolutionary origin of sense perception. A good example of Gibson's approach is the visual grasp of spatial dimensions. The retinal image is two-dimensional, yet we see the world as three-dimensional, and the standard view before Gibson had been that some extra cognitive processing is needed if we are to move to a three-dimensional view of the world. Gibson denies this, arguing that the information available in the world enables us to perceive it as three-dimensional.[11] Like Descartes, the traditional analysis focused on radiant light, in the form of light rays, reaching a stationary perceiver, but once we take into account the conditions under which normal vision occurs, what we should be concerned with is observers who move their eyes, move their heads, and indeed move their bodies, walking around their immediate environment. In this case, it is ambient light, not radiant light, that we use to identify objects and events in the world. What is crucial to the optics of vision is not radiated light, as with the optics of telescopes, but ambient light. This requires movement. Far from

being the canonical instance of vision, stripped of the compli-
cations and ambiguities that arise when something starts moving, vision without movement is something so impoverished at
the level of information as to be useless in understanding how
we can even associate vision with cognition. The whole point—
and the whole evolutionary point—of visual cognition on this
approach is that it works in an environment with particular
surfaces, enclosed spaces, open paths; an environment that
permits movement in some directions not others, containing objects that approach or recede; and the aim is to enable
observers to negotiate that environment.

There are a number of issues on which an account of visual
perception modelled on optical instruments differs from this
kind of approach. On the optical instruments model, the core
case from which one starts is that in which radiant light from
a stationary distant object is resolved into a sharp image which
is then interpreted so as to yield information about location
and features. Radiant light is harvested, so to speak, so that
as much light as possible enters the instrument, because the
more light, the clearer the image. But under normal circumstances of vision, the kind of focusing that the eye needs to
perform is less a question of generating a sharp image and
more a question of filtering out noise from information: once
the focus of attention in the case of vision moves from radiant light to ambient light, it becomes evident that filtering out
'noise' is going to be a significant feature of successful vision.
Unlike telescopes, where the aim is to bring all incoming light
to a sharp focus, vision, like hearing, can only work because it
is highly selective. It is part of a process of information seeking, and without treating some, perhaps the greater part, of
incoming light as 'noise' and excluding it, vision as we understand it (as opposed to mere sensitivity to illumination) would
not be possible. In short, it is not a question of harvesting as

much light as possible, but rather of filtering out as much 'noise' as possible.

Bearing these considerations in mind, let us return to the question of representation. On the optical instruments conception, the philosophical problems arise from the idea that what we are aware of in vision are representations and, because of the extremely limited amount of information that radiant light reflected from objects can contain, these must be subjected to extensive interpretation by the brain or mind, and only then can they yield a picture of the world. But because its effective starting point is the retinal image, the standing of visual perception is little more than that of enhancement of a proxy. As we have just seen, however, the optical instrument model makes a number of false assumptions about visual perception. Once we accept that the observer's eye is constantly moving in relation to what is seen in the world, exploring that world, that it is not seeking maximum light but maximum information, which means extensive filtering, cutting out light not harvesting it, then the information that reaches the eye, far from being a passive image of the world, is in fact highly processed. The fact that the amount of information that can be carried by light rays is minimal, a consideration that plays such a crucial role in representational accounts and which leads to the requirement of their interpretation by a higher faculty, in fact has no bearing on how visual information is yielded in perception. Above all, the idea that there are two discrete stages, the formation of the optical image followed by the interpretation of that optical image, bears no relation to the way in which information-seeking strategies are there right from the start, part of the process of exploration of the world.

From Descartes onwards, visual cognition has been located in the mind or brain, a correlate of the view that it is the mind or brain that sees. Descartes's optical instrument model of visual cognition directly gave rise to the idea that, in vision, what we see are representations, not what they are the representations of. These representations, unlike the things they represent, are in the mind, not in the world. In this way, representationalism created separate internal and external worlds at least as effectively as mind body dualism ever did. Indeed, many of the problems that have been associated with the metaphysical doctrine of mind/body dualism actually derive from a different source: an epistemological extrapolation from a mistaken and misleading account of vision, one that modelled vision on optical instruments. If one moves outside early modern metaphysics and accepts that it is people—not their minds or brains—who see, one can raise the question of where vision occurs, and the alternative is that vision occurs in the world, because it is part of an integrated sensory-cognitive package. This package is primarily a means of exploring and interacting with the world. The notion of an 'external' world as opposed to an 'internal' world makes no sense here. The observer is bodily located in the physical world, using this sensory-cognitive package to negotiate that world.[12] True, one can separate off components of that package, such as the visual focusing of radiated light. The mistake lies in treating the separated bits as a model for the whole. One must understand vision through an understanding of perceptual cognition, and the philosophical view that what we are aware of in vision are proxies, not real things in the world, is a clear lesson in what can go wrong if we proceed the other way around.

The problems here have arisen because vision has been subjected to a philosophical model in which the mind, or reason, has been given the task of understanding the world. On this model, it is natural philosophy that provides a scientific understanding that reveals the nature of the world to us, not sense perception, which is merely the medium that we are forced to employ in the first instance, and which we can bypass once it has done its work. Perceptual cognition, and knowledge more generally, comes to be modelled on scientific enquiry, one of the crucial instruments in which was the telescope.

Knowledge of the World

It is somewhat paradoxical that an account of perceptual cognition deriving from one of the formative discoveries of the scientific revolution, on the nature and behaviour of light, should end up not simply distancing us from the world but opening up a gulf between what we can know and what there is. But the representational account of perception quickly became a representational account of knowledge per se. Locke sums up the problem clearly in his *Essay Concerning Human Understanding*:

> 'Tis evident, the Mind knows not Things immediately, but only by the intervention of the *Ideas* it has of them. Our *Knowledg* therefore is *real*, only so far as there is a conformity between our *Ideas* and the Reality of Things. But what shall be here the Criterion? How shall the Mind, when it perceives nothing but its own *Ideas*, know that they agree with Things themselves?[13]

The dilemma described here was that which Malebranche took up. It was Malebranche's account of representationalism that was the most influential one for subsequent generations of philosophers. In the extensive discussion in Book 1 of his *Search after Truth*, he begins by distinguishing between our judgement of primary and of secondary qualities. He denies that the senses are trustworthy guides to the discovery of such primary qualities of objects as size, shape, motion, and location, but that we are not completely deceived about the characteristics of bodies, for we are right in believing that bodies have some size, shape, location, speed, and direction of movement, even if we are wrong in supposing them to have the ones they appear to our senses to have. The deception worked on our senses is much more complete in the case of the secondary qualities such as colour, warmth, sound, odour, and texture. These, Malebranche tells us, 'in fact are not and never were outside us'. Such secondary qualities are purely mental ones, and the fact we are more mistaken about secondary qualities, which are states of the mind, than we are about primary qualities, which are states of bodies, suggests to Malebranche that we have a clearer idea of extension than we do of mind: exactly the opposite of Descartes's view. Our mistakes in this respect arise because we confuse four things: the *action* of an object on our sense organ (e.g., the pressing of the minute parts of a body against our skin); the *effect* this motion has in our body (e.g., the transmission of impulses from our nerve endings to our brain); the *modification of our mind* that accompanies the event that occurs in our brain (e.g., the feeling of warmth); and a *belief* that arises naturally and involuntarily in us about this sensation (e.g., the belief that the warmth we feel is actually in the object touched and in the hand that touches it).

As well as sensory ideas, which exist only in our mind, there are for Malebranche also clear and distinct ideas which, he argues, exist in God. Drawing on Neoplatonist and Augustinian conceptions, he argues that what we know most clearly are eternal, unchanging essences, and these can only exist in something which is itself eternal and unchanging, namely God. God makes up a realm of unchanging archetypes. When we contemplate non-sensible, purely intelligible things, we contemplate them not in ourselves, but in God. Pure geometrical figures do not exist in our mind—they are not just our mental constructions. Rather, they have a completely objective independent existence in an intelligible world which Malebranche identifies with God.

Locke took issue with the doctrine that we see all things in God in an unpublished 1693 critique of Malebranche. His objection is that, if when we believe we see the sun what we in fact see is not the sun at all, but an image that God has caused to be in our mind, then because we cannot compare this image with the real sun, we are in no position to say whether it is an image of the sun at all.[14] The point seems generally applicable to any theory that holds that what we grasp in perception is a representation and not the thing represented. But if, as Locke maintains, the mind only perceives its own ideas, then it would seem that the objection he puts forward must surely count against his own view. What then is Locke's response to the question of how the mind, when it perceives nothing but its own ideas, knows that they agree with things themselves?

There are, he tells us, two sorts of idea. Complex ideas are what he calls 'archetypes of the mind', and do not represent anything. Simple ideas, by contrast, cannot be created by the mind and must be the product of 'things operating on the mind in a natural way'. Simple ideas are

> the natural and regular Productions of Things without us, really operating upon us, and so carry with them all the Conformity which is intended, or which our State requires: for they represent to us Things under those Appearances which they are fitted to produce in us, whereby we are enabled to distinguish the sorts of particular Substances, to discern the states they are in, and so to take them for our Necessities, and apply them to our Uses. Thus the Idea of Whiteness, or Bitterness, as it is in the Mind, exactly answering that Power which is in any Body to produce it

there, has all the real Conformity it can, or ought to have, with things without us. And this conformity between our simple *Ideas*, and the Existence of Things, is sufficient for real Knowledg.[15]

What is it that makes simple ideas true ideas here? Locke seems to be advocating a Cartesian view about what work ideas do. He talks of them being produced in the mind by things in a manner that accords with the way in which God, in his wisdom, wills them to be produced. The suggestion seems to be that God has made our minds in such a way that they respond to things by producing the requisite ideas, where what is requisite is something that God has determined, not something that we can settle by examining the relation between what is represented and the representation of it.

But there is a very significant difference between Locke and the Cartesian tradition here, and it will help to appreciate it to consider the Aristotelian account of the veridicality of ideas. Aristotle did not think that we establish the veridicality of ideas by comparing them with what they represent. Rather, as we have seen, he argued that nature has provided us with the sense organs we have so that we might know the world. On this approach, only once we have answered the question why we have the sense organs we do, can we ask what their veridicality consists in, and Aristotle's answer is that our sense organs are veridical when they are perceiving special sensibles under optimal conditions. Compare this with Malebranche's Cartesian account. Here again, a functional understanding of sense perception is prior to the question of veridicality. Our sense organs are designed to enable us to preserve our bodies, not to enable us to know what the world is like. Malebranche provides numerous examples to show that the senses systematically mislead us as to the nature of the world, but he is adamant that the error does not lie in the senses: rather it lies in our mistaken judgement that the role of the senses is to reveal the nature of the world to us. If we want to understand the nature of the world, then we must turn to natural philosophy (science).

But can the Malebranchean account bypass veridicality by comparison in the way that Aristotle's can? Aristotle's is what might be called functional veridicality, as opposed to comparative veridicality. The representation of the world is veridical to the extent that it completely satisfies a function; to the extent that it does exactly what it is supposed to do. The functional understanding offered in the Cartesian account is different: satisfaction of the function does not yield veridicality, but recognition of certain kinds of bodily need and how these needs might be satisfied. Such recognition is cognitive and representational, but not of a kind that involves veridicality. The problem for Malebranche is that he has a functional account of what perception does, an account that has nothing to do with veridicality. But he is also concerned to establish that there is such a thing as a veridical account of the world, namely that provided by the right natural philosophy. His functional understanding of perception is irrelevant for these purposes. In particular, it does not yield functional veridicality of an Aristotelian kind, because its function is different from that postulated by Aristotle: we have the perceptual faculties we do so that we might protect our bodies, not so that we might know the world. But if functional veridicality is not available, how is veridicality to be established? It would seem that all that is left for Malebranche to appeal to is comparative veridicality, yet this is ruled out by his doctrine that we see all things in God, which denies any causal connection, direct or indirect, between the object to which we direct our sensory faculties and the perceptual representation that we have as a result of this.

Representation is, then, a genuine problem for Malebranche. Locke also wants to establish veridicality, but he wants to establish it for sensation, which Malebranche has ruled out as too contaminated by secondary qualities, and wholly incapable of the clear and distinct grasp required for genuine knowledge. Locke's objection to Malebranche is a legitimate one, because it shows how Malebranche is not entitled to comparative veridicality, and we have seen that he cannot establish veridicality on functional grounds, that is, on the grounds of satisfying the function of sense perception. Locke, by contrast, does not attempt to establish comparative veridicality, so the objection to Malebranche does not apply to his own efforts. Instead, in Locke's case, everything rests on his ability to establish functional veridicality, and this is what he sets out to provide in his account of sensation.

He needs something on a par with the Aristotelian approach, along the lines that we know that our sensory ideas represent the world not because we are able to compare them with the world, but because the reason we have them in the first place is so that we might know the world, and, given this, their proper exercise secures such knowledge. Such an approach assumes that the function of our sense organs is indeed to reveal the nature of the world to us, that is, to provide us with a veridical representation of the world. But Locke manifestly could not have denied the inadequacy of the Aristotelian account of the transmission of species and the formation of an image on the crystalline humour. Moreover, he was resolutely opposed to the Aristotelian idea that we grasp essences in sense perception, and he certainly did not wish to deny that colour is a function of micro-corpuscular structure. How, then, could he defend functional veridicality? In particular, what of his question, in the passage from the *Essay* quoted above, as to whether 'the Idea of Whiteness, or Bitterness, as it is in the

Mind, exactly answering that Power which is in any Body to produce it there, has all the real Conformity it can, or ought to have, with things without us'?

How could one establish this conformity on a non-comparative basis? The answer is that we go through tests—whether through reason, evidence, or a combination of the two—to satisfy ourselves. The procedure is not unlike that in legal trials, natural history, and civil history, but also in some respects like astronomy, where we test claims against the evidence, and establish, where we can, one account as being the true one. The difference is that, in such cases, the evidence may be virtually limitless, allowing only a degree of probability, whereas in the case of sensation, the evidence is confined within a very narrow range: it is in effect just a question of securing optimal conditions for observation. Notice that Locke does not say that the idea conforms to the thing, but rather that it has all the conformity it can have, or all the conformity it ought to have. There is a scale or continuum, as it were, and sensation comes at the limit of the scale. The judgement we make is not one relative to how things are independently of our ideas of them, for that is impossible, but to how things are relative to evidence and reasons.

Does Natural Philosophy Replace Sense Perception?

A crucial ingredient in Locke's strategy is a construal of sense perception on which it has a degree of cognitive authority which Cartesians, and Malebranche in particular, denied to it. As we have seen, in the Cartesian tradition, perceptual cognition consisted of two processes: sensation and an attendant judgement. This latter should not be confused with the judgement that we might term post-perceptual reflection, or intellectual reflection, which is not at issue here, being accepted by both the Cartesians and Locke, albeit construed somewhat differently in the two cases. What we are concerned with here is something which is indispensable to perception itself. This turned out to be a very complex tangle of issues, and it cannot be said that all of these were resolved, but it is in this context that Locke in effect forges a new conception of the role of judgement in sense perception, a conception that vindicates phenomenal explanation.

If, on Locke's account of the veridicality of sensations of bodies and their qualities, there is no comparative judgement of the kind that Malebranche requires to establish veridicality, then the question of just what kind of judgement is involved in sensation must be raised. Malebranche treated perception as comprising sensation, a physiological process, and judgement, a completely separate mental act. Arnauld had in effect objected that Malebranche had confused seeing by means of representations and seeing representations: having a visual representation of the world and seeing the world are not two stages of, or two separate parts of, the one process, but rather just two ways of describing exactly the same thing, one in physiological terms and the other in mental terms. One way in which we might describe Arnauld's criticism, is to say that Malebranche has illegitimately broken a single act up into two parts, and then proceeded to treat each part separately, enabling him to hypostatize sensory representations, so that it looks as if the mental process is being applied to an independent physiological item. At the basis of Arnauld's criticism is the claim that the perceptual act must be unified, and this is exactly the conclusion that Locke seems to draw from Arnauld. What exactly Locke believed about the representational nature of ideas is obscure, but the crucial conclusion is that of the unity of perception. Arnauld used this to probe the nature of perceptual representation, but Locke moved in another direction. For Locke, the issues turn on whether there are separate ingredients in perception which we might label 'seeing' and 'judgement'. His own take on unification emerges in the doctrine that perception is simply successful sensation. The act of perception is single because it is identical with sensation. There is no separate or separable act of judgement involved in seeing the world: there is just one thing, sensation.

It is above all Locke's understanding of the functional veridicality of sensation that enables him to incorporate judgement into the very act of sense perception. For the Cartesian tradition, the physiological and physical details of what occurs in sense perception are absolutely crucial to our assessment of it as a source of knowledge, and this is what effectively makes sense perception an unsuccessful competitor to a micro-corpuscularian natural philosophy. But this is not how Locke construes the matter: the whole point is that sense perception and natural philosophy are not in competition. How the action of bodies affects our sense organs is something that, Locke believes, we do not understand and may never fully understand: sense perception cannot reveal to us the nature of whiteness, nor the role that primary qualities play in its production. The thrust of Locke's argument is that, whatever the physical mechanisms by which sense perception occurs, these cannot cause our idea of whiteness to fail to conform to whatever it is in nature that causes us to have that idea. In this way, the credentials of sense perception are secured against the claim that it might be replaceable by something else.

If we compare the role of philosophy in Descartes's legitimation of a Copernican natural philosophy with Locke's vindication of sense perception, it is evident that, to the extent to which we are concerned with an exercise in reconciliation, there is a significant shift both in what philosophy is being used to reconcile, and in the means of reconciliation. In the first case, Copernican natural philosophy and the claim that only Church teaching can establish the motion of the Earth are brought into line by subordinating them both to an overwhelming metalevel philosophy, one that rises above natural-philosophical and theological argument by translating the issues into one of the foundations of anything that could be counted as knowledge, of whatever kind. This goes further than the Thomist project, giving metaphysics a degree of autonomy which is absolute, something Aquinas did not envisage. But structurally, there are parallels with the Thomist project, and in this respect what Descartes is doing is a variant on a more traditional philosophical undertaking.

Locke's project, by contrast, although it is a reaction to Cartesianism, does not by any means continue in this traditional philosophical undertaking. The terms of the reconciliation are now science or natural philosophy and a non-philosophical, non-theological form of judgement, which will later be termed common sense. In other words, instead of reconciling science and religion, the role of philosophy now becomes that of reconciling science and common sense. But the philosophy that occupies this role is not philosophy as traditionally conceived, that is, metaphysics. It does not stand over science and common sense, and judge them with a bird's eye view. Nor does it provide foundations for knowledge, as Leibniz was urging.

In particular, representationalism is a metaphysical doctrine, such a core one in early modern thought that worries about representationalism begin to infect metaphysics per se, and Locke moves away from thinking through the question in metaphysical terms, preferring to give precedence to the phenomenology of vision. It is with Locke that the credentials of philosophy as a second-order form of activity come to be questioned, a questioning that will come to fruition in the rejection of reason (as a second-order activity) in favour of sensibility (a first-order form of activity) in the French Lockeans, as we shall see in the next chapter; and in Hume, who shows how self-defeating is the idea that there is any metaphysics that can stand in judgement over other disciplines, as we shall see in chapter 7.

CHAPTER SIX

Reason versus Sensibility

WITH LOCKE'S DEFENCE of the reliability of sensation as a guide to understanding the natural world, we encounter the beginnings of a general shift in the nature of philosophical engagement with the world. The reintroduction of Aristotelianism in the thirteenth century had established sense perception as our means of understanding the world, but it was a systematized sense perception comprehensively subordinated to reason. This is the model that Descartes follows. And it is a model that Locke qualifies, in his denial that natural philosophy is the only source of philosophical reflection about the world. The development of the Lockean approach is to be found primarily in his French followers such as Condillac, Bonnet, Buffon, and Diderot.

In the *Encyclopedia* of d'Alembert and Diderot, the first volumes of which began to appear in 1751, there are two main entries for '*sensibilité*' (sensibility/sensitivity/sensation), one coming under the rubric of 'morals', the other under the rubric of 'medicine'. The former defines sensibility as the 'delicate and tender disposition of the soul that makes it easily moved and affected'. Sensibility 'imparts a kind of wisdom about propriety, and it goes further than the penetration of the mind alone'. The other entry, that falling under the rubric of 'medicine', describes *sensibilité, sentiment* as 'the faculty of sensing, the sensitive principle', defining it as 'the basis and conserving agent of life, animality par excellence, the most beautiful and most singular phenomenon of nature'. Sensibility, we are told, 'is in the living body', and is 'a property by which certain parts perceive the impressions of external objects, and in consequence of this produce motions in proportion to the degree of intensity of this perception'. Although the two entries are separate, there is no doubt that the connection between the phenomena described is not merely accidental. By the mid-century, in the work of writers such as Diderot, sensibility/sensitivity/sensation is a unified phenomenon having physiological, moral, and aesthetic dimensions, and it lies at the basis of our relation to the physical world: it is what natural understanding has to be premised on. Not only that, but it has come to encompass dimensions of natural processes such as those discovered in physiology, as in the phenomenon of irritability whereby, when touched, muscles contract with a force much greater than the original cause. Nature seemed to harbour a power and responsiveness that was capturable in terms of some broad notion of sensibility/sensitivity. If natural philosophy was to provide a general cognitive model, it had to adapt its explanatory resources to these phenomena, and to become part of the programme of sensibility. In the course of the eighteenth century, it was increasingly considered that it was only in doing so that a plausible account of our relation to the natural world could be achieved.

Contact with the World

The problem of what kind of relation we stand in to the natural world had been raised in an acute form in Descartes. In his attempt to undermine ordinary beliefs about the natural world and replace them with a mechanistic picture, he used an epistemologized metaphysics, that is, a metaphysics which doesn't investigate how the world is, but investigates rather how the world is *independently of us*. This makes an investigation of 'us' mandatory. In the first instance, what the doubt pushes us into is subjectivity, and indeed epistemological doubt centres on the perspective of the subject. Descartes explored this in a distinctive way. Pyrrhonism had made constant reference to subjective states, and it made what one believes relative to a whole range of subjective states—anger, love, familiarity, habits, religious views, and so on—which Descartes never even mentions. Yet he manages to make the whole question of legitimation turn around the subject. Although he is concerned with such questions as that of what in perception is due to the perceiver and what is due to the world, this in itself would not generate a concern with subjectivity. The Epicureans were particularly concerned with this problem, for example, but they did not think of the perceiver as something separate from, or removed from, the world. But just as important is the fact that naturalism pervades doubt in antiquity. Pyrrhonist doubt, for example, did not end up distancing us from the world. On the contrary, as we have seen, it shows that we are so integrated with the world that its very particular features shape our experience of it, making it impossible to transcend this particularity.

Cartesian doubt pushes us in the other direction, and Descartes achieves this by developing and transforming Montaigne's conception of subjectivity. Montaigne probably initiated his project of self-exploration with the traditional aim of discovering a universal human nature, but what he ended up doing was something completely different. He discovered himself, his thoughts, feelings, emotions: something cut off not just from the empirical world, but cut off from other subjects. Descartes deploys this view of the self—a self which has an identity in its own right, an identity that is independent of the relation in which it stands either to the empirical world or other selves—in an epistemological context, so that the locus of knowledge of the empirical world is now something removed from that empirical world. Because of the way in which he puts Montaigne's notion of subjectivity to use in this new context, subjective appearances are now not so much a feature of human cognition generally, as a feature of *my* cognition. It is not that my cognition is significantly different from that of others, but rather that one experiences one's own cognition as a subjective process, whereas one experiences that of others quite differently. It is this that allows hyperbolic doubt, for a gap is opened up between the self and the empirical world, or, as it is now beginning to become, the 'external' world.

For Descartes, a crucial difference between humans and animals is that the animal has no unified cognitive life, and to this extent such cognitive life as animals have is modularized. Human beings, by contrast, because they possess a rational soul, are able to stand back from their cognitive representations of the world—mirroring the way in which metaphysics as a second-order discipline is able to stand over and judge other disciplines—and recognize them as *their* representations, make judgements about them, and exercise free will in respect of them. These are requirements of moral agency, language use, and various other distinctive features of human beings in Descartes's view. Human beings are able to transcend modularity because they are able to stand back from and unify their mental life, and it is this unified mental life, this unified locus of subjectivity, the self, that enables them to stand in a relation to something that is not them, namely an independent world. An independent world comes with a sense of self.[1]

The transcendence of modularity is also crucial for Locke, but he has a more difficult task, because the unification now takes place at the level of sensation itself. For Locke, perception is not sensation plus something else, but simply successful sensation: the perceptual unity of the thinking thing that engages in the perceptual judgement of the world is just the phenomenal unity of perceptual experience, and we cannot infer anything from this alone about the ultimate unity or simplicity of any further underlying self.[2] Considered from a Cartesian point of view, on this Lockean account of perception we would be denied the ability to see the world as independent: for the Cartesian, a separate act of conscious judgement is required for us to grasp that our perceptions reflect a physical reality independent of us. Nevertheless, the idea of a unity of sensibility plays much the role that unity of subjectivity plays in Descartes. It provides us with access to something that goes beyond the capacities of our particular sense organs, even if this access only establishes the existence of something independent of us, not its nature.

Yet there is a shared ground that has almost always been overlooked in comparisons of the two. Once we ask what unity of subjectivity amounts to in Descartes, it soon becomes clear that we are dealing with questions of the unity of the person, and the issues are not restricted to cognitive states, but essentially include affective states and questions of morality. The unity of subjectivity comes into its own in Descartes's criticisms of the habit of scholastic psychology of breaking up the mind into higher and lower faculties. What he fears is 'fragmentation of the soul': how can we hold ourselves responsible if there is not something that lies behind our cognitive and affective states? Unity of subjectivity is, however, not in fact something that comes naturally, and it is rarely achieved fully. Indeed, a good deal of Cartesian moral philosophy consists in advice on how to shape oneself into a unified self, so that one can take control of one's passions, use them fruitfully, and thereby form oneself as a fully morally responsible agent. The transcendence of modularity, the forging of a mental unity, is above all the shaping of a moral persona. The question of a unified subjectivity is intimately and essentially bound up with questions of affective states as well as cognitive ones, and it is intimately and essentially bound up with moral questions. Similarly with the Lockean unity of sensibility, as the development of Locke's doctrines in the French Lockeans makes clear. The claim of the French Lockeans is that it is sensation or sensibility that puts us in contact with the world, and that this has consequences not just for our cognitive but also for our affective relation to the world and to each other. With respect to cognition, the principal target of this way of proceeding as regards cognition was the idea that cognitive grasp exclusively inhabited the realm of reason, something that was the mainstay of metaphysics, in that it enabled one to rise above the phenomena and judge them. This is what the French Lockeans resolutely oppose. It was not just our cognitive relation to nature that was at issue, however, but nature itself. Reason might be thought to reflect nature, but how could sensibility reflect nature?

The introduction of a comprehensive Lockean philosophy in France came—in the wake of the effusive praise of Locke in Voltaire's *Philosophical Letters*—in the writings of Condillac. In his *Essay on the Origin of Human Knowledge* (1746), as in his subsequent *Treatise on Sensations* (1754), Condillac went beyond straightforward epistemological questions and developed a more general notion of sensibility which had consequences for a far broader range of issues, building on themes that had been developed by Diderot in his *Letter on the Blind* (1749), where exploration of sensory handicaps is used to reveal that what we take as given in perception is the result of a complex learning process, involving construction, abstraction, and language use. In these works, of Diderot and Condillac alike, questions of cognition are removed from the confines of a narrowly conceived, sceptically driven epistemology, so that affective states and moral questions are caught up in the enquiry. What happens, in effect, is that affective states come to underpin cognitive ones.

In his *Treatise on Sensations*, Condillac goes beyond Locke's enquiry into how ideas come into our mind, asking also about the origins of our mental faculties themselves. Starting from a Lockean account of the nature and origin of our ideas of the world, the problem is to discover how we could know anything outside our own mental states. Condillac asks us to imagine a statue which we bring alive, as it were, by attributing, one by one, various sensory faculties to it, asking what its experience of the world would be like.[3] Let us say, for example, that we give the statue the power to smell. We place a flower in front of its nose, and the statue experiences the odour of a rose, or a carnation, or whatever, depending on what object stimulates it. The olfactory sensation is not experienced as being that of an external object, however, but simply as an experiential state. Suppose that we give it the power to hear, so that it can experience the full range of auditory variation in pitch, tone, and intensity. Again, there is nothing in this experience that would lead the statue to imagine that that experience had an external source. Vision likewise: the statue would experience light and colour, but there is nothing in this experience that would even suggest an external source of the experience. To gain a general idea of 'sensation', the statue must reflect on the qualities it senses, without reference to the five ways in which the bodies are affecting its organs: that is, it must run together all the individual sensations it receives to form a single class. Nevertheless, even a statue with all five of the senses, which was able to compare, reflect, remember, and accomplish the other intellectual operations, would not be led, on these grounds alone, to imagine that its states were anything but internal and self-contained. Despite having a grasp of spatial relations, for example, the statue would be solipsistic: its sensory experiences would not project it into, or connect it with, the world. It would remain isolated and self-contained. How, then, could we develop a conception of the world as independent of us, on the sensationalist view? Condillac's answer is that a sense of reflection emerges from the sensations, allowing us to distinguish our own body from the sensations themselves, by combining the sensations and making something new out of them, in which the various objects of sensation can be compared under different descriptions. How this sense of reflection arises is left unexplained, however.

Diderot takes a different tack, expanding Lockean sensationalism into a fully fledged sensibilism. In his *Letter on the Blind*, the question that interests him is how the 'mentality' of a blind person, not just his perceptual states, differs from that of a sighted person, and what this tells us about sensibility in general. His interest focused on two cases, the Cheselden report and Nicholas Saunderson.

The Cheselden report appeared in 1728 in the *Philosophical Transactions* of the Royal Society. It was a report by an English surgeon, William Cheselden, 'An Account of some Observations Made by a Young Gentleman, who was Born Blind, or Lost his Sight so Early, that he had No Remembrance of Ever Having Seen'. Cheselden had, over a twelve month period, removed cataracts from each eye of the patient, and his report contained a reasonably detailed account of the recovery. In his *Letter on the Blind*, Diderot combines consideration of the Cheselden case, which explores what happens when sight is restored, with another, that of Nicholas Saunderson, in which the implications of lack of sight are explored. Saunderson was Lucasian Professor of Mathematics at Cambridge and the author of a large, posthumously published, two-volume *Elements of Algebra*. The striking thing about Saunderson is that he was blind, and Diderot, drawing on the memoir by his friends that prefaces the *Elements*, makes him the primary subject of the *Letter on the Blind*. In effect, what Diderot does is to use the case of Saunderson to pit unity of sensibility against a Cartesian unity of subjectivity, arguing that the unity of sensibility, properly construed, is essentially something socially responsible that encourages a well-formed persona, whereas the Cartesian is insensible to the world and works merely in abstractions. It is Saunderson's very blindness that in effect denies him a fully developed unity of sensibility. A deficient sensibility is primarily a question of an emotional, aesthetic, and moral challenge for Diderot. Because of their impoverished sensibilities, the blind turn their minds inwards and are drawn to thinking in terms of abstractions. Jessica Riskin puts the point well, noting that 'this made them natural mathematicians and rationalists: in a word, Cartesians. Conversely, Cartesians' abstract, inward focus made them insensible to the world outside their minds: philosophically blind.'[4] This leads Diderot to suggest that both the blind and Cartesians, because of their solipsistic cast of mind, were inhumane. The blind offer a crucial case study for Diderot, because he believes that their abstract manner of experiencing pain in others weakens their sense of sympathy for the suffering of others. The situation is in effect the analogue of what in the

Cartesian case would be someone who, lacking the ability to unify his or her mental life (perhaps because of melancholia, or what we would now think of as various forms of neurosis), thereby failed to shape him/herself satisfactorily into a moral persona, and whose moral agency, and humanity, would thus be deficient in comparison with someone (an *honnête homme*) who had achieved this shaping.

What is ultimately at stake for Diderot is the sensory basis of civic life, where the contrast is between sensibility and the solipsistic rationalism that he considers indicative of the abstract, second-order approach of metaphysics. The general question underlying this is that of where the ideas that regulate our lives—our moral, emotional, social, political and intellectual lives—come from. The consequences for language, culture, and history of the Lockean claim that all knowledge derives from sense perception had been drawn in detail by Condillac in his *Essay on the Origin of Human Knowledge*. Later, in his *Treatise on Sensation*, his uncompromisingly sensationalist epistemology was employed in the service of the reform of social and political ideas, fundamentally recasting the origins of human abilities and capacities in an effort to reject all outdated sources of authority. This approach is strengthened in a radical way in Diderot, who goes far beyond anything advocated by Condillac, in his distinctive effort to separate morality completely from religion and to rebuild it on a sensationalist basis. It is axiomatic to the sensationalist project that one begins life with a tabula rasa, and the question is not just how one develops a cognitive, affective, and moral life on this basis, but whether, having grasped that this is the context in which development occurs—that is to say, having grasped that traditional sources of authority, most notably religious authority, can no longer play this role—, there are any guidelines that we can follow in cultivating responsible citizens.

In dealing with this question, there are two extreme alternatives that he rejected. The first was associated with mechanism, more specifically biomechanics. The classical ideas of *passion* and *émotion* which Descartes had explored in his *Passions of the Soul* were grounded medically, and indeed his general theory of the passions is built very much around a medical understanding of the passions. This approach was subsequently developed in detail by Antoine Le Camus, in his *Medicine of the Mind* (1753), in which all defects of the understanding are treated as being ultimately a matter of the flow of animal spirits, and hence their cure falls within the compass of biomechanics. It is not surprising that Diderot would have rejected this approach, but the second alternative, which is the polar opposite of this, is a different matter. This is the theory we find in Helvétius's *On the Mind* (1758), whereby the human mind is wholly determined by the sensations it receives, so that it is simply a question of controlling the environment in which the child is reared and educated to the greatest possible degree. Diderot certainly agrees with Helvétius that education is the basis on which to form morally and socially responsible citizens, but he does not agree that the mind is determined simply by the sensations it receives. More generally, he is critical of the 'analytical method' whereby one isolates individuals and then adds them together in a kind of social arithmetic, and he draws lessons for the psychological realm from this was well.[5] One's psychological life is determined by an equilibrium between, or internal organization of, the constituent parts, and this equilibrium will vary from person to person, affecting their responses to their environment. The human being is a collection of separate parts, each conserving its particular function, but at the same time sympathizes naturally, or through habit, with others.[6] In his early *Essay on Merit and Virtue*, Diderot borrows an architectural metaphor from

Shaftesbury, noting that, just as a building requires a careful balance between its constituent parts, the passions of a person form a system in which it is the balance, rather than the individual passions, that matters. Helvétius had maintained that one's sensibilities are wholly determined by one's environment, but Diderot, arguing from the organic complexity of bodies and the need for an internal organization, had no difficulty showing that the environment is just one element that shapes one's sensibilities. Nevertheless, this does not alter the fact that, for Diderot, our relation to the world depends very much upon how we arrive at that relation, and one assimilates cognitive information in a process which is always and necessarily social, cultural, and has moral implications, so that what is shaped is not merely a cognitive sensibility, but a sensibility in which cognitive, affective, and moral questions are inextricably tied together.

We can see this development as the outcome of two currents of thought, one distinctive of the Enlightenment, the other something which has pervaded philosophical discourse from its origins. The first is the project of establishing how we come by our social and moral ideas once the mind has been naturalized in the sensibilist fashion, that is, once non-sensory sources of authority have been eliminated as inauthentic. The contrast drawn is a sharp one. On the one hand, there is the development of a persona which reflects on its own ideas, asking whether there is anything physical that corresponds to these ideas, a paradigmatically Cartesian procedure: it is a mind complete in its own right, enquiring into the world only as it needs. On the other, there is the sensibilist position whereby the development of a unified persona starts with experiences in which there is no neat separation of cognitive, affective, and moral factors. Proceeding in this way offers a striking alternative to the analysis of our cognitive and affective lives in second-order 'philosophical' terms.

The second current of thought is that of the shaping of the persona of the philosopher. Here we have a tradition that goes back to the origins of philosophy, in Plato's definition of the philosopher in the early Socratic dialogues. In Diderot's *Encyclopedia*, considerations of a philosophically appropriate persona are drawn out in a number of entries, notably those on eclecticism and the *philosophe*. While there are some very traditional tropes here—self-knowledge and self-control remain core issues for example—there are two distinctive features that are comparatively new. The first is the move away from the idea that the ideal persona is restricted to an elite group. Rather, the qualities manifested in such a persona are available to all, at least in theory. In particular, they are not connected with esoteric philosophical training, as was the case with the ancient philosophical schools, or with membership of a particular social group, as Descartes's *honnête homme* had been, for example. The second feature is directly connected with the first. It lies in an explicit commitment to a life of social engagement and political reform, by contrast with a life of withdrawal from the world and contemplation. The second feature, by itself, had been an explicit part of a number of conceptions of the philosophical life, from Plato to Bacon, but its combination with the first feature results in something distinctive. The package of the two together brings both a rejection of cognitive authority vested in a particular group and a rejection of political authority vested in a particular group. The radical democratic politics that issues from this package is a distinctive feature of French Enlightenment thought, but it is certainly not the only direction in which a concern with sensibility drives Enlightenment thought in general. A different kind of approach, one which explicitly eschews any form of political radicalism, is that of Hume, whose philosophical work was celebrated more in France than in Britain in his own time, but who thrived in a political culture—which can be traced to the 1688 Revolution—of toleration quite different from that of France, and who was a staunch and conservative defender of this political system, which he did not doubt was the best that had ever come into existence. At the same time, Hume probes more deeply into the questions of reason and sensibility than anyone else, although he has no qualms about raising profound issues even if he cannot provide an answer to them.

Moral Diversity and Moral Complexity

We saw in chapter 1 that the kind of reason-based ethics that predominated in classical and Hellenistic antiquity was poorly equipped to deal with moral complexity, which became particularly manifest at the two end points of morality: at the traumatic level, represented in the violent tragedies of Greek drama, and at the mundane level, where it was a question of the ethics of office. In both cases, the problems arose because of an inflexibility in the second-order approach to questions of ethics that was constitutive of philosophy. Greek drama highlighted the need for a grasp of affective states in considering how moral decisions are made under conditions of uncertainty and duress, while the conflicting demands of different offices highlighted the need for moral decision making on a case by case basis. Neither of these forms of engagement worked in terms of second-order considerations, and it would seem that it was in this that their success lay.

The question of moral complexity came to the fore in a new and shocking way early in the eighteenth century, in Mandeville's *Fable of the Bees*. Mandeville's argument presented a moral dilemma, and offers an instructive test case on the merits of a sensibilist approach, a casuistic one, and attempts to reinstitute a second-order philosophical resolution. Mandeville argued that the qualities, such as avarice, that encouraged the kind of successful commercial society which was to everyone's benefit, were the opposite of those that were universally lauded in the case of individual morality. As Mandeville himself puts it,

> It is certain that the fewer Desires a Man has and the less he covets, the more easy he is to himself; the more active he is to supply his own Wants, and the less he requires to be waited upon, the more he will be beloved and the less trouble he is in a Family; the more he loves Peace and Concord, the more Charity he has for his neighbour, and the more he shines in real Virtue, there is no doubt but that in proportion he is acceptable to God and Man. But let us be Just, what Benefit can these things be of, or what earthly Good can they do, to promote the Wealth, the Glory and worldly Greatness of Nations? It is the sensual Courtier that sets no limits to his Luxury; . . . the profuse Rake and lavish Heir, that scatter about their Money without Wit or Judgment, buy every thing they see, and either destroy or give it away the next Day . . . : It is these that are the Prey and proper Food of a full grown Leviathan.[7]

The basic dilemma, then, was that the demands placed on behaviour by those collective goals that bring with them economic and political well-being were in conflict with the moral demands that shape the individual behaviour that we value most. This is a problem that goes back at least to Machiavelli, who had warned that virtue, humility, and modesty would lead to disastrous results in collective civic action. To believe otherwise, Mandeville argues, is to follow those 'silly people' who imagine that the good of the whole is consistent with the good of every individual. A crucial point here is that responses to Mandeville's account were generated within attempts to come to terms with commercial societies, and this, more than anything else, is what marks out the dilemma from traditional problems in moral philosophy. The moral dilemmas Mandeville highlights are not problems in moral philosophy, conceived as an abstract enterprise. They arise as a result of a particular socio-economic transformation of society.

Mandeville does not offer a solution as such, but he does think of the issues in terms that parallel those of the duties and responsibilities of office. The argument proceeds not in terms of one set of values gradually eclipsing another, but rather associates different values with different offices. This is a question that has a significant history before Mandeville. In the sixteenth and seventeenth centuries, moral agency was tied to realms of responsibility: mothers, judges, and princes, for example, had different responsibilities, and the moral demands placed on them derived from their office. There was an awareness that what was due in one capacity might conflict with what was due in another, and one form of response to this was the various forms of moral pluralism, in Hume and Adam Smith for example, although this was not necessarily associated with questions of office. Mandeville's argument is that we should evaluate the behaviour of people by different criteria depending on 'the Usefulness and dignity of their callings, their capacities, with all qualifications required for the exercise or performance of their functions'.[8] Extreme examples of such callings would include military and ecclesiastical professions. Military values had occasionally become dominant throughout societies in times of war, and there was a persistent view in the eighteenth and nineteenth centuries that war was necessary to revive the life force of societies that had been made effete by

urban luxuries. At the other extreme, there was a rejection of
what were conceived of as monastic values for society in general, because even though, for many in Catholic societies, these
values embodied the highest ideals of Christianity, by the eighteenth century they were deemed inappropriate in the general
case. In both cases the relevant values have immediate moral
implications, with which everyday individual morality and/or
commercial values may conflict.

The idea that the situation mirrors that of the demands
of conflicting offices, and as such should be resolved by casuistry, is not helpful here, because it does not indicate *how* we
might reconcile the conflicting demands. Mandeville assumes
that the conflicts are unchanging, but one way in which one
might attempt to resolve the dilemma is to see the conflicts
as temporary. Marx took such a route. Like Rousseau, Marx
believed that communities had evolved towards the kind of
commercial society, capitalism, that Mandeville describes, but
he insists that capitalism is characterized not by a single collective entity, but by a number of economically defined classes,
the antagonism between two of which define the nature of
the society. One of these is the economically and politically
dominant class. The other is the class identified with wage-
labourers, that is, those who earn their living by selling their
ability to labour. For Marx, capitalism is not the end point
of the evolution of society, and it is the dynamics of the relation between these two classes that determines not only the
fundamental shape of capitalist society, but also the possibility of its future transformation. This future transformation is
largely a function of two factors. First, what lies at the heart
of the antagonism between the two main classes is the kind of
economic relation in which they stand to one another, namely
the purchase by members of one class, not of the products
of labour, but of the ability to labour for a specified length

of time. This results in a specific kind of dependence of one class on the other which, Marx considers, inevitably generates fundamental antagonisms. Second, Marx has a conception of labour as a form of self-fulfilling activity. This acts as an absolute model, on which a satisfactory form of society can be envisaged, one in which one's labour can be genuinely fulfilling and one's life is not prevented from being satisfying by the kinds of factor that militate against this in capitalist society. Marx conceives this form of society not only as a genuine goal, but also as a direction in which the antagonisms between capital and labour will inevitably lead.[9] Note that it is a society in which morality effectively returns to the individual level, one in which non-antagonistic interests replace those of class: antagonistic values are ultimately resolved in the form of a set of universal individual values which others, such as Hume and Smith, would have been happy with. In short, on this view, moral diversity arises only while society is evolving, but it diminishes as moral values now themselves come to reflect genuine human needs and goals. The problem is that, until such a state of affairs is brought about (assuming it ever can be), political considerations effectively replace moral ones, with potentially dire consequences.

If, on the other hand, moral pluralism is to be embraced, two things are needed. First, the idea of the unity of virtue, a core Platonic doctrine, needs to be jettisoned. Second, some way needs to be found of making sure that moral pluralism does not simply degenerate into moral relativism, of the kind traditionally ascribed to the sophists.

Smith offers a form of moral pluralism, and his discussion takes place in the context of two sets of issues. The first is consideration of the traditional question of the unity of virtue. The second is consideration of the merits of 'sympathy' on the one hand, and 'self-interest' on the other. Following Hume, he rejects the unity of virtue, telling us that '[b]y running up all the different virtues too to this one species of propriety, Epicurus indulged a propensity, which is natural to all men, but which philosophers in particular are apt to cultivate with a peculiar fondness, as the great means of displaying their ingenuity, the propensity to account for all appearances from as few principles as possible'.[10] But if the various virtues do not form a unity, nor are they wholly independent of one another. The question arises, for the moral pluralist, of what the balance between the various virtues consists in, and here Smith parts company with Hume, telling us that a 'system which places virtue in utility, coincides too with that which makes it consist in propriety. According to this system, all those qualities of the mind which are agreeable or advantageous, either to the person himself or to others, are approved of as virtuous, and the contrary disapproved of as vicious.' The difference between such a view and Smith's own is that 'it makes utility, and not sympathy, or the correspondent affection of the spectator, the natural and original measure of this proper degree'.[11]

In countering Mandeville's promotion of self-interest and avarice by advocating moral pluralism, the crucial thing for Smith to provide is some way of balancing the competing claims of various virtues. For Smith, it is sympathy—a capacity through which we understand, and identify with, what others are feeling—that lies at the basis of our behaviour as moral agents, and it is sympathy that acts as the common measure of the virtues.[12] Sympathy rests above all on the ability to place oneself in the position of another. In this respect, it would seem to be the exact opposite of self-interest. Yet at times Smith makes not sympathy, but prudence, the foundation of values. In the *Wealth of Nations*, he writes that 'though the principles of common prudence do not always govern the conduct of every individual, they always influence that of the majority of every class or order'.[13]

Self-interest is a species of prudence, but not constitutive of it, and in any case, it is only one among of number of interests that Smith identifies as influencing people's behaviour. What then is the relationship between prudence and sympathy? On Smith's account, they have different standings. Prudence, along with justice, humanity, generosity, and public-spiritedness, for example, is a virtue. But sympathy is not a virtue as such. Rather, it provides a criterion by which one judges the appropriateness of behaviour. Whether self-interested behaviour is appropriate in particular circumstances is something to be determined on the basis of sympathy, in the form of the judgement at which an impartial spectator would arrive. In particular, what is essential to any society, including a commercial one, is not a virtue such as benevolence, but justice: this is what the impartial spectator provides.[14]

This approach enables one to 'tame' prudence, in the form of self-interest, rather than simply denying it a role, by controlling the role it can play. Self-interest is subject to a moral constraint which balances various interests and virtues. The problem is that a fixed range of moral values, with a single form of control—sympathy as manifest in the impartial spectator—regulating the appropriate balance, does not appear to leave much room for variation. Moreover, his form of moral pluralism is too limited to take account of the moral diversity uncovered in the travel and historical literature. The difficulty becomes more evident when we consider that the dilemma of conflicting values that Mandeville poses is a problem generated by a transition from an agricultural society to a commercial one, and the shift in values that this transition brings with it, rather than a problem that has a purely synchronic dimension, as if it were confined to a conflict of values within a particular society. Yet Smith's solution is very much within the latter genre, paralleled by the fact that he treats morality in terms of individual morality.

The approach of Smith and Hume was to revise and broaden the scope of individual morality through the advocacy of forms of moral pluralism. This was in line with the traditional view which, if only implicit, had been that only individual behaviour has a moral dimension. Individuals are able to form intentions and act upon these, and this would seem a prerequisite of moral behaviour. By contrast, the role of intentionality in collective behaviour is difficult to fathom. The natural home of morality, so to speak, lies in the realm of the individual. On such a view, while it is true that empires, nations, and states can act in various ways that attract moral sanction or approval, and can be subject to moral maxims such as that of the doctrine of just war, moral responsibility is properly ascribed not to a state as such, but to the ruler. For the kind of approach taken by Mandeville, by contrast, collective activity has a moral dimension, one that conflicts with individual morality, and it is far from clear that the language of intentionality is applicable to collective or aggregate behaviour.

The sensibilist approach of Smith and Hume has two distinctive features: it allows moral pluralism, and it treats intentions and character as the source of the morality of behaviour. But Smith and Hume are not extending the resources of philosophy. They are devising new resources to replace those of philosophy, which in effect they are treating as a failed exercise. We shall return to this question below. Our immediate concern is to ask whether there is a way of rescuing philosophy. To do so, a very different kind of approach was needed, and this was supplied by Bentham, who offers an account which, in direct opposition to the sensibilist understanding of morality, denies moral pluralism and bypasses intentions and character completely in accounting for the morality of behaviour.

It is helpful to see Bentham's account as a response to the dilemma posed by Mandeville. One important feature of Mandeville's account is the way in which he refuses to subordinate the collective values of a commercial society to individual morality. This is also a feature of Bentham's account, which provides a solution to Mandeville's dilemma by granting to collective values the autonomy that individual values traditionally had. Rather than trying to make sense of collective goals in a vocabulary borrowed from the study of individual morality, Bentham sets out to formulate an independent account of collective values. The account has a number of striking features. First, unlike those of Mandeville and Smith, for example, it rejects the idea that sensibility, or sentiment, or passions are what motivate and regulate morality, making it depend entirely upon reason, a move in the opposite direction to that in which British thinkers had gone. Second, it severs the connection between morality and intentionality, which had been one of the fundamental premises of moral philosophy. Third, in severing this connection, it opens up morality to a quantitative assessment. Bentham's solution is not something that derives from within an autonomous philosophical tradition, as later defenders of utilitarianism in general and consequentialism in particular have urged, in an attempt to decontextualize utilitarianism and make it a purely conceptual, ahistorical form of ethics. The move to commercial society has a general political dimension: it is a manifestation of the move from the idea of governments conforming to absolute standards of virtue and justice to *raison d'état* or 'national interest' conceptions whereby the concern of government is with the preservation and enlargement of the state. It is the central role of commerce in the latter that makes the shift to commercial society part of a fundamental transformation.

Bentham's primary concerns were with the improvement of the decisions of politicians and legislators—with punishment and reward, legal reform and codification—within a broadly moral context, as the title of his best-known work, *An Introduction to the Principles of Morals and Legislation*,[15] indicates. In the *Principles*, Bentham set out a number of distinctive positions. A key argument, one on which a good deal else depends, is his rejection of natural law theories, which he labels 'nonsense on stilts'. Natural law theories typically held that moral values derived ultimately from the nature of human beings and their interaction with the world: the task of all accounts of human behaviour, from moral theory to legislation, is to identify and promote these values. Moreover, legislation is intimately tied to moral philosophy, in that its principles must be consonant with those that moral theory derives from natural law. This is where the link between personal morality and legislation traditionally came, for the principles enunciated in theories of natural law were very much those of individual morality, and this was what secured the authority of laws. Bentham severs the connection between an independently given morality and legislation, arguing that the authority of law cannot be due to its satisfying moral constraints deriving from some assumed natural law. The law needs no external source of legitimacy for Bentham, whether natural or divine. Simplifying somewhat, rights, in particular, do not exist prior to the legislation of the sovereign or government: they are created by the command of the sovereign or the government. Theories that posit an initial social contract from which basic rights derive, Bentham argues, are not only completely fictional, but get matters the wrong way round, ignoring the fact that such rights could not be enforced unless there were already a government.

If the rules that govern the political and legal realms can only be conventional (by contrast with divine and natural law theories), then these cannot rely on any anterior principles of personal morality. Moreover, since they are features of state behaviour, which is collective rather than individual—and clearly not representative of any universal norms on Bentham's account—, they are autonomous with respect to individual morality. Individual morality not only loses its power to regulate the kind of collective behaviour at stake in political and legal decision making, however. It also loses its conceptual centrality in our understanding of what morality is. To the extent to which collective decisions or agreements on political and legislative matters have a moral dimension, a model taken from individual morality is clearly inappropriate. Yet collective activity does have a moral standing for Bentham. The key lies not in intentionality, but in consequences. The assessment of whether an action is right or not is simply a function of the consequences of that action. It is a matter of using the consequences of various forms of behaviour to appraise their moral standing.

Such an approach depends on two factors. We need to identify what it is that we assess the consequences of behaviour with respect to. And, something distinctive of consequentialism, we need a means of determining how successfully we have achieved this. On the first question, Bentham adopts a criterion—pleasure and pain—that had been adumbrated at various times in the history of moral philosophy, most notably by Epicurus in antiquity, and by Hobbes and Hume in the modern era. But the way in which he deploys it is quite original. He combines this with a second criterion, 'the greatest happiness of the greatest number', again not original, but again deployed in a novel way. On the account he proposes, not only does the moral value of an act depend on its consequences, but the value of these consequences is a function of the pleasure or pain that they provide. This connects directly with his answer to the second question, for the importance of pleasure and pain in Bentham lies in the fact that he considers them to be, if not straightforwardly quantifiable, then at least amenable to quantitative comparison, and this allows him a comparative measure of value. Accordingly, he can then argue that those actions are best that maximize benefits. However, in determining the value of some action, we do not restrict ourselves to benefits for us: it is a fundamental principle of his utilitarianism that benefits for us must count equally as, must be of equal value to, similar benefits for any other person.

Seen as an answer to Mandeville's dilemma, this approach has a number of strengths. Not least, it attempts to allocate moral value to collective behaviour in a coherent way. It is not a question of a triumph of commercial values at the collective level, but rather a matter of how one accounts for how values are generated outside the individual realm. Moreover, in accounting for the generation of collective values, Bentham can avail himself of the fact that collective behaviour is quantifiable in a way that individual behaviour is not. This gives him an absolute standard, sweeping to one side worries about moral relativity, because there now is a single procedure for the moral worth of actions that is universal. Because ethical behaviour, as in Kant, is a function of a set of abstract universal rules or maxims, rather than being concerned with concrete prohibitions or injunctions, problems of moral diversity do not arise, because there is no varying content that they have to come to terms with.

Collective behaviour is naturalizable and quantifiable in a way that individual behaviour is not. As such, it is able to offer a new route to the unification of ethics that was not open to Mandeville, one that avoids Mandeville's dilemma. Instead of trying, *per impossibile*, to extrapolate from the individual level to collective values, consequentialism works in the opposite direction, extrapolating from collective to individual values. Just how far Bentham himself was prepared to follow the path that he sets out is a matter of dispute. But whatever Bentham's own hesitation, a utilitarian consequentialism of the kind that Bentham sets out was subsequently developed into a general account of ethics by utilitarians such as James Mill, John Stuart Mill, and Henry Sidgwick. This account was general in the sense that it covered collective and individual morality without distinction. In this unified understanding of morality, it is an account that is developed to resolve problems in the collective case that becomes the general model. Questions of intentions and character are jettisoned in favour of something far more straightforwardly observable, namely the consequences of acts.

Beyond Philosophy?

When Smith writes that 'it is altogether absurd and unintelligible to suppose that the first perceptions of right and wrong can be derived from reason' but must be traced to 'sense and feeling', and when Hume writes that 'reason is, and ought only to be the slave of the passions, and can never pretend to any other office than to serve and obey them',[16] and that morality 'is more properly felt than judg'd of', they are not suggesting an expansion of the resources of philosophy, but making it clear that philosophy has failed to provide a plausible account of morality. Similarly Marx's solution depends on a theory of history rather than second-order reflection on the nature of morality. In general terms, there are two directions in which one can go in response to this. The first is to revise philosophical resources radically, so that the morality of behaviour is judged against criteria that secure a single criterion of morality, eschewing any kind of pluralism: a traditional aim, but at the cost of abandoning the idea of the morality of one's behaviour being determined by one's character and intentions. Of course, deontological accounts try to mitigate these consequences, and indeed the bulk of the philosophical discussion of them is devoted to refinements designed to mitigate unwelcome consequences. But for accounts of morality such as those of the sensibilists, abandoning considerations of character and judgement takes us too far from what had always been intrinsic to morality, and on which our natural, untutored moral judgements are based.

Accordingly, the other direction in which we might go is to abandon any claims to a purely philosophical understanding of morality. That is, the approach is to develop forms of understanding that replace philosophy, and to deny that morality is the kind of thing that is fruitfully subject to second-order enquiry, to the extent to which such enquiry claims to capture the essential aspects of morality. The issues here are not specific to moral philosophy. The general question is whether it is conceivable that there should be any area of concern not subject to fruitful second-order enquiry. For Hume, as we are now about to see, the limits of philosophical reasoning are far more extensive than those at issue in morality.

PART III

The Decline of Philosophy and Its Re-Purposing as Metascience

CHAPTER SEVEN

The Retreat from Philosophy

IN THE 'EPISTLE TO THE READER' that opens his *Essay Concerning Human Understanding*, Locke offers an understanding of what it is to be a philosopher that is radical in its modesty, for, as he tells us, it is 'Ambition enough to be imploy'd as an Under-Labourer in clearing Ground a little, and removing some of the Rubbish that lies in the Way to Knowledg'. The view of the philosopher as under-labourer formed a very powerful current of thought that had Voltaire and Hume among its major advocates. What had seemed one of the perennial and most secure features of philosophy, namely its proclivity for system building, had become highly contentious, and with this the aims and aspirations of the philosopher were being transformed. Just how momentous this transformation was becomes evident when one considers that the original characterization of a philosopher in Plato depends crucially on the systematic nature of philosophical enquiry, for the failing of the sophists lies in their seeking simply to win arguments or show off their ingenuity, whereas the truth that the philosopher seeks requires systematic connections. It was in large part the systematic nature of philosophy that prevented the decontextualized form of argument for its own sake that characterized the sophists' practice. Yet it is this very systematicity that is now called into question on the grounds of intellectual honesty, as the persona of the philosopher is turned inside out.

The Perils of Metaphysics

Reason is 'nothing but a wonderful and unintelligible instinct in our souls', Hume writes in his *Treatise of Human Nature*, and he offers a very Lockean deflationary account of what we can know, writing that it is 'certain we cannot go beyond experience; and any hypothesis, that pretends to discover the ultimate original qualities of human nature, ought at first to be rejected as presumptuous and chimerical'.[1]

The *Treatise* was written in France, and some of the central concerns of the work turn on the questions at issue between Locke and Malebranche that we looked at in chapter 5. Malebranche is treated by Hume as the archetypical systematic metaphysician: which he was, given that the systems of his two competitors, Spinozean and Leibnizian metaphysics, by the 1730s had each been largely marginalized (outside Germany at least, in the latter case). Hume does not argue against the Malebranchean position, however, but sets it out as an apparently coherent way of approaching its subject matter, to the extent that it may look as if he is actually adopting this position as his own. In fact he does reject it: it is just that the Malebranchean position is taken as indicative of philosophical reasoning per se, and Hume's point is to draw attention to the limits of a particular kind of philosophical enterprise. To the objection that he is using philosophical arguments to criticize

philosophy, he replies that '[r]eason first appears in possession of the throne, prescribing laws, and imposing maxims,
with an absolute sway and authority. Her enemy, therefore, is
oblig'd to take shelter under her protection, and by making use
of rational arguments to prove the fallaciousness and imbecil-
ity of reason, produces, in a manner, a patent under her head
and seal.'[2]

Consider the most striking case of this: Hume's treatment
of causation in Book 1 of the *Treatise*.[3] Here, the account of
cause that Hume sets out is straight out of Malebranche.[4] As
well as extensive passages that précis Malebranche's *Search for
the Truth*, there are other passages that can only be described
as word-for-word translations of Malebranche.[5] Hume reit-
erates the Malebranchean doctrine that we obtain no idea
of power from our notions of body, mind, or the union of the
two, and he uses the same example as Malebranche to show
the vacuity of an appeal to powers and forces; he repeats Malebranche's view that we are not aware of a power in ourselves
when we move our arms, as well as using his example of a par-
alytic person willing his arm to raise without the effect being
produced; he follows Malebranche explicitly in arguing that
the variety of philosophical opinions about power is evidence
that we lack a clear idea of it. Malebranche explains that a true
cause is a 'necessary connection', a distinctive doctrine which—
by contrast with Descartes, Locke, or Berkeley, for example—
he stresses on a number of occasions, with a view to arguing
that there are no such necessary connections between natural things: a view that Hume, who likewise stresses the idea
of cause as a necessary connection, adopts. The one significant difference between the two is that Malebranche believes
that there are indirect connections between things, which are
determined by God, a doctrine that Hume ignores, leaving us
with no connections.

There is much dispute over Hume's degree of commitment to the rejection of necessary connections, and whereas earlier commentators had construed him as denying any real causation in the world, asserting that there is merely constant conjunction, there has more recently been a move to see Hume as a 'sceptical realist', that is, someone who accepts that there are real causes in the world, but who denies that we can have a philosophical grasp of them.[6] This makes a good deal of sense of his use of Malebranche. Hume is not plagiarizing Malebranche: not only does he refer to *The Search for Truth* in passing, but Malebranche was a very familiar philosopher to both French and English audiences (more familiar than Descartes, for example), and one whose views on causation were well known. Rather, Hume employs a slightly pared down version of Malebranche's view to represent the epitome of philosophical reasoning on this question.

Hume's approach can be compared with that of Locke. On the Lockean account, there are forms of enquiry in which one can seek underlying causes, but there are realms of enquiry in which this is the wrong way to proceed, not only because it gets nowhere but, more importantly, because it cuts off productive avenues of research which a phenomenal approach reveals. Hume's argument is that one can always pursue systematic enquiry, and it remains a perfectly legitimate exercise: indeed, he characterizes this kind of philosophical search as something that is part of human nature. However, one ultimately pays a price for pursuing this path, and in the case of causation, as in the more general case of scepticism, the price of drawing matters to their logical conclusion is a denial of something that we not only know to be the case, but without which we could not proceed in our daily lives. Systematic metaphysical enquiry takes on a life of its own, becoming increasingly disconnected from the world as it proceeds: Malebranche, Spinoza, Leibniz, and Berkeley had all been criticized in these terms, but Hume is the first to offer a considered diagnosis of what has gone wrong.

There are two connected questions at issue here that can help us understand what Hume is proposing, the first touching on the nature of scepticism, the second on the relation between reason and sensibility. On the question of scepticism, as we have seen, it is important to draw a distinction between Pyrrhonism, which is doxastic, that is, it is concerned with beliefs, and Cartesian scepticism, which is epistemological, that is, concerned with knowledge. Hume is as concerned with Pyrrhonism as he is with epistemological scepticism, and what is distinctive about his approach is that he runs together doxastic and epistemological considerations in an idiosyncratic way. It is not that he simply conflates the two: rather, what he does is to assess the value of doubt generally, with respect to both doxastic and epistemological criteria. The oddity of this way of proceeding is that hyperbolic doubt comes to be assessed by doxastic criteria, which of course it fails to satisfy. Consider the case of cause. One can question whether one's belief that there are necessary connections meets the highest standards of justification, and indeed one may conclude that they do not, if only because these standards of justification, for whatever reason, can never be met. But one cannot, on philosophical grounds, genuinely believe that one is mistaken about necessary connections, any more than one can genuinely believe that one is mistaken about the existence of an external world. By applying doxastic criteria to hyperbolic doubt, Hume inevitably finds himself in a dire position where 'I am first affrighted and confounded with that forelorn solitude, in which I am plac'd in my philosophy, and fancy myself some strange uncouth monster, who not being able to mingle and unite in society, has been expell'd all human commerce, and left utterly abandon'd and disconsolate'.[7] Philosophical speculation can lead to such a state of psychological distress, due to the inability to associate or align reason and sensibility.

In fact, the issue of the nature and limits of human enquiry turns in Hume as much on sensibility as on reason. In *An Enquiry Concerning the Principles of Morals*, Hume takes issue with Montesquieu, who he tells us 'supposes all right to be founded on certain *rapports* or relations'. Since such an approach 'excludes all sentiment, and pretends to found everything on reason, it has not wanted followers in this philosophic age'.[8] That there is a more general point at stake here is evident from the remark in the *Treatise* that 'the understanding, when it acts alone, and according to its most general principles, entirely subverts itself, and leaves not the lowest degree of evidence in any proposition, either in philosophy or in common life'.[9] Trying to live in accord with reason alone is misguided:

> Philosophy on the contrary, if just, can present us only with the mild and moderate sentiments; and if false and extravagant, its opinions are merely the objects of a cold and general speculation, and seldom go so far as to interrupt the course of our natural propensities. The CYNICS are an extraordinary instance of philosophers, who from reasonings purely philosophical ran into as great extravagancies of conduct as any *Monk* or *Dervise* that ever was in the world. Generally speaking, the errors in religion are dangerous; those in philosophy only ridiculous.[10]

Yet the solution to this does not lie in renouncing abstract, systematic reasoning, for to do so would be to 'cut off entirely all science and philosophy' and would 'subvert entirely the human understanding'.

How then should we proceed, on the Humean account? On the title page of the *Treatise*, Hume announces that the work is 'an attempt to introduce the experimental Method of Reasoning into Moral Subjects'. This approach raises two fundamental issues. First, there is the question of whether there is any single form of critical enquiry that allows one to stand back from the various kinds of cognitive project and pass judgement on them, and in particular whether this is a task to which philosophy, in the form of metaphysics, is fitted. Hume argues that there is no such single form of enquiry. Second, where such a question had been answered in the affirmative in those eighteenth-century projects traditionally associated with the Enlightenment, it was on the assumption that such a critical task was the duty of 'reason', however that was identified. But Hume raises the fundamental question, inherent in the eighteenth-century sensibility tradition, as to whether understanding of the world and our place in it is exhausted by reason, and he answers that it is not. Reason requires marshalling understanding of the world into a propositional form, but Hume argues that understanding is in fact a balance of propositional and non-propositional forms of engaging with the world, where the latter include desires, expectations, anxieties, fears, hopes, goals, raw beliefs, and so on.

Hume approaches these questions in a distinctive way, in terms of the relation between religion and philosophy, which he considers are unified in the form of Malebranchean metaphysics. He offers what he calls a 'natural history' of religion, and then applies this to philosophy. The natural history of philosophy provides him with a largely non-philosophical way of understanding just how philosophy operates, what it can and cannot do. Although the term 'natural history' does not denote a history in the modern sense, that is, a diachronic account, it is worth stressing from the outset not only the important role that history proper—diachronic history—plays in Hume's thinking, but also the importance of identifying just what role this is. Hume's approach was resolutely historical, but by contrast with those of contemporary French philosophers such as d'Alembert and Diderot, in which the aim was as often as not a reduction of Christianity to a 'conspiracy of priests', his treatment of religion was more along the lines of the experimental or phenomenological versions of natural philosophy. That is to say, it was primarily a matter of establishing connections between phenomena, and paramount among the phenomena connected were religious and philosophical thought and practice, for it is one of the distinctive features of Hume's treatment that Christianity, in its contemporary forms, turns out to lie at the intersection of philosophical and religious thought and practice. What is distinctive about his account is that he uses this historicization of religion and philosophy to open up questions about the nature of propositional understanding. He manages to transform what at first looks like yet another criticism of the limits of systematic understanding into a far more profound and difficult form of enquiry, an enquiry into the limits of a propositional understanding of the world. The appraisal of sensibility in our understanding of the world and our place in it no longer hinges on the existence or otherwise of innate ideas, but is now a conceptual issue about the forms of understanding available to us, and in what circumstances it is appropriate to draw on them.

The procedure Hume uses can be glimpsed most fully in what is by far its most elaborate version, his history of British politics. Following the lack of response to his *Treatise*, he turned his intellectual talents to essays—concentrating on political and economic questions—and a multi-volume history of England: these, especially the latter, were very successful, and it was through them that he was known. *The History of England* provides a concrete narration of the practice of politics (including ecclesiastical politics), in which the theme of liberty and authority discussed in the *Treatise* and in the *Essays* is developed in a distinctive way. The treatment is twofold. Hume explores the origins of liberty, both in human nature and in the contingent circumstances of the history of England, with a view to building up the concept on a firm basis, from which he can then criticize what he considers to be mistaken conceptions of liberty, particularly those espoused by radical democratic elements among the *philosophes*. What emerges from the *Essays* is the idea that there must always be a balance between liberty and authority, and the *History* shows that that balance is shifting, depending on the historical circumstances, and always precarious. As for the writing of history itself, in his essay 'Of the Rise and Progress of the Arts and Sciences', Hume develops his idea that the relation between cause and effect is a matter of inference rather than direct perception, arguing that such connections are more easily established when changes in human conditions produce changes in large-scale human behaviour, as in the case of the rise and progress of the arts and sciences, or that of the rise and progress of commerce, rather than on an individual level, and he distinguishes two forms of history, corresponding respectively to cultural change and to individual actions. Given his broader aims, the idea of finding a way to accommodate or balance competing considerations, rather than forcing a choice of one set over another, is not simply an issue about how to write history, but an integral aspect of Hume's conception of what understanding the human condition consists in. The example that he works out in detail along these lines is that of the British constitution, which is not the work of conscious design: rather he sets out to show that its provisions were largely unintended results of painful and unwilling adjustments forced by over a century of political chaos.[11]

To understand how this approach works in the case of religion and philosophy, it will be helpful to begin by considering the two fundamental questions that Fontenelle had opened up, and which were to provide a focus for much eighteenth-century anthropological thinking about religion. The first was whether modern religion might in fact be a form of superstition: a criticism that Christians had unhesitatingly used to dismiss other religions is now turned on Christianity itself. The idea was that perhaps superstition was not a perversion of Christianity after all, but in large part constitutive of it, as Hobbes and Spinoza had earlier argued. Hume is not particularly concerned with this question, not because he does not identify various beliefs as superstitions, for he does, but rather because the issues do not turn on the question of reason versus superstition for him.

Second, Fontenelle had argued that myths are important, because they reflect a universal human tendency to project into nature one's own experience, so that gods and goddesses emerge as magnified anthropomorphic projections. The interesting thing about these projections is that they reflect particular fears and aspirations, and in tracing the origins of religion to such myths, he rules out the idea of a primitive monotheism. The very idea that polytheism might be a, or even the, original form of religious belief historicized Christianity, and opened up the possibility that it might merely be a stage in human development. In *The Natural History of Religion*, Hume explores—in a way that an account which focused on superstition could not—the advantages and disadvantages of polytheism. His concern, he tells us in the Introduction, is with the origin of religion in human nature, not with any rational grounds that might be adduced for or against it. Religious belief, he notes, is and has always been widespread, but not universal, and, more importantly, the content of the belief has varied so radically that there are no two cases where it has been identical. But one thing, he argues, is manifest from the literature on 'primitive' religions: the original forms of religion are always polytheistic.[12] He sets out, therefore, to reconstruct why this might have been the case, and why we witness a subsequent transition to monotheism. Primitive religion arose, he argues, not from a search for fundamental truths, but as a practical way of dealing with and controlling the fear and dread arising from a hostile environment. It results from a form of projection of human qualities onto inanimate things, and the move from polytheism to theism has nothing to do with rational argument. There is no general progress towards 'reason' in the development of religious belief. This is evident in the present day, he argues, and 'since the vulgar, in nations which have embraced the doctrine of theism, still build it upon irrational and superstitious principles, they are never led into that opinion by any process of argument, but by a certain train of thinking, more suitable to their genius and capacity'.[13]

This prompts the question of why monotheism has replaced polytheism. In weighing the benefits and disadvantages of polytheism and monotheism, Hume devotes considerable attention to the inherent toleration of polytheists and the lack of it among theists, noting that 'if, among Christians, the English and the Dutch have embraced the principles of toleration, this singularity has proceeded from the steady resolution of the civil magistrate, in opposition to the continued efforts of priests and bigots'.[14] Moreover, the idea of an infinitely superior God fosters submission and abasement, whereas when gods are conceived as only finitely superior, the virtues which flourish are those of 'activity, spirit, courage, magnanimity, love of liberty'. Given that there are such significant social benefits to polytheism, and given that polytheism is such a natural system, we can imagine its having flourished, so Hume asks why it has not in fact flourished. The chief objection, he argues, is 'that it is not ascertained by any just reason or authority', whereas where 'theism forms the fundamental principle of any popular religion, that tenet is so conformable to sound reason, that philosophy is apt to incorporate itself with such a system of theology'. The problem is that philosophy soon finds itself 'unequally yoked with her new associate; and instead of regulating each principle as they advance together, she is at every turn perverted to serve the purposes of superstition'. It is perhaps not remarkable that, when Hume then turns, in the *Dialogues Concerning Natural Religion*, to a philosophical account of the nature of a single God, something that sums up Christian theology both in content and tenor, it is Malebranche's account that he quotes.[15] Again it is Malebranche who is the archetypal metaphysician, just as he was on causation. And the conclusion is the same in both cases: 'All the philosophy, therefore, in the world, and all the religion, which is nothing but a species of philosophy, will never be able to carry us beyond the usual course of experience, or give us measures of conduct and behaviour different from those which are furnished by reflections on common life.'[16]

By tying in his account of religion with an account of philosophy, Hume, in a stroke of genius, makes the critical evaluation of religion feed into a critical evaluation of philosophy, conceived no longer simply as the language of criticism from which it itself is immune, but rather as something deeply problematic in its standing, for philosophy must retain an autonomy as the vehicle of criticism of non-philosophical thought, while at the same time taking its place as a form of practice which, like religion, has its roots in human nature and as such develops in various ways which can be opened up to investigation. The new task that Hume identifies is not to analyse philosophy at the level of doctrine, however, for this is uncontentious and is indeed part of any philosophical programme, but rather to undertake an analysis at the level of the philosophical enterprise itself, an analysis that describes things phenomenologically—as a 'natural history'—rather than acting as a neutral arbiter; for, as we have seen, Hume deems the latter enterprise impossible, and not just in the guise of metaphysics, but simpliciter. It is helpful to understand the parallels with the investigation of religion here. For one important strand in the late seventeenth-century historicization of religion, that exemplified in Bayle for example, the point was not to investigate the development of religious doctrine, something that scholars had been doing for centuries, but rather to enable one to stand back from religion in general, and Christianity in particular, and to consider it as an object of study without any assumptions as to the validity of its claims to truth. Hume in effect adapts this procedure, suitably refined, to philosophy: that is, to metaphysics, which he treats as constitutive of philosophy for these purposes. This is not to deny legitimacy to metaphysics, or more generally to an a priori systematic discourse, however. Hume thinks that to do without systematic enquiry would be to 'cut off all science and philosophy', and this is something that he is not prepared to give up: the difference between barbarism and civilization is that between living what Hume terms the 'common life' unreflectively, and engaging critically with it. The point is rather that putting ourselves at a critical distance, devising a language and a set of resources by which we can analyse the respective merits of natural philosophy and Christian teaching, for example, cannot be a matter of metaphysics, or indeed any single form of enquiry. Hume's view on metaphysics, and philosophical reflection generally, is that it puts us in a position to participate critically in our culture. Indispensable as it is in this respect, however, it is not unique. Moreover, participation is quite different from, and indeed stands in contrast to, the idea of an autonomous discipline standing above others in judgement on them.

Hume's use of principles in his examination of the limits of philosophy—principles devised in his constitutional history and above all in the 'natural history of religion'—resulted in a powerful deflationary account of the aspirations of philosophy. But his was not an isolated criticism. Quite the contrary: there was widespread disillusionment with the pretensions of philosophy, all the more striking because this had different sources and was pursued in different ways. In the middle and later decades of the eighteenth century, there were larger-scale and more influential movements in Germany and France, in which moves to supersede philosophy were successful over a number of decades. What is interesting is that the immediate motivations for these movements are not only quite different from that of Hume, but also from one another. This goes to support the idea that there was a general and widespread malaise of philosophy and a rejection of its aspirations. In the French case, there was a concerted attack on the qualifications of the philosopher to address traditional philosophical questions, notably those on the nature of the mind. In the German case, there was a concerted attack on the persona of the philosopher, as being someone out of touch with reality. In both instances, replacement of the philosopher by someone more qualified or better suited to dealing with the important questions was advocated: the *médecin philosophe*, 'philosophical physician', and the *Popularphilosoph*, 'popular philosopher'. And in both cases, the underlying criticism is that there is something distinctly *unhealthy* about the philosopher.

Medicine of the Mind

What do we have to know to understand the cognitive and affective states of a human being? Compare Condillac's statue-man with Bonnet's similar version of a statue-man, which he set out after, but independently of, Condillac's account. There is a crucial difference between Condillac's approach and that of Bonnet. While they agree on a number of fundamental issues, Bonnet, who had begun his career in natural history, becoming one of the outstanding microscopists of the age, only began to consider philosophical issues after his sight gradually became so impaired that he had to give up microscopy. He identifies the difference between his approach and that of Condillac as lying in metaphysical versus scientific/observational approaches.[17] Drawing on up-to-date anatomical research on the brain and the nervous system, he rejects any approach to the faculties that works in purely conceptual and philosophical terms as inadequate. In effect, Bonnet replaces philosophical treatment of the faculties with a physiological account, and although he strays from philosophy less than he might lead us to believe, his approach prompts the question whether, once we abandon innate ideas and start exploring what kind of information the sense organs provide and how this is synthesized, we need to shift from a second-order discourse to one that works within anatomy and physiology. And once we move to the issues that philosophers had drawn from their purely conceptual forms of investigation of human faculties, particularly those on the nature of the soul, we find that we are led in a wholly new direction. Bonnet asks, for example, whether we need to introduce a soul for the statue-man to become a human being. The problem was that the introduction of the soul would seem to add nothing to our understanding of human cognitive and affective states. If we

have successfully constructed our fully functioning statue-
man, Bonnet asks, what would happen if we then introduce
a soul into this automaton? The answer is that all the feelings, and all the faculties, such as memory and imagination,
would remain as they were, for these are all a function of the
behaviour of the fibres in the brain, which are 'independent of
the soul'. Moreover, if we placed the soul of a native American
Indian in Montesquieu's brain, the Indian soul would have the
same sentiments, perceptions, and abstract ideas as Montesquieu, as well as speaking French and writing *The Spirit of the
Laws*.[18]

This is a development with radical consequences. As Anne
Vila has pointed out, there is a move here from sensibility as a
power to be observed to a vision of sensibility as a power to be
harnessed and redirected, for 'if the development and successful conduct of the intellect could be shown to be determined
entirely by the action of fibers in the common sensorium, then
the soul could be completely marginalized from discussions of
human nature. It was now the body that, through its inherent
reactive properties, seemed to offer the most effective site of
intervention in the moral, intellectual, and physical constitution of human beings.[19] What we act upon when we proceed in
this way is sensibility, not reason. The French vitalist physician
Théophile de Bordeu emphasizes this new standing of sensibility: 'The reign of feeling [*sentiment*] or sensibility [*sensibilité*] is among the most extensive; feeling is involved in all the
functions; it directs them. It dominates over illness; it guides
the action of remedies; it sometimes becomes so dependent
upon the soul that the soul's passions take the upper hand over
all the changes of the body; it varies and modifies itself differently in almost all the parts.'[20]

This is instructive, for in its new expanded domain, sensibility no longer looks like something for which physiology

or psychology alone could account. Rather it is medicine—
a form of medicine in which control of sensibility holds the
key—that now becomes the primary tool of investigation. In
his *Encyclopedia* entry on 'prognostic', for example, the physician Jean-Joseph Ménuret argues that the medical technique
of prognosis enables the physician to lift 'the thick veil that
obscures future events', and 'guided by the brilliant torch of
repeated and well-judged observation, he sees with a confident
eye both objects that exist now and those that will emerge'.
It is no longer physiology that replaces philosophy, but medicine, for the new focus on sensibility vastly expands the range
of phenomena to include both cognitive and affective states,
and mental and bodily states. These are not only connected,
but require explanation as connected phenomena, and a new
discipline was being forged to achieve this, which we can term
philosophical medicine, where the 'philosophical' part comes
not from a shared approach, but quite the opposite: from a
wholesale takeover of areas in which philosophy had claimed
as its own but had failed to provide anything.

In this respect, the principal significance of the work of
Louis de la Caze, and the feature that secured the promi-
nence of his *The Idea of Man, Physical and Moral* (1755) in
the decades to come, was, as the title intimates, his explic-
itness in drawing out the moral and social consequences of
this newly conceived medical science. His starting point is a
revival of the doctrine of 'non-naturals', whose first systematic
formulation can be traced back to Galen's *Ars medica*. Factors
relating to health are divided there into the naturals, the non-
naturals, and the contra-naturals. The naturals were structural
and functional elements innate in each body, such as the tem-
peraments, humours, parts of the body, faculties, and functions. The non-naturals were those factors that determined
the state of the body without being controlled by the natural

functioning of the body: ambient air, food and drink, move-ment or exercise and rest, sleep and waking, excretion and retention, and the passions of the soul. The contra-naturals comprised diseases, and these could result from an internal imbalance in the naturals or from an imbalance between naturals and non-naturals. Health on this account was the result of a proper ordering of the naturals and a proper regi-men of the non-naturals, brought together under the general notion of 'hygiene'. Since one cannot avoid the effects of the non-naturals, in the Galenic tradition they were included in the curriculum of the medical schools, and physicians were required to learn about them not only to treat diseases, but to preserve health and to prevent diseases. This Galenic conception was revived in eighteenth-century medicine in France. Popular medical manuals of the period were writ-ten directly for a bourgeois reading public, and stressed the perils to health of misuse of the non-naturals, particularly for those with a sedentary lifestyle. The theme is pursued with vigour in Diderot's *Encyclopedia*, above all in the articles on 'non-naturals', which are identified as preserving health, so long as they are used properly, and they are seen in terms of the healing power of nature. The basic medical concern in the doctrine of the non-naturals was care, not cure, and the physician's primary role has now become that of pedagogue and advocate.

One non-natural that was of particular interest to many physicians was the passions of the soul. La Caze set out to establish connections between physiologically characterized sensibility and affective states in terms of a general notion of health as a harmonious 'animal economy'. The crucial thing about this animal economy was that sensations were not just physiological in nature, but were pleasurable or painful, with an intensity corresponding to the needs of the animal economy. Our moral habits are determined by this animal economy, in terms of the pleasure or pain with which particular behaviour is associated. But although this means that there is no direct social shaping of behaviour, for example, there is nevertheless an indirect influence, because the 'constitution' of the body, and hence its animal economy, are themselves shaped by the 'constitution' of society, which La Caze argues is variable: regionally, in terms of the social distribution of tasks, and in terms of whether the society is in a savage state, where muscular action is at a premium, or civilized, where sensibility may become too refined.[21] The definition of health as harmony and balance is now extended to the social realm: for any kind of excess disturbed bodily harmony, promoted 'disorder', and put the all-important connective tissue into a state of 'vicious sensibility'.[22]

The issues that are at stake here form the core of disputes in the second half of the eighteenth century over the extent to which human faculties and behaviour can and should be shaped by social and medical intervention. Beginning in the 1750s, there was a burgeoning stream of literature advocating the use of medicine in these matters, duly accompanied by a number of warnings about the over-stimulation of sensibility. It is in this context that the *médecins philosophes* thrived, for their interests transcended those of traditional medicine and projected it firmly into the moral or human sciences.

The key early figure in this development was not French, however, but Dutch. It was the *On the Governance of the Mind* (1747) of Jerome Gaub, professor of medicine and chemistry at the University of Leiden, that transformed—and indeed naturalized—the philosophical question of the mind–body relation so that it turned on the relationship between the mind and the body in health and in disease. Gaub argues that there are two sets of circumstances in which the physician should intervene:

where a condition of the body causes a mental disturbance, or, where this is not the case, it can nevertheless best be dealt with by treating the body; and where the mind is the cause of the disease, or, where this is not the case, it can nevertheless best be dealt with by treating the mind. The comparison of healthy and unhealthy states plays a crucial role in his discussion of mind–body interactions. But so too does the more radical thesis that the 'physician's duty is to care for the whole man; mind and body are abstractions'. The idea that the 'whole man' is prior to the abstractions of mind and body has some significant consequences for treatment, for the physician is now encouraged to treat the body to deal with maladies of the mind, and to treat the mind by means of agents acting on the body. *On the Governance of the Mind* opens with a characterization of health in terms of harmony between the mind and the body, and a malady is anything that disturbs this harmony. Consequently, it is not just the form of treatment advocated that is radical, but the range of issues with which the physician is now called upon to deal.

In his *Medicine of the Mind* (1753), Antoine Le Camus sets out to develop the idea of the medically conceived connection between the mind and the body, pursuing Gaub's mind-body holism in terms an investigation of sensibility, which he treats as the key to understanding the connection between mind and body. He begins by arguing that the sensationalist tradition is, as it stands, insufficiently developed to provide the kind of understanding needed. In particular, he urges that sensation not simply be taken as primitive, as those in the Lockean tradition do, but must be traced back to sensibility, of which it is just a particular manifestation. He then takes up the argument that sensibility must be traced back to its origins. In the second book of *Medicine of the Mind*, he identifies the causes affecting our mind and will: generation and heredity, sex, climate and seasons, regimen, age, and degree of health. These factors affect the blood and thereby have an effect on the size of vessels and the elasticity of the fibres, which in turn affect mental powers and character. The key lies in the cultivation of sensibility, which, like health more generally, is a matter of harmonious balance, and over-cultivation can be injurious. The balance is secured through such factors as diet, hygiene, and moderation. These are the subject of the third book, where detailed instructions are given as to how to adjust climate, education, and regimen so as to remedy excesses or deficiencies in sensibility.

The idea of a harmonious state was generally perceived as a 'natural' state, both in the case of the correct balance of the naturals, and in the case of the balance between the naturals and the non-naturals. The task was that of guiding individuals to the achievement of a natural state. Personal regimen remained the preferred option, and cultivation of sensibility was what this personal regimen involved. But just what the cultivation amounted to was contested. Above all, questions began to be raised about 'the perfectibility of man'.

With the publication of Rousseau's *Émile* in 1762, this question had been thrust into the forefront of the Republic of Letters. Rousseau, in the imaginary educational experiment to which he subjects Émile in the novel, sets out to show how we might cultivate the kind of sensibility that enables us to act morally. As Anne Vila puts it, 'Rousseau's *morale sensitive* would provide the key for making people virtuous not by training their minds, but rather, by carefully controlling the impressions made upon their bodies—or more precisely, upon their sensitive systems.'[23] This is of particular importance in Rousseau's account in *Émile*, because it is the excessive stimulation, the constant excess of impressions, that is the cause of a distorted mode of experiencing and understanding our relations with others. Consequently, one needs to moderate one's exposure to this excess of impressions, by choosing with care one's society, occupations, and pleasures. The sensationalism that drives much of the programme, in Rousseau for example, enables one to include, not just the traditional elements of formal education here, but also the whole social and cultural milieu in which one lives.

The new understanding of sensibility was one that was thoroughly integrated with questions of nervous sensitivity and muscular irritability. Rousseau is in fact exceptional in pursuing the questions he does without—or at least without very much—attention to these physiological questions, even though he is adamant that excess stimuli work through the whole body. His criticism that modern urban sensibility is out of alignment with nature is pursued in terms of comparison with a hypothetical state of nature. But such lack of alignment can also be thought of in physiological terms.

There were a number of physicians who combined a Rousseau-like worry about excessive stimulation with a concern with nervous sensitivity. Particularly influential was the Swiss physician Samuel August Tissot, author of one of the best-selling medical advice books of the eighteenth century. Tissot launched an attack on the over-cultivation of sensibility: accepting that intellectual processes are generated and regulated by the activity of sensible fibres, he rejected the prevalent view that one could perfect one's sensibility by engaging in the arts and sciences. He argues that, on the contrary, such activity had deleterious effects on health, producing delicate, over-sensitized individuals who are unable to deal with daily life in a satisfactory way. The route to health for sickly scholars such as philosophers is not more reading in the arts and sciences, but more attention to the advice of their physician.

Philosophy and the Shaping of Character

The characterization of traditional philosophers as 'sickly scholars' would have resonated increasingly in the German states from the middle of the century. Academic scholarship for its own sake was becoming widely ridiculed in Germany from the middle of the eighteenth century onwards, beginning with Lessing's 1748 play *Der junge Gelehrte*. The contrast between the systematic metaphysics or *Schulphilosophie* of the followers of Christian Wolff—typified for its critics in the *Stubengehlerte*, the anti-social and argumentative learned man who spent his all his time alone in his study—and the advocates of *Popularphilosophie* is not a simple one between content and presentation, but something that explicitly went to the heart of what it meant to be a philosopher. A number of images were used by the *Popularphilosophen*. The problem with the professional philosopher, writes Johann Feder, is that he is 'locked in his closet, buried under his books, withdrawn from the world' and preoccupied solely with 'people in his head'.[24] Christian Garve compares the academic philosopher to the traveller who, concerned only with reaching his destination, takes the shortest route there, without any interest in the fields and farmlands that he traverses, whereas the *Popularphilosoph* is like someone who enjoys and enlightens himself on his stroll, taking in everything around him with no particular destination in mind.[25]

Popularphilosophie was in some respects a continuation of a Wolffian programme, one aimed at a cultivation of knowledge and virtue, even though the audience at which it was directed was different, as were the means by which it was achieved. Its aims were the cultural and ethical cultivation of members of the educated classes, as opposed to a university audience, and the means of cultivation lay not in metaphysics, as it did for Wolff and *Schulphilosophie*, but in areas such as history, aesthetics, and pedagogy, with a strong commitment to a literary culture, broad learning, and the art of conversation. Although a few of the *Popularphilosophen* were professors of philosophy, most were not, and many earned a living outside the university system. Given this lack of adherence to any philosophical school, of the kind one finds in the university system at the time, it is not surprising that there was no consensus on substantial philosophical issues among the *Popularphilosophen*. But there was one theme that did unite them: a commitment to an anthropology, a 'science of man'. As the *Popularphilosoph* Karl von Irwing put it, 'presently one can incorporate almost our whole philosophy, and not without profit, into the science of man'.[26] What is at issue here is not a question of Enlightenment versus Counter-Enlightenment, nor is it just a question of the standing of metaphysics. Science too is subjected to severe criticism in *Popularphilosophie*, basically along lines dictated by Rousseau. Kant, for example, early in his career, tells us that science 'cannot make up for its own discontents', and its practitioners 'become increasingly harmful to themselves and useless to the public'; science itself 'tears us away from pleasures'.[27]

The difference between 'School philosophy' and 'popular philosophy', between the almost exclusive pursuit of metaphysics and the pursuit of a broad understanding, is crucially tied up with the German idea of *Bildung*—the notion of cultivating a particular kind of educated, cultured, and enlightened persona for oneself. The division is not merely between different styles of pursuing intellectual enquiry, but above all between different personae for the practitioner of these forms of enquiry. The question of the persona of the philosopher is, as we have seen, something not restricted to philosophy in antiquity: the question of who had the appropriate qualities and attitude to pursue philosophy in a serious way was a pressing concern for early modern philosophers. In a culture in which *Bildung* gave a focus to one's life, the idea that the pursuit of philosophy as practised in an academic environment could not only fail to contribute to, but hinder personal development was a devastating criticism.

The Collapse of the Standing of Philosophy

The combination of the attacks of Hume, the *médecins philosophes*, and the *Popularphilosophen* marks a collapse and replacement of philosophy on a par with that of the fifth century. The forms of philosophical practice in the two are different in many respects, but they are both second-order forms of enquiry, and they both satisfy the requirements of genuine philosophical discourse, on the criteria deriving from Plato, that we looked at in our first chapter. In both cases, they face a twofold threat. There is a threat to the standing of the philosopher, a questioning of whether the philosopher has the qualities and knowledge requisite to pursue the questions to which philosophy deems itself directed. There is also an associated threat that derives from forms of enquiry or learning that offer an alternative approach to these questions, one that is typically empirical in orientation, and eschews the idea that a form of second-order enquiry is remotely plausible as a guide to the issues, let alone a means of resolving them.

The question of the standing of philosophers might seem an odd one to modern ears. This is because, unlike their eighteenth-century forbears, since the 1950s modern Anglophone philosophers, for example, have no public standing qua philosophers. They are simply members of a university discipline. Scientists, by contrast, do have a public standing. Even in relation to scientific matters outside their own specialty, their opinions are taken seriously in their capacity as scientists, and they are listened to. The opinions of individual philosophers on moral and political matters, for example, might be taken seriously, but this is because they are able to offer intelligent commentary, just like any highly educated person, not in their capacity as philosophers as such. But in the early modern period the standing of philosophers—by contrast with theologians and statesmen for example—was something that was highly contested and fought for, just as the standing of the philosopher had been in antiquity, from Socrates onwards. It reflected the seriousness and distinctive thoughtfulness of the claims of the discipline.

The challenge of the *médecins philosophes* is particularly significant, because it prefigures a broad threat from science to philosophy that emerges in the nineteenth century. It bears directly on the competence and aspirations of philosophy per se. The charge that philosophical accounts of the mind dealt with an idealized 'normal healthy mind', without taking into account the range of deviations from this state, was particularly apposite at a time when health was beginning to be considered a statistical norm rather than some natural state of the body. This reinforced the idea that what philosophers had picked out as the mind was doubly problematic: it was not only an idealization, but failed to reflect anything in nature. In fact, some philosophers had shown some awareness of the issues here, particularly in the moral bearing of the idea of a healthy normal mind. Descartes, in his correspondence with Princess Elisabeth, had understood how those suffering from melancholia may lack the ability to unify their mental life, thereby failing to shape themselves satisfactorily into moral personae. As a consequence, their moral agency, and even humanity, may be deficient in comparison with someone (an *honnête homme*) who had achieved this. For Descartes, brought up on writers like Seneca, with his techniques for overcoming the passions, morality was about preparing oneself for full moral agency: it was about shaping character, and this meant that attention had to be paid to those factors (corporeal as well as mental states) that retarded or prevented the shaping of character.

Descartes himself was not averse to a medical understanding of such factors, but the *médecins philosophes* were able to develop an elaborate empirical account of the environmental and personal factors inhibiting the appropriate combination of conditions that fostered the formation of a balanced personality. Here we have a new factor bearing on the understanding of morality. We have already noted two such factors that second-order enquiry misses: the constraints of acting under the duress and uncertainty highlighted in tragic drama, and the conflict of responsibilities of office. We now have a third complicating factor: the need to take deviations from an idealized mental/psychological norm into account (perhaps abandoning this idealization), and to treat these as part of the psychological make-up of moral agents, thereby considering degrees of moral responsibility that have mental, corporeal, and environmental determinants.

It is important to stress here that it is not the competence of some particular philosophical account in the understanding of the mind and of morality that is being questioned, but the competence of philosophy per se. What is in question is the ability of a second-order form of enquiry, one that assumes the exclusiveness of reason in understanding mental processes, including moral judgements. This is something that, in the eighteenth century, could reasonably be understood to have brought philosophy to an end, and this is perhaps no better evidenced than by the fact that Kant, the person who will reinvent philosophy from scratch as it were, himself began his intellectual journey by holding this view. In his pre-critical days, for example, he had few doubts about the dangers of pursuing metaphysics and science, and his characterization of them is in terms of something unhealthy: in an essay of 1764 he highlights metaphysical speculation in an account of mental illness and its cure.[28]

Ten years later, in his lectures on logic dating from the early 1770s, Kant distinguishes 'dogmatic' from 'critical' philosophy. The dogmatic philosophers identified are Descartes, Malebranche, Leibniz, and Wolff. Among the critical philosophers, Hume figures prominently in Kant's account, although only Locke is identified here. Summing up the influence of the two approaches, Kant tells us that 'the critical philosophy thrives most, and in this the English have the greatest merit. For the most part the dogmatic method has fallen into disuse in all sciences; even morals is not expounded dogmatically any more, but more often critically.'[29] In aligning himself with 'critical' philosophy in these lectures, Kant is not using the term as he will after his 'critical' turn in the 1780s. The distinction drawn here between critical philosophy and dogmatic philosophy is different, and it reflects a number of deep divisions in European intellectual culture in the second half of the eighteenth century. In its starkest terms, the choice can be seen as that between modelling oneself on Wolff—the systematic metaphysician cloistered in the university and writing in a dry style exclusively for a university audience—and Rousseau—the 'free agent' who sees little if any value in the education provided by universities, and who writes in a personal and engaging style for men and women of letters.

CHAPTER EIGHT

The Search for a Theory of Everything

MARIONETTA [*worried that her sweetheart cousin has come under the spell of the Kantian philosophy*]: *Will you oblige me, Mr Flosky, by giving me a plain answer to a plain question?*
MR FLOSKY [*Kantian philosopher*]: *It is impossible, my dear Miss O'Carroll. I never gave a plain answer to a question in my life.*
MARIONETTA: *Do you, or do you not, know what is the matter with my cousin?*
MR FLOSKY: *To say that I do not know, would be to say that I am ignorant of something; and God forbid, that a transcendental metaphysician, who has pure anticipated cognitions of every thing . . . should fall into so empirical an error as to declare himself ignorant of any thing.*

THOMAS LOVE PEACOCK, *NIGHTMARE ABBEY* (1818)

BY THE MIDDLE DECADES of the eighteenth century, the choice for philosophers was beginning to become one between a theory of everything and (what was considered to be) a Humean-style nothing. The former was slowly emerging as the answer to the decline of the standing of philosophy, a decline to be checked by the emergence of a form of philosophy of unparalleled ambition. This is evident in the title of Christian Wolff's widely reprinted 1720 metaphysics textbook, *Metaphysics or Rational Thoughts on God, the World and the Soul of Man, and on all Things Whatever*. The 'all things whatever' comprised ontology, rational theology, rational cosmology, and rational psychology. On these questions, there was competition from theologians, who had never wholly abandoned the aspiration to a theologically based theory of everything. There had been remnants of Scotist metaphysics among seventeenth-century theologians, and Francisco Suárez's synthetic works in this genre were popular among both Catholic and Protestant theologians, particularly in the Low Countries. Here the aim could be described as a theological theory of everything. But there were also attempts to offer something along the lines of a philosophical theory of everything in two metaphysical systems, those of Spinoza and Leibniz. In his *Ethics*, Spinoza set out to show that a philosophical programme based in mechanist natural philosophy could supply us with an understanding of the world and our place in it which was a comprehensive alternative to that offered by Judeo-Christian teaching and aspirations. Spinoza's pantheism was seen, by some in the eighteenth century, as highly religious in orientation, and Novalis talks of Spinoza as someone 'intoxicated by God' (*Gottrunkener*).[1] The difference is that Spinoza's God is something metaphysical rather than something religious, and wholly at odds with the Judeo-Christian understanding, of which he had provided a devastating criticism in his earlier *Tractatus Theologico-Politicus*.

Leibniz's conception of God, by contrast, is comparatively orthodox, especially on questions such as providence, as is evident from his *Theodicy* (1710), and even though he appears to want to ground the divine in his metaphysics, unlike Spinoza he still wants to maintain a (conventional) distinction between the natural and the supernatural. Wolff took up Leibniz's project, translating its disparate fragments into a systematic account. In one sense it is this project that Kant takes up too, but the Wolffian version is in effect a false start for Kant, who deploys philosophical resources that are so far removed from traditional metaphysics that, in his *Metaphysical Foundations of the Doctrine of Right*, he could announce that philosophy had only begun in 1781, with the publication of his *Critique of Pure Reason*.

How did Kant conceive of what he had achieved in the *Critique* such that this made it the beginning of something quite new? Clearly, given that his stated aim was to examine the very possibility of metaphysics, the examination could not itself be metaphysical. A crucial point about metaphysics for Kant is its claim to a priori knowledge of objects, and in a set of lectures given just after the publication of the first *Critique*,[2] he tells his students that his transcendental philosophy differs from metaphysics in that, in the former, 'reason determines nothing, but rather speaks always of only its own faculty'. Transcendental philosophy, by contrast with metaphysics, has nothing to do with ontology: 'it is concerned with the sources, extent, and the bounds of pure reason, and pays no regard to objects'. This is part of Kant's 'Copernican Revolution'. Up to now, he writes in the Preface to the second edition of the *Critique*, it has been assumed that all our cognition must conform to objects, but this has manifestly failed, so we must try to see whether we might have greater success in supposing that objects must instead conform to our knowledge, thereby proceeding along the lines of Copernicus, who, failing to account for celestial motions on the assumption that the observer was stationary, reversed this and made the observer active, moving around stationary stars.[3]

Actually, starting from the knowing subject and asking what kinds of object match our clear and distinct conceptions is a device that had been used by Descartes and Spinoza. And they, like Kant, had been inspired by mathematics in this respect. But such considerations led Kant in the direction of a novel form of enquiry, an investigation into our capacity to know anything by employing our reason alone, in isolation from everything else.

The *Critique of Pure Reason* starts from sensation, but the aim is to examine the pure or a priori representations proper to each faculty, beginning with that of sensibility, which falls under the rubric of the 'transcendental analytic'. The treatment is distinctive: space and time are, Kant argues, not features of the empirical world, but ways of imposing form on sensation such that its contents can be presented to consciousness. In Kant's terminology, it comprises those things that can be intuited but not thought. An example that stimulated his thinking on this was his 'incongruous counterparts'. It began as a counterexample to Leibniz's theory that space is just the relations between things, so that if there were no things, there would be no space. Incongruous counterparts, the example of which are left-hand and right-hand gloves, are identical in respect to size, proportions and dispositions of their parts, but despite this they do not have boundaries in common, and therefore do not coincide. We can grasp the difference immediately—it can be intuited—yet it cannot be 'thought': we have no conceptual account of the difference. Reflection on this case leads Kant to consider what the difference is between intuition and conceptual understanding, and how such intuition works. It is sensibility that enables us to connect our representational states with an object presented in a particular way. But my representations are in me, not in the world, and the space that they invoke is not in the world either. Space is not an empirical representation, in the sense of something abstracted from external objects. It does not have an empirical origin, for it is a presupposition of my ability to distinguish myself from anything else in the first place. It is the condition of possibility of my having representations at all:

> We can accordingly speak of space, extended beings, and so on, only from the human standpoint. If we depart from the subjective condition under which alone we can acquire outer intuition, namely that through which we may be affected by objects, then the representation of space signifies nothing at all.[4]

Similarly with time: like space, it is a 'form of the intuition', in this case an 'inner' intuition, by contrast with the 'outer' intuition of space. The idea of transcendental philosophy is premised on the treatment of space and time as forms of sensibility, that is, as something 'non-conceptual', in Kant's sense.

The conceptual structuring proper comes with the 'understanding'. While the faculty of sensibility presents the contents of sensation, it presents them as unconnected, and it is the understanding that imposes conceptual structure on these. Concepts are rules for combining certain representations and excluding certain others. The structuring comes in the form of twelve 'categories', such as cause and substance, without which our experience could not result in knowledge of any kind. As well as the categories, however, there are 'principles', which establish necessary connections between our experiences. The necessary connection between cause and effect here becomes something intrinsic to the kinds of experience we have. This is a form of argument we encounter regularly in Kant—something that cannot be demonstrated in its own right is established as a condition of possibility of our having the kind of experience that we have—and, as we shall see, it is used in several different contexts. Finally, Kant distinguishes the understanding from 'reason', a third faculty that, divorced from sensation in the form of 'pure reason', attempts to go beyond the limits of the understanding. Here the procedure is to show how such attempts generate antinomies, cases where both an argument and its negation can be equally asserted, showing what happens when reason alone tries to go beyond experience. The argument is especially effective since the antinomies are generated on basic issues such as space and time, divisibility, causation, and God.

For Kant, it is essential that examination of the three faculties set out in the first *Critique* provide us with a complete understanding of cognition, something possible because of the restriction that there can be no empirical input into the enquiry. It is 'nothing but the inventory of all we possess through pure reason, ordered systematically'.[5] But the *Critique* deals with theoretical knowledge, and the kinds of issue raised are quite different from those relevant to morality, for example. The central problem of theoretical philosophy is the move from an object to my representation of it. Things move in the opposite direction in the case of morality: I modify the present state of the world, in that the object of my moral behaviour is realized on the basis of my representation of what ought to happen. At the time he wrote the first edition of the *Critique*, Kant thought that morality was relatively unproblematic, philosophically speaking, but he rethought his account of morality in his *Groundwork of the Metaphysics of Morals* (1785), and the second edition of the *Critique* (1787) reflects his growing concern with questions of morality.[6]

A complete account of theoretical reasoning will in itself not tell us about morality. Nor will it tell us about religion. Yet in terms of its scope, Kant sets out to offer a theory of everything, something to replace the Leibnizian/Wolffian metaphysical theory of everything, and Leibniz and Wolff had incorporated morality and religion into their accounts. Kant is not just abandoning the resources of traditional metaphysics. Part of this abandonment lies in his distinction between those things that fall within the boundaries of theoretical reason and those that do not. But if morality and religion are identified as falling outside the bounds of theoretical reason, how could they be included in a theory of everything?

Philosophy as a Theory of Everything

The immediate importance of Kant's 'critical philosophy' for his contemporaries lay in a correlate of his establishment of the limits of reason: namely, an understanding of what can be said and done about those things that fall outside the limits of theoretical reason, for it is here that all the ingredients of the 'everything' that is the subject of a theory of everything are locked in. The gap cannot be bridged by metaphysics, and it cannot be the work of pure reason, but nor can areas that fall outside the limits of theoretical reason, such as morality and religion, be allowed to fall outside philosophical enquiry simpliciter. They are subject to second-order enquiry, and this is what allows them to fall under the rubric of a *philosophical* theory of everything. Indeed, for Kant, if morality and religion were to survive, this was on the condition that they could be successfully assimilated into a philosophical model. But what kind of assimilation could second-order enquiry effect? Kant spells out the answer in the *Groundwork of the Metaphysics of Morals*:

> Indeed there is really no other foundation for a metaphys-
> ics of morals than the critique of *pure practical reason*,
> just as that of metaphysics is the critique of pure specu-
> lative reason, already published. . . . I require that the cri-
> tique of pure practical reason, if it is to be carried through

completely, be able at the same time to present the unity of practical with speculative reason in a common principle, which must be distinguished merely in its application.[7]

But morality was indissolubly caught up with religion for Kant and his contemporaries. On Kant's view, morality would simply make no sense without religion, and he will offer a defence of the existence of God and an afterlife as the condition of possibility of our experience of morality. It was as a response to growing uncertainty about what the legitimacy of religious belief consists in that Kant's critical philosophy was transformed from something marginal and thrust to centre stage.

The limits of reason in defending religion was an especially pressing question in German thought from the 1750s onwards.[8] One group, the 'rationalists'—predominantly followers of Christian Wolff—effectively based religion on natural theology, holding that fundamental theological questions, such as the existence of God and the doctrine of personal immortality, were open to rational demonstration, and that scripture was at best allegorical, and at worst mythical. The 'pietist' or 'fideist' response to this approach (the tradition in which Kant himself was raised) was to argue that such questions were a matter of faith, and quite independent of reason, and consequently could only be illuminated through the study of scripture and revelation.

The most prominent defender of reason in the Leibniz/Wolff metaphysical tradition by the 1780s was Moses Mendelssohn. His aim was to offer a middle way between materialism on the one hand, and zealotry, irrationality, and counter-Enlightenment on the other. For Mendelssohn, all judgements—whether theological, aesthetic, exegetical, or philosophical—have a single form, for their conclusion/

predicate only ever makes explicit what is contained in the premises/subject. Of course, judgements invariably seem to reveal to us something new, but on Mendelssohn's account this is only because we have not analysed them fully: such an analysis would show that, in true judgements, the conclusion is always contained in the premises, whereas in false ones it is not. Because of this, reason in the form of metaphysics is able, simply through analysis, to establish the truth or falsity of any judgement. The problem was that this seemed to put in jeopardy principles believed to be necessary to moral conduct or to our happiness, but whose truth we cannot establish. To accept this discrepancy would in turn undermine the duty that we have to follow those principles. Mendelssohn responds by distinguishing sharply between moral and intellectual standards. The reasons that we have to find something morally compelling are simply incommensurable with the reasons we have for believing something true or false. The former are dependent on our beliefs and on acts of will, whereas the latter are not, for whether something is true or not is completely independent of us. In contrast to his opponents, Mendelssohn dissociates moral questions from theological ones. Theological questions—those concerning God's existence, personal immortality, and providence for example—*are* matters of truth and falsity, and they are a matter for metaphysics, even if metaphysics is unable to provide definitive answers to such intractable questions.

The most radical consequences of rationalism surfaced with regard to the issue of the standing of revelation. The 'neologist' school of biblical interpretation rejected the idea that revelation formed a coherent whole, and instead set out to examine dogmas one by one. Original sin, predestination, supernaturally efficacious grace, the damnation of heathens, Christ's atonement for human sin, and the eternality of punishment were all thrown into question in Johann August Eberhard's *New Apology of Socrates* (1772), and in Hermann Samuel Reimarus's posthumously published *Apology or Defence of the Rational Worshippers of God*, especially the fuller 1777 edition, which questioned the concept of a historical revelation, denying that the Bible is a doctrinal text, and arguing that it was simply a collection of ambiguous and contradictory documents.

If rationalism was a radical position, the kind of alternative offered by the *Popularphilosoph* Johann Hamann was no less so. The core argument of Hamann's *Socratic Memorabilia* (1759)[9] is that reason is propositional knowledge, but that there is another kind of knowledge, that of faith, which is non-propositional, and this is superior to propositional knowledge. Hamann develops the claims for non-propositional knowledge by examining the contrast between Socrates and Jesus, traditionally taken to be diametrically opposed advocates of reason and faith respectively. He reinterprets Socrates as a critic of reason, a precursor of Jesus, taking Socrates's attacks on the sophists as a repudiation of those who believe that everything can be grasped through reason: it is the sophists who are the rationalists, whereas Socrates is presented as the antithesis of the sophists, someone for whom the recognition of one's own ignorance is the highest form of knowledge. On Hamann's reading, the crucial thing about Socrates, by contrast with the sophists, is that he is inspired, and it is his inspiration that enables him to grasp the truth. By assimilating this inspiration to faith, Hamann is able to treat faith as a special kind of knowledge. It stands in contrast to propositional knowledge: it is intuitive as opposed to 'rational' knowledge, and, unlike rational knowledge, it is unmediated.

Hamann's writings nicely illustrate the intricacy of the perceived threat to reason, the complexity of its motivations, and the diversity of the proposed solutions. This is important because reason, along with free will, had traditionally been treated as the distinguishing feature of human beings, so any revision to, or threat to, its standing manifestly had profound consequences for how the human realm was conceived. Above all, it had consequences for what resources were drawn on in the attempts to understand human behaviour.

For those who wanted to assert the primacy of reason and at the same time adhere to basic Christian precepts, the problem was how, without treating it in terms of metaphysics—whose ability to secure theological claims had been, and remained, a deeply problematic enterprise—, an account of Christianity could be devised which established that Christianity was not a matter of blind faith, and accordingly something that had a form of legitimacy, one different from metaphysical truths and not inferior to them. When the questions came to a head in the mid-1780s, it emerged that there was an elaborate proposal for a solution to this problem that had been overlooked, in the *Critique of Pure Reason*. The *Critique* was a difficult work, an academic treatise of a kind that was out of fashion, in a genre which Kant himself had rejected in the 1760s and 1770s. It was written at such a level of abstraction that it seemed unconnected to the concerns of the day. To make matters worse, in the same year as its publication, the German translation of Berkeley's *Three Dialogues between Hylas and Philonous* appeared. In the first review of the *Critique*, its advocacy of transcendental idealism was identified with Berkeley's denial of the existence of matter, which was dismissed as nonsense, and at the same time questions were raised as to whether Kant's employment of reason alone, in isolation from everything else, enabled him, for example, to distinguish between the content of experience and that of dreams.[10] The first edition of the *Critique* quickly went out of print, but the 'critical philosophy' received a new lease of life when a one-time Jesuit pupil of Kant, Karl Leonhard Reinhold, underwent what can only be described as a conversion to Kantianism in 1785, and began publishing a series of letters on the *Critique* from the beginning of 1786. Reinhold translated the critical philosophy from an academic treatise into a series of popular essays, renouncing any claims to systematic exposition or demonstrative argument.

To gauge the appeal of this, it is important to remember that Kant's project in his three *Critiques* was not just to fix the limits of reason, but also to explore in a systematic way what could be said about matters that fell outside those limits, and this project was crucially tied up in that of providing a solution to the question of the legitimacy of religious belief. This is the context within which we should situate Kant's solution to the problem of religious understanding: that is, to what one needs to do to make philosophy a theory of everything. But it was a solution that only gained a general currency with Reinhold, whose focus was on whether Kant's critical philosophy could show us how belief in the existence of God, personal immortality, and divine providence can be vindicated. In particular, Reinhold set out to show that, through Kant's doctrine of practical faith, it has a unique claim to success in this. His argument was that the critical philosophy was able to save reason from the scepticism/fideism dichotomy, and to help integrate theology and science into a unified comprehensive vision grounded in metaphysics, or, more properly speaking, that transcendental form of enquiry that has replaced traditional metaphysics for Kant.

On the face of it, the account of the conditions of possibility of experience seems to reinforce the sceptical conclusion as far as religion is concerned. Even worse, by attempting to solve the problem of the standing of religion by offering a general account that removes space, time, and causation from the world, and makes them forms of intuition or forms of structuring the world, religion seems to follow science along a non-realist path. The general difficulty here arises from the fact that, for Kant, all our knowledge is constrained by the way in which the world must appear to us. There is no way in which we can grasp how things are prior to this structuring, so we cannot ask whether there really is a God, independently of an experience that is the product of our own minds, any more than we can ask whether space and time really exist independently of our experience. On Kant's account, metaphysicians, in striving to provide answers to the questions of how things really are, have attempted to use the resources of pure reason to establish how things are in themselves, but in doing so, they have attempted to step outside the boundaries of possible experience. We only have access to appearances, so the task should rather be that of understanding how critical reflection on appearances can reveal something about those things that go beyond them.

The way in which experience is generated is crucial here, for Kant's elaborate argument is that this experience, and the conditions under which it is generated, are universal: the world *must* appear to us in a particular way, and it must appear to all of us in this way, because the conditions of possibility of its appearing in this way are universal. If experience were not constrained by something universal, the critical philosophy would be no better placed than metaphysics in establishing basic truths. But the universal constraints are not all there is to our experience of the world. Equally important, for Kant, is the freedom and autonomy of the subject. Our experience is organized not only by sensory and intuitive structuring over which we have no control, but also by self-imposed conceptual rules. In other words, this structuring of our experience is both a manifestation of something that we simply have to take as given, and at the same time a manifestation of our freedom from an order in the world that simply discloses itself to passive agents.

A key ingredient in Kant's armoury is the use of transcendental arguments. These are deployed not only within the sphere of theoretical reason, but also outside it, in the realm of practical reason. Here Kant sets out to show that the existence of a personal God is a condition of possibility of our having the kind of experience we have, although what is at issue now is not our experience of the natural world, but our experience of morality. The arguments are set out in Kant's writings on practical philosophy.[11] The issues turn in the first instance on the question of freedom, specifically on what he considers to be the undeniability of our freedom. This is simply asserted, and he offers no consideration of problems of moral complexity that we examined in earlier chapters, maintaining rather that we can always distinguish between free and determined behaviour, and that this difference can be captured in the idea that free actions are regulated by a normative principle: unlike determined actions, we can say of free ones that they are correct or incorrect, right or wrong. This is so intrinsic to our behaviour that our freedom is a necessary condition of our acting in the way we do. Note that this freedom is not established by theoretical reason—in the antinomies of pure reason Kant had shown that theoretical reason (in the form of metaphysics) cannot establish whether our behaviour is free or determined—but by practical reason. Our desires and inclinations may be motivated by considerations and principles that have been determined outside our control, but we choose which of these principles to act upon, and we unhesitatingly experience this activity as guided by self-imposed principles. I can always distinguish between the normative question of what I should have done in some particular case, and the factual question of what I did do in that case. That I cannot demonstrate that I am in fact free, as opposed to merely believing that I am free, is a limitation of theoretical reason. What practical reason shows is that my standing back from the world, as it were, and taking a position on what to do and what not to do—or, to put it in different terms, being a genuine agent as opposed to merely part of a deterministic world—is only possible on the condition of freedom.

The principles on which we act when we act freely are not merely subjective, however. When we distinguish between what we did and what we ought to have done, the latter judgement may reflect two different kinds of practical principle: those that we actually act upon, and those that reflect a general criterion for behaving morally or appropriately. The important difference between the two lies in the fact that, in the former case, we would not extend the principles to the behaviour of others, whereas in the latter case we would, in the form of a command or imperative. Kant asks whether any of these imperatives could be unconditionally binding, whether there might be something that binds every rational agent independently of any particular tastes, inclinations, or purposes that guide their behaviour, and he concludes that while this cannot be a substantive principle, it can be a formal one, namely the principle of universalizability: to act only on principles that you would want to become universal. The only way in which ethics can proceed, on Kant's account, is to identify an *unconditional* or absolute good, and this maxim is designed to capture that.

One of the most controversial features of Kant's account of morality was that it appeared to sever the connection between morality and Christianity. But in fact he conceives there to be a form of transcendental connection between morality and God. As it turns out, he would in any case seem to need this connection on independent grounds, because of a very problematic aspect of his account: the relation between morality and happiness, or morality and the 'good life', things which are tightly connected in the Aristotelian tradition of virtue ethics, for example, seem to have come apart in the Kantian picture. The demands of his principle of universalizability—the 'moral law'—override any concern with happiness, yet if the moral good led us in a completely different direction from happiness, then the plausibility of Kant's account of moral behaviour and its motivations would be severely diminished, as he recognized. Instead of acknowledging this as a failing of his account, however, he turns it into a strength, using it to show the necessity of a religious basis for ethics. His solution is to argue that, given we are in fact motivated by the moral law (amongst other things), and given that the moral law does not guarantee happiness in this life, then to explain our moral behaviour, at a motivational level, we need to invoke a kind of idealized 'highest good', something on which morality and happiness converge. We need to act as if this convergence were possible, and two things must be the case for it to be possible: we need to postulate continued existence after this life, that is, personal immortality; and we need to postulate the existence of a personal God who correlates virtue and happiness in due proportion. In short, given the insights into the nature of morality that Kant believes he has provided, we need to invoke the existence of God and personal immortality if we are to make sense of our moral behaviour. The argument does not establish the existence of either personal immortality or God, for it was one of the basic errors of 'pure' or theoretical reason to believe that these were things that could be demonstrated. Rather, it is designed to show that we have no option but to believe in these things: we must act (and in effect always do act, in Kant's view) as if they were true.

The answerability of reason—a union of both theoretical and practical reason—to itself alone is a crucial ingredient in Kant's understanding of the completeness of his theory of everything, for it means that reason carries within itself its own ends. Because it sets ends for the understanding, it is inherently teleological, something explored in detail in the *Critique of Judgement*, the third and final of the series. It is this teleology that binds the parts into a single whole, and it is on the question of the systematic unity of this single whole that the fate of Kant's transcendental philosophy hinged.

All or Nothing

The veridicality of our representations of reality had preoccupied early modern philosophers, but Kant moved the concern of philosophy away from this. On his account, our cognitive powers are answerable to themselves alone, and the task is the establishment of the unity of these cognitive powers: the unity of reason. This is the framework of idealism, and the move from Kant's transcendental idealism to the absolute idealism of Schelling and Hegel was a continuous one, in which the task, to make reason answerable only to itself, was completed. Accordingly, just as Kant had claimed that philosophy had begun only with the publication of his *Critique of Pure Reason* in 1781, we should not be surprised to see Hegel declaring in 1806 that, with the publication of his *Phenomenology of Spirit*, philosophy had now been completed, and come to an end.[12]

The move to absolute idealism was a response to a perceived failure of systematicity in transcendental idealism, without which there was no unified theory of everything. The aspirations of the Kantian programme remained largely intact, especially the idea that reason was answerable to itself alone, but there was a widespread belief among advocates of a Kantian programme that Kant himself had failed to secure it. Kant had speculated on the idea of a single first principle to ground his philosophy, writing that sensibility and understanding perhaps spring from a common root.[13] He had clearly considered such a single source unknowable, however. Yet to have something unknowable at the basis of a comprehensive account of reason was understandably regarded as unsatisfactory, rendering the whole system incomplete. The root of the problem in Kant, on the account of his erstwhile popularizer, Reinhold, was his failure to investigate the principles and procedures underlying the acquisition of transcendental knowledge, and without this we can have no confidence in the theory founded on them. In his 'foundations of philosophical knowledge', Reinhold sought a single first principle on which to ground the whole enterprise in a 'principle of consciousness' which would secure a unified faculty of representation. At the same time, he insisted that philosophy must be systematic if it was to achieve this task, and that it must take the form of phenomenology, offering a presuppositionless account of consciousness.

Reinhold relates that his discomfort with Kant came when he was teaching the critical philosophy, and found that disputes between Kant's defenders and detractors were no more resolvable than the old disputes between 'dogmatists'.[14] Kant had claimed that the *Critique of Pure Reason* finally resolved all the debates between philosophers, and accordingly a deep lack of agreement on basic concepts went to the heart of the transcendental philosophy. Repair was urgently needed, and for Reinhold this meant going back to a fundamental concept of the *Critique* which Kant had left egregiously undefined: representation. The concept of knowledge presupposed that of representation, and the idea of synthetic a priori knowledge that stood at the centre of the *Critique* depended crucially upon it. Reinhold therefore sets out, in his *Essay on a New*

Theory of the Human Capacity for Representation (1789), a new theory of representation—a theory of consciousness as such—and proceeds to deduce all the results of the *Critique* from it. But equally important to Reinhold's reformulation of the critical philosophy was the question of systematicity. Kant's procedure, he argues, was analytic, in that it moves from the parts to the whole, in what he considers a random way. What is needed is something truly synthetic, something that begins with the idea of the whole and then proceeds to deduce the necessary order of its parts. In this way, we should be able to establish the unity of our faculties, a key criticism in Kant's idealist successors, and something generally understood among them to be necessary for a successful realization of the project of transcendental philosophy.

The requirements both of representation and of systematicity played a guiding role in subsequent attempts to reform the Kantian schema, and although Reinhold's solution quickly fell out of favour, his rethinking of what was needed to realize the Kantian project inspired attempts, over the next forty years, to offer a theory of everything. A theory of everything is the ultimate in ambition, and, as Kant himself was aware, if the fundamentals can be questioned, then the project comes to nothing. The target of attack for his idealist successors—notably Fichte, Schelling, and Hegel—was his contentious separation between the sensibility and the understanding, which he had not only failed to elaborate upon, but had treated as if it were a given, beyond investigation. The unity of philosophical understanding is the core issue here. The separation between sensibility and understanding not only looks purely contingent, as opposed to being the result of a single philosophical understanding, but involves a separation between form and content which the idealists saw as the source of problems in Kant, and which they accordingly merged. The form of our representations has its source in the subject, and this merging means that the matter of empirical objects, which forms the content of our representations, also has its source in us. This idealist solution has a welcome consequence for what was the sticking point of Kantian philosophy for its advocates and critics alike: things-in-themselves. For Kant, we deduce the existence of these from the fact that we know that something not constituted by the forms of sensibility must occupy the conceptual space outside experience. But this in turn hinges on a separation between form and content, and when the two are merged, the need for things-in-themselves disappears.

The search for a single principle underlying the whole also means that the separation between theoretical and practical reason, and correspondingly that between nature and freedom, is dissolved. The subject comes to the fore here. It does not merely condition the world in accordance with the understanding; it is wholly responsible for the world. In Fichte, this means that the subject comes to understanding by 'positing' itself, and the self-understanding that results is ipso facto an understanding of the world as well, for this comes with the positing. For Schelling, Fichte's subjective idealism fails to do justice to the fact of an external objective world, and he develops a 'philosophy of identity' in which the subject and object emerge as products of a self-division in a primordial unity, the Absolute, and on this conception it does not matter whether we derive the self from nature or nature from the self. Finally, in the most influential of the idealist schemes, that of Hegel, all objects of knowledge are deduced in a highly systematic way from a descendent of Schelling's Absolute: Spirit (*Geist*). But just what this consisted in was obscure: was this Spirit a universal interpersonal subject of thought, which enclosed all individual subjects, or was it a quasi-Platonic realm to which subjects had access?

What we have in Kant and the idealist attempts that, driven by the Kantian vision, sought to develop or replace him, is a set of varied efforts to establish the most comprehensive understanding of the world possible. This, of necessity, was conceived as taking the form of a single system, a single philosophical source of understanding, something whose only precedent (in the West) was the Christian understanding of the world that found its fullest statement in Augustine. But the Christian project and the philosophical one were not the only theories of everything. There was one more to come, and it was in many ways a direct response to the failure of the philosophical theory of everything.

Science as a Theory of Everything

German philosophy effectively had the field to itself in continental Europe in the period from the last decades of the eighteenth century up to Hegel's death in 1831. For most German philosophers, Kantian thought had been surpassed first by that of Fichte and Schelling, and then by that of Hegel. Orthodox Hegelians had considered that Hegel's work was the culmination of philosophy, and so had brought philosophizing to an end. With the rapid decline in the standing of Hegelian philosophy in the wake of his death, however, a vacuum opened up, and it did indeed begin to look like philosophy had come to an end, if not for the reasons that Hegelians had supposed. A certain style of philosophizing, which had begun with Kant, but which had been transformed in quite a radical way in classical German idealism, had collapsed under its own weight, and there was no alternative with anything like its breadth of vision and standing. In Germany, there were a number of reactions to this, some involving a politically radical materialist reworking of Hegel in the writings of the 'Young Hegelians',[15] others involving a revival of Schopenhauer's largely forgotten idiosyncratic reworking of Kant.[16] The crucial development, from the point of view of our concerns, is that the collapse of speculative idealism occurred at the same time as a significant rise in the fortunes of science, and the interplay between these is what distinguishes the developments that followed. This is not a peculiarly German development, but the debates in Germany were particularly influential, and more than any other developments shaped how science and philosophy were conceived well into the twentieth century.

On the face of it, there is a straightforward division in mid-nineteenth century German thought between those who considered that philosophy no longer had any role to play, and those who thought that philosophy was needed to rationalize and understand just what science is and what its achievements are. With the demise of idealist philosophy, the view emerged that science could take over all the questions with which philosophy had concerned itself, and could begin to explore them in an empirical way, with the aim of establishing materialism.

We can distinguish two broad kinds of materialism devoted to the replacement of philosophy by science. First there is the group of self-styled 'scientific materialists', such as Karl Vogt, Jakob Moleschott, and Ludwig Büchner, who argued that there was nothing that could not be explained in materialist—either physico-chemical or physiological—terms. The second group, in which we can include Hermann von Helmholtz, Emil du Bois-Reymond, Rudolf Virchow and others, argued that everything that we can explain could be explained in materialist terms, but that there were limits to knowledge. Consciousness provided a point of division between the two groups. For du Bois-Reymond, for example, the lesson is clear: in the case of consciousness, we simply have to concede that some things might be inexplicable.[17] In allowing the idea that there might be areas that fall outside purely scientific understanding, du Bois-Reymond and others were not suggesting that there could be other forms of study that would allow these areas to be opened up. There was no understanding that was not scientific understanding for them: it was just that such understanding could not be exhaustive. As he put it in an 1876 talk,

> For us the only knowledge is mechanical knowledge, no matter how poor a surrogate for true knowledge this may be, and consequently there is only one true scientific form of thought, the physical-mathematical. Because of this, there can be no mistake more serious than to believe that one has explained the purposefulness of organic nature by appealing to an immaterial intelligence, conceived in our image and acting purposefully. . . . As soon as one leaves the realm of mechanical necessity one enters the boundless foggy regions of speculation, gaining nothing.[18]

For the scientific materialists, by contrast, the effective postulation of an unknowable realm came suspiciously close to commitment to a Kantian noumenal realm. The division between the two groups had a political and religious dimension, the first tending towards political radicalism and atheism, the second towards conservative politics and an unquestioning attitude (at least in public) to religious orthodoxy. Moreover, the scientific materialists, who were marginalized in the scientific community, thrived in the genre of popular science, by contrast with Helmholtz et al., who had an authoritative voice within the scientific establishment, albeit one that they occasionally had to struggle to maintain as Prussian politics shifted ground.

The materialists were divided in this way amongst themselves on the question of whether science could answer every question. But the two groups were united on the issue of what explanatory resources were legitimate: namely, those limited to science. In particular, they were united in opposing the philosophical speculation that had come to a head in German idealism, and for them this meant an end to philosophy per se. Philosophy, in the form of German idealism, had had totalizing aspirations, subsuming all forms of knowledge, including science. For the materialists, these totalizing aspirations were not abandoned with the collapse of German idealism, but were transferred to science.

The 1850s was the decade in which scientific materialism flourished in Germany. In the writings of the scientific materialists, reductionism was presented as the way to dispense with the Kantian distinction between the noumenal and phenomenal realms, and Vogt, Moleschott, and Büchner are very much in the ontological tradition of French eighteenth-century materialists such as La Mettrie and d'Holbach, where what was at issue was the question of the primacy of matter. This forms the basis for the association of their programme with atheism and radical anti-clericalism, through the denial of the existence of any spiritual substance, or spiritual realm more generally. But the programme of scientists such as du Bois-Reymond and Helmholtz had no such radical consequences. On the contrary, it studiously avoided them. Its proponents were not interested in denying the spiritual, but concerned with proceeding in scientific enquiry in a way that demonstrated no need for any appeal to the spiritual.

Ethics was a different matter. Even the group of scientists associated with du Bois Reymond and Helmholtz saw science, rather than philosophy or religion, as a model for ethics. In 1858, du Bois-Reymond's colleague Virchow was one of a number of physiologists and others calling for ethics to be guided by science, and, in an 1873 talk on 'The Sciences and Their

Importance for the Ethical Education of Humanity', he argued that, for progress and prosperity, natural scientists must participate in applying the scientific method 'to problems of the spirit, and of the conscience; we demand that each from his own standpoint help to develop morality as an empirical science according to the rules which general natural science has constituted'. Meanwhile, in Britain, Francis Galton was calling for a 'scientific priesthood' to tend to the health and welfare of the nation, and Thomas Huxley was arguing that scientific progress had laid 'the foundations for a new morality'. Herbert Spencer was urging that ethical principles be derived not from religious precepts, but from scientific ones, in his *The Principles of Ethics* (1892). By the early decades of the twentieth century, there was if anything an increase in the number of calls for science to act as the basis for morality, summed up later in the century in E. O. Wilson's claim that the time might have come for 'ethics to be removed temporarily from the hands of philosophers and biologicized'.[19]

The Quantification of Morality

By contrast with general and speculative projects for the reform of ethics along scientific lines, there was one scientific approach to ethics, utilitarianism, that emerged in the nineteenth century and has seemed to a number of philosophers since to be able to offer what was needed. Eighteenth-century thinkers had naturalized sensibility—subjecting it to empirical investigation, on the model of the sciences—by relying primarily on developments in the physiology of sensation and in the study of the nerves. As we saw in chapter 6, the French Lockeans had argued that it is sensibility that provides us with access to the external world, and the route to naturalization of cognitive and affective states was through sensibility.

Reason was considered unnaturalizable, but at the end of the eighteenth century, Bentham's utilitarianism rejected all talk of sensibility and offered what looked like a direct form of naturalization of reason. Bentham initiated the naturalization of moral reasoning, arguing that the morality of behaviour was to be assessed in terms of observable consequences, and John Stuart Mill subsequently extended the naturalization programme to all forms of reasoning, construing logical inference in terms of a combination of naturalistic psychology and empirical generalization.

Utilitarianism embraced consequentialism, a quantitative form of ethical decision making designed to replace traditional moral philosophies, which had construed ethics in terms of the intentions and the character of the agent, considerations discarded in consequentialism. Political economy and utilitarian ethics were in the vanguard of the naturalization of economic, political, and moral discourse, and Mill unified ethics and political economy into a single scientifically inspired utilitarian project. Having translated ethics and economics into a 'scientific form', the utilitarian unification formed what was perhaps the most ambitious of any of the unity of science projects of the nineteenth century. Moreover in carrying out this project, Mill offered an integrated account not only of ethics and political economy, but also of the empirical sciences, logic, and mathematics, and thereby opened up new and unprecedented questions about the nature and limits of scientific understanding, questions that were to preoccupy philosophy to such an extent that enquiry into the standing of science came to be one of its defining features from the second half of the nineteenth century onwards.

Mill's original concern was, nevertheless, not with questions of science, but with political ones, in particular the elaboration and defence of a radical politics. But his debates with

William Whewell raised deep issues about the epistemological standing of the 'moral sciences', particularly ethics and political economy, and the question arose of how one should discuss morality. Whewell had located his discussion in the context of knowledge generally, and had contrasted it with scientific knowledge in crucial respects. In taking up questions of scientific knowledge, Mill engages the issues on the terrain that Whewell sets out. Drawing on Kant, Whewell had postulated the existence of 'fundamental ideas' which guide our empirical investigation of nature. These are objective, not just in the sense that they capture something in nature, but because they correspond to archetypical ideas existing independently of any particular beliefs that humans have. In the context of the moral sciences, these 'fundamental ideas' are used to provide a grounding for traditional conceptions of political and moral conservatism. This is the pivotal point of Mill's disagreement with Whewell, and, against fundamental ideas, he pits induction as the source of our knowledge and understanding of the world.

Both Whewell and Mill sought objectivity in our moral and scientific judgements. The basic reason behind this agreement is that both see morality in terms of the exercise of reason, not sensibility as Hume and Smith, for example, had advocated. Consequently questions of objectivity and truth are paramount. The contrast between the two lies in the fact that induction appeals to an external standard, whereas Whewell's 'intuitionism' seeks a priori support for moral ideals. Mill advocates abandoning the idea of a priori support and making the whole of knowledge subject to external standards.[20] Induction is the external standard in the case of the sciences, consequentialism in the case of morality. The answer to the problem of moral diversity and conflict—between different societies or (as was becoming a pressing problem) between individual morality and commercial culture—cannot lie in the kind of moral pluralism advocated by Hume and Smith. There must be a single moral code. But to specify this moral code in terms of a particular content, as Whewell does, seemed to Mill to involve an unjustified, and indeed unjustifiable, choice of content. How then could objectivity be secured? One answer was that it must consist in eschewing questions of content and elaborating a rule. Kant had proposed such a rule—universalizability, the criterion by which the morality of an action depends on whether it could become one that everyone could act upon in similar circumstances—, but this was an internal rule, whereas Mill, following the utilitarian tradition of Bentham and James Mill, wants something external, namely the consequences of the act, to serve as the criterion by which to decide morality. It was not the character of the person acting, the person's intention, or the universalizability of the act that mattered, but the observable consequences. If the act had harmful consequences, then it was immoral to act in that way. A great deal of qualification and fine-tuning was necessary to establish the plausibility of consequentialism between its formulation in Mill, and that of successors such as Sidgwick, but the crucial point was that consequences were external and observable. This, combined with the fact that they were calculable, in that one could compare actions in terms of the amount of benefit or harm they caused, gave consequentialist morality a quasi-scientific standing: an independence from particular habits, prejudices, or ill-formed beliefs, and a decision procedure that—unsurprisingly, given its connection with political economy—was not unlike a form of economic calculation.

What was new here was the way in which the standing and application of science lay at the foundation of the debates. Bentham and James Mill had not connected their programmes for moral and political reform with science, nor had their opponents, the defenders of conservative morality and politics. Whewell changed this, propelling the epistemological and methodological standing of science into the centre of the question of how we are to live our lives. Mill's strategy was to demonstrate that fundamental ideas were not needed, in either the physical or the mathematical sciences, so Whewell's proposed justification for his moral theory in the role of fundamental ideas in the sciences fell flat. But Whewell's account had two apparent strengths. First, bare induction, from particular facts to general conclusions, is unlikely to yield fruitful scientific results: the idea that induction might be guided by 'fundamental ideas', indistinctly grasped at first but gradually coming to light in the course of the enquiry, provides a means by which induction might be led along fruitful paths. Second, for Mill, while it is external standards that secure objectivity in the cases of the natural sciences, in the form of induction, and morals and politics, in the form of consequentialism, it is not clear what provides these standards in a deductive discipline such as pure mathematics. Whewell could rely on a variety of fundamental ideas to secure mathematical truths, maintaining that they correspond to ideal archetypes. But these are internal criteria, as is Kant's construal of mathematical truths as synthetic a priori. If Mill were to make a general case for external criteria, then he had to provide an account of what these would be in the case of an apparently purely deductive endeavour such as mathematics or logic.

This Mill set out to do, in one of his most ambitious philosophical exercises, offering a novel theory of logic. On this theory, inference is the process by which we move 'from known truths, to arrive at others really distinct from them'.[21] Logic 'is the entire theory of the ascertainment of reasoned or inferred truth', and it divides into two forms, induction and deduction (the latter of which he calls ratiocination): when 'the conclusion is more general than the largest of the premises, the argument is Induction; when less general, or equally general, it is Ratiocination'. Induction and deduction share fundamental characteristics on this conception, and both fall under Mill's general account of truth, whereby 'truths are known to us in two ways: some are known directly, and of themselves; some through the medium of other truths. The former are the subjects of Intuition, or Consciousness; the latter, of Inference'. Directly known truths are sensory experiences, unlike Whewell's archetypical ideas, which are purely intelligible, that is, non-sensory. They allow scientific inference to meet an external criterion of objectivity.

In short, not only had Mill quantified morality, but at the same time he had incorporated moral reasoning into a form that closely paralleled scientific reasoning, presenting them as part of a unified enterprise. Well might Quine, a century later, maintain that 'philosophy of science is philosophy enough'.[22]

CHAPTER NINE

Science Assimilates Philosophy

SCIENCE AS A THEORY OF EVERYTHING, ubiquitous as it now is, is not a distinctively twentieth-century phenomenon. Rather, it emerges in the mid- to late nineteenth century, and it took up a project to which theologians, eighteenth-century metaphysicians, and then Kant and his idealist successors had devoted their resources. And just as theology had to scale back its ambitions as philosophy took over, so the ambitions of philosophy had to be radically realigned with those of science as the latter took up the mantle. In this final chapter I want to consider the early development of two of the most significant ways in which this realignment altered philosophy, both taking their cues, in different ways, from problems deriving from Kant. The first is the attempt to find a place for philosophy as a metatheory of science. Here philosophy becomes an underlabourer of science, as Locke had suggested, but in a way that he couldn't have envisaged. The second is the attempt to provide a scientific foundation for philosophy, for example by replacing epistemology by formal logic, effectively attempting to make philosophizing a non-empirical form of scientific enquiry, something of equal standing with science. Nevertheless, despite what seems to be a significant divergence in aims, in practice the two projects are often difficult to separate: the overriding goal is that philosophy be associated with science, and how this is achieved varies.

Philosophy as a Metatheory of Science

In the wake of the collapse of a philosophical theory of everything and its replacement as the master discipline by science, philosophy had to be radically reconfigured if it was to survive as a significant enterprise. There remained a metaphysical reading of Kant, gradually built up in the later decades of the nineteenth century. But by far the predominant interpretation was the epistemological one developed by the Marburg School of neo-Kantians, which, in the final decades of the nineteenth century, offered a vision of philosophy as a metatheory of science. It comprised an attempt to re-purpose Kantian epistemology to a new role, making it undergo a radical transformation from a theory of everything to something approaching Locke's under-labourer conception of philosophy. The aim was to 'complete' scientific enquiry, by providing it with legitimating foundations that science itself was unable to provide, but which, the neo-Kantians argued, it needed if its goal as the ultimate form of understanding were to be achieved. Philosophy here was wholly devoted to rationalizing and legitimating science, which had now become the paradigm form of enquiry.

For Hermann Cohen, the leading light of the Marburg School, Kant provided a systematic method for philosophizing, and it is the systematic nature of this method that Cohen is eager to preserve. Starting from the natural sciences, the aim is to discover what gives scientific theories their unity and coherence, reconstructing and analysing them so as to identify the conceptual basis on which we are able to group phenomena together and unify them under general causal laws. These general causal laws are mathematical and logical, and they display the 'presuppositions and foundations' inherent in the facts of science. Cohen sees the uncovering of the basic philosophical principles underlying science not merely as a reflection on science, but as contributing to its progress, by clarifying the relation between science and mathematics and identifying their common goals.

In one of his last pieces, Cohen asks, 'What is science?', and 'What is cognition?'.[1] Answering the first question, he supplements the examination of the facts of science as revealed by its history with the provision of a philosophical grounding for science. He then links this to the second question, arguing that providing a philosophical grounding for science is the same as providing a philosophical grounding for knowledge more generally. Philosophy, in the form of the new Kantian-inspired discipline of epistemology, and science are now part of the same endeavour. For Cohen, the natural sciences are no less constitutive of knowledge than they were for the scientific materialists, but there is nevertheless a role for philosophy, in the form of epistemology: namely, that of providing a systematic understanding of the success of science, and thereby making sense of it, that is, making sense of why a scientific understanding of the world is understanding per se. 'In the final analysis', he asks, 'what does philosophy want to accomplish? It wants to represent the progressive connection of philosophical problems to the whole of human culture.'[2] This progressive connection must be one grounded in science.

Cohen arrives at this conception by means of a radical reworking of Kant. In 1902, in his *Logic of Pure Understanding*, the first volume of his 'System of Philosophy' (the three volumes of which mirror Kant's three *Critiques*), things-in-themselves are stripped of any existence outside the mind and construed merely as objects of thought: they become regulative concepts of scientific discovery. The model here is Cohen's elaborate account of infinitesimals in mathematics, which he argues mirror things-in-themselves. Infinitesimals originate in, and are generated purely by, mathematical operations. They are not independent of mathematics, and provide an analogy for how things-in-themselves are not independent of thought, but are internally generated limits. The consequences of this dependence on thought are drawn for Kant's distinction between sensible intuitions and concepts. Kant had argued that sensibility must precede the application of the categories to experience. There must be 'an orientation in thought', on a par with our orientation in space and time, which provides us with a starting point, as it were, from which our understanding of the world begins. This starting point is prior to the application of the categories which we use to come to an understanding of the world. The categories themselves are the work of reason. But this does not mean that our orientation in thought, subsequently intimately connected with sensibility, is pre-rational, or not rational in some other way. Kant himself does not provide a definitive answer, though he proceeds as if it were guided by reason. Cohen offers a clear-cut solution, ridding sensibility of any separate role, and subjecting all aspects of experience to the dictates of reason. The consequence of losing a separate faculty of sensibility is that knowledge is no longer a relation between the mind and something independent of it: all knowledge now becomes something internal, a doctrine that Cohen calls 'critical idealism'. Truth is no longer a matter of correspondence, but becomes a question of internal relations. Accordingly, it is the coherence of internal relations—the unity of a philosophically construed science—in which the understanding of science now consists, and neither psychology nor ontology have any place in this understanding. At the same time, such a move makes epistemology the sole arbiter of experience, and for the Marburg School generally, epistemology is essentially a metatheory of science.

Philosophy is completely reconfigured on Cohen's conception, and it has aspirations to offering a totalizing form of understanding, but no longer in its own right. On this account, what the philosophy of science sets out to establish is the basis for the unity of science. Science must be a single form of understanding if it is to occupy the intellectual role that he sees for it, and if it is a single form of understanding, then this is something that must be established beyond dispute. The legitimacy of science as the pre-eminent form of understanding the world, and of the understanding of our place in the world, depends on its unity, but it cannot establish this simply by relying on its own resources: for that, philosophy, qua theory of the foundations of science, is needed. Philosophy *completes* science, by establishing its unity on an a priori basis. Without philosophy, science would risk decomposing into an unruly mixture of disciplines (which is in fact what it is, as I have argued elsewhere[3]). Marburg neo-Kantianism binds itself to science, providing a protective perimeter, while effectively having no identity outside this role.

Yet, in his last writings, Cohen began to consider that the idea of philosophy as simply a guarantor of science might be too narrow, and in his 'philosophy of symbolic forms', Ernst Cassirer, following what he took to be Cohen's lead, attempted to include a wide range of attempts to come to terms with the world, from myth and religion through aesthetic forms, which he brought under a general theory.[4] The general theory ended up as a genealogy of reason, however, with the various forms of engagement with the world following a historical sequence, each gradually being superseded so that what we end up with is science at the pinnacle. Although the exercise is supposed to show how non-scientific forms of understanding can be accommodated to a general model, and despite not only Cassirer's insistence that no one region of human experience could claim priority over any other, but also his emphasis on the aesthetic dimension of Kant's work, it becomes an exercise in the progress of reason, and the progress of reason could have no other outcome but science. Both critics and supporters of Cassirer had problems reconciling the idea that myth, for example, was autonomous with Cassirer's conception of science. The question accordingly arises as to why Cassirer should have tried to incorporate everything within propositional understanding. Why could he not allow that there are legitimately non-propositional ways of engaging the world: 'legitimate' in that they cannot be judged by the standards of science, or treated as if they must ultimately converge on scientific understanding? The answer is that Cassirer's is ultimately an Enlightenment project, more specifically a Kantian Enlightenment project: reason overcomes bigotry and prejudice, it secures cosmopolitan values, and in the form of science it provides the motor of civilization. To sacrifice this project would in effect, for Cassirer, have been to sacrifice civilization. A Kantian Enlightenment understanding of the central role of rationality in the moral and political spheres is a crucial aspect of neo-Kantianism. But this rationality has now become one explicitly identified with science, philosophy itself having become simply a metatheory of science.

The Logical Structure of the World

A second response to the challenge of science replacing philosophy was the elaboration of a 'scientific' form of philosophy, the aim of which was to translate the concerns and procedures of philosophy into as scientific a form as possible. The origins of this approach can be traced to Mill, who conceived of logic in such a way that it provided a unifying basis for every sphere of cognitive activity, from the natural sciences and mathematics to morality and economics. The core philosophical problem for Mill is that of objectivity, and how it is to be secured. In *A System of Logic*, he argued in some detail that mathematical truths were empirical generalizations which were widely applicable and widely confirmed. His attempt to establish a general account of the objectivity of reasoning makes philosophy a form of science, with the same canons of reasoning applied to both. The two are continuous, and philosophy, despite its distinctive subject matter, is assimilated to science.

One upshot of Mill's reconstruction of philosophy on a scientific model is that epistemology becomes assimilated to logic. But Mill's own logic could not carry the weight of the new projects that emerged at the turn of the century. His psychologistic conception suffered from insuperable problems. In arguing that psychology studies thought, for example, he set out to discover the empirical laws that regulate thought, for if it were to have a scientific standing, he argued, it must then be subject to external criteria of evidence. But how could what is involved in mathematical operations—calculations or proofs— be captured in empirical-psychological laws of thought? To claim that what we treat as valid proofs or correct calculations is a fact about how our minds work perhaps makes sense in Kantian terms, where the fact is a conceptual one about what it is to think, but it is difficult to see what rationale there could be for it as an empirical feature of thought. Moreover, it is difficult to understand what justification there could be for Mill's claim that we discover logical, geometrical, and arithmetical truths experimentally. Above all, Mill's emphasis on generality in terms of the compression of many truths, in geometry, for example, in an economical and fruitful way is revealing, because it indicates that his way of thinking about deduction is really about geometrical truths—what makes them true—, not about deductive inference as such. The traditional question of logicians, namely which inferences are truth-preserving and why, has a minor role in Mill's discussion.

But truth preservation is exactly what those logicians who thought, in the wake of Boole, of logic in algebraic terms, considered the essence of logic. Such considerations were probably what motivated both Frege and Russell to be attracted initially to Kant's view. Both held, against Mill, that mathematics was a priori. But both subsequently abandoned the theory that it was synthetic a priori: that is, that it was not empirically true, so much as presupposed by the very possibility of experience. Independently of one another, they moved to the view that arithmetic is analytic. It might seem that this raised the problem of how one secures objectivity, but Frege argued in detail that the psychologistic view—whereby mathematics ultimately becomes a branch of empirical psychology—, rather than stopping relativism, actually invites it, because it offers no way of separating subjective ideas from objective thoughts. At the same time, on Frege's account of numbers, Millian questions of objectivity simply do not arise. Numbers had been traditionally treated as properties, so that the question arises of whether these are objective properties. But on Frege's account, they are not properties at all, but particular kinds of abstract object: not predicates, but names.

Frege held that geometry was synthetic a priori, as Kant had argued. On arithmetic, however, he rejected the Kantian view, and set out to show that arithmetic is analytic. Logic had traditionally been seen in this light: it was conceived to be the study of general laws of reasoning which were operative in every sphere of knowledge, and needed no support from empirical facts. Frege's first task was to show what was wrong in the Millian view of logic. *The Foundations of Arithmetic* (1884) sets out to show that logic had to be reformulated if it was to bear the weight of arithmetic. The discovery of a basic underlying structure to mathematics and logic was Frege's central project. Once this structure has been discovered, he argued, we will see that logic underlies mathematics. It is the basic form of inference. That is to say, it is the basic form of reasoning.

Now we reason with thoughts, and if our account of reasoning is to be complete, it must include an analysis of thoughts which reveals their structure. Boole had formulated logic in a way that resembled arithmetical equations, and he had taken Aristotelian syllogistic, which was constitutive of logic at that time, and tried to think it through in algebraic terms. But Aristotelian logic worked with a subject–predicate form, and Frege realized that the attempt to capture all inference in subject–predicate form breaks down in a number of significant cases. He concluded that the language of thought is not of subject–predicate form. The basic syntax of logic needs reformulating, and for Frege, syntax is motivated by semantics: syntax enables meaning to be conveyed, and it is subject ultimately to the constraints of semantics. So what is needed is a universal grammar which captures logical form adequately.

For example, the syllogism 'All men are mortal, Socrates is a man, therefore Socrates is mortal' is a valid argument not merely in virtue of the inference form, but also in virtue of how the component parts of the premises and conclusion bind together into a deductive argument. But how does one identify the role of the component parts: how do 'is' and 'a' and 'man' contribute to the validity of the argument? We need to have an account of their logical role. In other words, we need not only a logic that tells us about the relations between propositions— a propositional calculus—but also a 'predicate calculus':

something that tells us about the internal composition of propositions. Aristotle had tried to pursue the latter, but Frege thinks an algebraic analysis of propositions shows that he got it completely wrong. The question is how our thoughts are put together. What we need is an account of how their constituent parts are functionally related, so that they can be put in inferential relations with one another. And since to be put in inferential relations with one another they must be true or false, we need to know what it is that makes them true or false. It's here that we get the transition from a question of mathematics or formal logic to the deep philosophical questions about the nature of thought and what makes thoughts true.

In exploring the logical structure of thought, a pressing question is that of objectivity. Mill had assumed that objectivity requires that there is an association between proper names and what they refer to, a view that trades on the idea that the world is already differentiated, so that the point of the exercise is to identify and label already differentiated components. Frege retained the naming model of meaning, whereby meaning consists in a relation between something linguistic and something extralinguistic, but he revises it in a fundamental way: he argues that sentences, not words, are the minimal units of meaning. In making sentences the minimal unit of meaning, he is able to avoid equating meaning with what the linguistic items refer to, whether this be ideas or things, while at the same time he is still able to make it consist in a relation to something extralinguistic, namely truth conditions: to know the meaning of a sentence is to know the conditions under which that sentence is true. Truth conditions are Frege's way of providing meaning with the requisite objectivity and freedom from psychological reduction. Such an account is not possible if one retains the traditional view that words are the minimal units of meaning, for words are not the kinds of thing that have truth conditions, and on a Fregean account, insofar as one can talk of the meanings of words, it consists in the contributions they make to the sentences in which they appear. If we can provide a 'conceptual notation' that captures the essential meaning of terms that link propositions together, such as 'if', 'and', 'or', 'not', and the terms that operate within propositions, such as 'there is', 'some', 'any', 'all', then we can show how the truth value of a complex proposition depends on its component propositions.

Mill had to all intents and purposes replaced epistemology by logic—inductive logic or 'scientific method' in this case—but this proved implausible. The logic with which Frege replaces epistemology not only yields a theory of meaning, however, but shows how meaning underlies our thought about the world. Kant had offered an epistemological theory of the structure of thought, and he and his idealist successors had extrapolated from this to the structure of the world. A parallel move is exactly what we now see in the wake of Frege: an attempt to infer the logical structure of the world from the logical structure of thought. This is a project grounded in a scientific model, but it has every appearance of being a reformulation of a Kantian idealist project.

Frege's reform of logic and his corresponding theory of meaning provided the key to two new philosophical projects, phenomenology and analytical philosophy. As far as phenomenology was concerned, the aim was to provide a 'scientific', that is, a presuppositionless, account of the structure of consciousness, based on a Fregean account of the structure of language. In his phenomenology, Husserl argued that it was intentional acts that had meanings, and linguistic acts were simply a species of these. His postulation of a single class of meaning entities—noematic 'senses'—that play a role not just in language, but in all acts that can generally be construed as intentional, is of central importance here, because it allows him to conclude that linguistic activities generally are based upon underlying intentional phenomena which they express. His argument is that, when we understand an utterance, there is an inner mental process that accompanies the utterance, and this is what constitutes the act of understanding. The mind lies behind both language and perception, which are representations of mental processes. It is here that the phenomenological and analytic traditions diverged. For the analytic tradition, the Fregean notion of sense or meaning is intrinsically linguistic. Language does not *express* thought: it is the medium of thought. There is no separate mental meaning which is subsequently represented in linguistic meaning.

Nevertheless, both the phenomenological and analytic projects have a strong Kantian element in them, moving out from what thought must be like to what the world must be like. Analytic philosophy has its origins in the translation of epistemological questions into logical ones, and from Russell onwards there were various attempts to move from the logical structure of language to the 'logical structure of the world'. Indeed, it is striking that, although the developments in which Frege's analytic successors were engaged were part of a concerted reaction to the pretensions of idealist philosophy, what resulted could easily be mistaken for a variation on the idealist projects. Just as Kant and the classical idealists had projected the structure of the mind onto the structure of reality, so Russell and Wittgenstein in particular worked on the basis of an isomorphism between thought and reality, so that knowledge of the former provided knowledge of the latter, or at least gave us all we could know about the latter.

Russell's programme came explicitly to engage a number of metaphysical and epistemological questions. His doctrine of 'logical atomism', published after a long gestation period in a book of that title in 1918, develops the metaphysical and epistemological aspects of his earlier theory of descriptions. The theory of descriptions was part of a project, very like that of Frege, to replace various syntactic forms of ordinary language, particularly the subject–predicate form, with a semantically motivated syntax. The problem he tackled was how one held to the principle that every individual linguistic expression, if it was to have meaning, must refer to something, while at the same time accounting for non-referring expressions, without positing non-existing objects for these to refer to. His solution was to argue that the subject of a true proposition need not have any ontological properties if it wasn't *really* the subject of the proposition at all. The theory underlying this approach lay in his theory of descriptions, set out in his essay 'On Denoting'.[5] The sentence 'The present king of France is bald', for example, uttered at a time when there was no longer a king of France, clearly has a meaning, but in that case what does it refer to, if not a non-existent object? In 'On Denoting', Russell shows how to reformulate sentences containing denoting phrases so as to retain the meaning of the original sentence without employing any denoting phrase.

His subsequent turn to what he termed logical atomism fleshes out the underlying precepts of the theory of descriptions in epistemological and metaphysical terms. The idea is to clarify reasonable knowledge claims that lack clarity or complete justification, showing how they can be formulated in terms of relations between simpler, more intelligible, more undeniable entities. If, when formulated in these terms, there is decisive justification for the claims, then we should accept the reformulation, and the entities to which it commits us. We begin with those entities whose existence is indubitable because they are given in immediate experience—the self, colours, sounds, smells, tactile qualities, and so on—and then we try to construe all other discourse about everything else in terms of these. We build up our new metaphysics out of the simplest elements. In *The Philosophy of Logical Atomism*, Russell spells out a crucial principle underlying this metaphysics: there must be an isomorphism between the structure of an ideal language and the structure of reality. What began as a way of investigating mathematics has now become a way of investigating the world. If we can describe in outline how the world would be described in an ideal language, we will have (in outline) an account of what the world is like. There are many different ways of stating the facts, so the restriction to an ideal language is crucial, since only this will reflect the real structure of the world. Russell's aim is to construct an ideal language out of atomic sentences and their truth-functional compounds.

He was aware that there were intractable problems with his attempt to base knowledge on truth-functional compounds, but the idea of atomic sentences set out an ideal which might be aimed at. It was revised and systematized by Wittgenstein in the *Tractatus*, and by the logical positivists, particularly by Carnap, who set out a much more elaborate version of the doctrine of atomic sentences.

In the notebooks that were to form the basis for the *Tractatus*, Wittgenstein writes, 'The great problem around which everything that I write turns is this: Is there an order in the world a priori, and if so what does it consist in?' The a priori nature of the exercise is crucial here, just as it was for Kant and Hegel, in whose tracks he follows in his claims to be the first and only real philosopher: 'What has history to do with me? Mine is the first and only world.'[6] Wittgenstein believed that the method of a logically perfect language could be cut loose from mathematics, where it had in fact come to a dead end with Russell's discovery of the set-theoretical paradoxes, and he set out to generalize it to the whole of philosophy. And whereas Russell approached ontological questions through a combination of epistemological and logical concerns, Wittgenstein completely abandoned epistemology as a foundational discipline. Logic, he writes, 'must take care of itself',[7] and it directs you straight to ontology, epistemology becoming just a question of drawing the consequences of this metaphysical programme for the philosophy of science.

The original problem for Frege had been that of psychologism in mathematics; for Russell it had been the metaphysical problem of non-existent objects; and for Wittgenstein it had been how to conceive of the logical structure of thought in such a way that it reflected the logical structure of reality. The logical positivists introduced ingredients from each of these into their conception, seeing the last in particular as a means of realizing a more traditional anti-metaphysical programme: nineteenth-century positivism. It is the logical positivists who bring out most clearly, because most explicitly, the attempt to accommodate philosophy to a scientific model, and to rebuild the world in a scientific image.

There were two distinctive features of early positivism. First, there is the search for pure experience, that is, experience purged of illegitimate additions and preconceived ideas, and metaphysics is identified as the prime culprit here. Second, there is a rejection of a traditional feature of empiricism, namely the idea that objectivity lies simply in reflecting an independent reality. For thinkers such as Ernst Mach, who began as a Kantian, the philosopher or scientist is an active organizer of experience, imposing categories on experience which enable us to organize the world in the simplest way. But Mach soon rejected the notion that there could be synthetic a priori knowledge. Science, he argued, is continuous with common sense. It is a systematizing of experience, and thought is a specific part of human practical activity, an organic response or a process of adaption to the environment. If, discarding all metaphysical assumptions, we reflect on the nature of what we find in experience, what we encounter are complexes of elements which are neither mental nor physical, but neutral. We call these elements 'things' to the extent that we link them together in permanent combinations and study their properties, and we call them 'impressions' to the extent that we relate them to the body that perceives them. In scientific investigation, we simply select and symbolize ingredients of experience, not in order to uncover the structure of reality, but in order to make predictions. For Mach, scientific theory replaces philosophy, and offers a form of practical understanding that philosophy was never able to aspire to. Unlike metaphysics, its aim is not to explain but to predict: scientific explanations are just descriptions of unfamiliar items in terms of familiar ones, where the things that are most familiar to us are our elementary sensations.

The great attraction of positivism for subsequent philosophers was twofold. First, it was becoming increasingly difficult to adjudicate the claims of competing philosophical systems, by contrast with empirical science, which had standards for the assessment of the merits of competing theories, amongst which prediction played an absolutely crucial role. Second, if the empirical sciences exhausted the legitimate questions of truth about the extralinguistic world, what was left for philosophers? Not some higher or transcendent realm, but language: the aim of the new philosophical movement was to clarify language and make it more precise, thereby simultaneously exposing the traditional 'pseudo-problems' of philosophy and exhibiting the exact nature and extent of genuine theoretical issues.

Rethinking the Nature of Philosophy

The assimilation of philosophy by science, whether in the form of an attempt to develop a scientific form of philosophy, or in the form of construing philosophy as a metatheory of science, did not go unchallenged. The Fregean reasoning that drove the move from the logical structure of thought to logical structure of the world came in for criticism in both its phenomenological version and its analytic one. In his *Being and Time*, for example, Heidegger offered two main criticisms of Husserl. The first focused on Husserl's attempt to construe language as being simply one species of intentional act, and to give an account of meaning and intentionality in terms of an examination of the structure of our conscious experience. This, Heidegger argues, is to get things the wrong way round. Rather, it is public behaviour and shared standards that provide the basis for understanding what meaning consists in. The second criticism is that Husserl's account ignores various social practices and the like which do not have intentional content and which are not reducible to systems of belief, yet are a condition of possibility of abstract meanings. This kind of objection has also been pursued within analytic philosophy, by John Searle, who rejects a Fregean account of meaning on the grounds that truth conditions cannot be a complete account of meaning, because the truth conditions of an assertion are always relative to a background, and this background—of skills, practices, discriminations, and suchlike which are not themselves intentional states—does not form part of the semantic content of a sentence.

At the same time, and on similar grounds, in his later work, Wittgenstein came to abandon the radically simple picture version of language offered in the *Tractatus*, and started to consider the variety of uses to which language is put: the way we use words to describe, but also to command, commend, greet, thank, joke, and so on. The metaphor of a picture is replaced by that of a tool. According to the *Philosophical Investigations*, philosophical puzzles arise when philosophers overlook this range of practices, or 'language games' as he calls them. Each of these has its own logic and one cannot attempt to force all of language into a single mould. The task of the philosopher, as Wittgenstein came to see it, is not to devise theories to deal with these problems, but to 'dissolve' them by calling attention to the way in which language works, something he compared (using the same kind of homely image we find in Heidegger) to the untangling and mending of fishing nets: it requires practice, patience, and dexterity. The atomism of the *Tractatus* had been offered as a theory that went beyond the surface structure of language and offered a description of its deep structure, and correspondingly, it went beyond the surface structure of reality to its deep structure. But Wittgenstein became aware of various counterexamples to the idea of an underlying comprehensive logical structure, such as Moore's paradox. The paradox takes the form of the statement 'It is raining but I do not believe that it is raining', and the problem is that, while it seems that no one could consistently assert such a sentence, there is no *logical* contradiction between the two parts of the sentence, because the first is a statement of fact about the weather and the latter a statement of belief about the weather. Wittgenstein was intrigued by such seeming paradoxes, which he came to believe derived from the search for deep structure. He gradually came to believe that the logical structure of reality might actually be visible on its surface: revealed in the ordinary uses that we make or words in ordinary situations. As he will put it later in the *Blue Book*,[8] the attempt to model philosophy on science 'is the real source of metaphysics, and leads the philosopher into complete darkness'. Urging a rethinking of the nature of philosophy in the *Philosophical Investigations*, he writes that philosophy 'just puts everything before us, and neither explains nor deduces anything.—Since everything lies open to view there is nothing to explain.'[9] Here we have an abandonment of a second-order form of enquiry. This is not to deny that some have interpreted Wittgenstein's notion of 'philosophical grammar', for example, as a way of filling out conceptual analysis, considered as the core of philosophy.[10] And this is compatible with the idea that philosophical problems are not genuine problems, but pseudo-problems that arise because of a misuse of the language in which they are expressed.[11] But the ties of philosophical grammar to the idea of a 'language game'—'a system of reference by means of which we interpret an unknown language'[12]—and with 'forms of life', which are dependent on culture and context, suggests a different direction, one that departs radically from philosophical thought. One might substitute 'philosophy' for Karl Kraus's definition of psychoanalysis: 'it is the disease for which it takes itself to be the cure'.

The criticisms of the idea that language, or consciousness, has a logical structure which mirrors the logical structure of the world, go hand in hand with a rejection of the idea that philosophical understanding must model itself on scientific understanding. Such criticisms begin with a development within neo-Kantianism. As with the Marburg School, the overriding goal for the Southwest German version of neo-Kantianism was the defence of philosophy. But once we go beyond this, significant differences emerge. The chief representative of the Southwest School, Windelband, distinguishes between the natural sciences, which establish laws about what is the case, and philosophy, which he argues is a normative realm, determining standards of judgement for what ought to be the case. In an 1882 essay on norms and laws of nature, Windelband argues that these are two activities which treat the object from different perspectives, and so are complementary.[13] The basic claim raised by proponents of the distinction is that the kinds of understanding that we seek in accounting for human behaviour are different from those we seek in the natural sciences, because the kind of thing that we want to understand is different. One way in which this contrast can be expressed is in terms of the distinction between reasons and causes: giving the reasons someone has for doing something—interpreting that person's behaviour—and giving the causes of that behaviour are two different things. The difference is that between interpretation of the behaviour and explanation of it. The former has to capture how the actors themselves conceive of what they are doing, whereas the latter does not. While it might be appropriate to 'stand back' from phenomena in the natural sciences to achieve objectivity, this is inappropriate in the case of the human sciences, where we are dealing not with an objectified realm, but with human beings who have intentional states, emotions, the ability to exercise judgement, and so on. These are attributes that they share with the investigator, and which the investigator is therefore in a position to interpret and make sense of. This is clearly something quite different from what we do in the natural sciences. The argument is that the natural sciences have been wrongly taken to provide a model of objectivity per se, something that can simply be exported to any other area of study. This is not to deny that objectivity in the sense of impartiality is appropriate in the human sciences. Rather, what is at issue is whether criteria of objectivity, or guides as to how objectivity might be achieved, can simply be imported from the natural sciences into cases where it is not a question of discovery of causes, but of the interpretation of behaviour.

A different kind challenge to the standing of scientific explanation is more profound, for what is in question is not the scope of scientific explanation, but whether science has the legitimacy claimed by its advocates. Dilthey, for example, treated understanding—*Wissenschaft*—as dealing not only with knowledge, but more generally with human experience and the meaning of human action in history.[14] What is distinctive about Dilthey's hermeneutic conception is his rejection of the search for an a priori ground for our knowledge of human culture. Knowledge is always bound up with the culture that it attempts to know: there is no absolute starting point for knowledge.

A theme in a work by Dilthey's student Heidegger, *Being and Time*, is a rejection of the idea that the values of science, as articulated by the Marburg neo-Kantians through epistemology, are universal cosmopolitan values. For Heidegger, these values have failed, science and technology having resulted in tools of war and unthinking consumerism. He rejects not only cosmopolitan values, which reflect only a thoroughly rationalized and inauthentic view of humanity, but also their associated notions of freedom and spontaneity. The latter were integral to the neo-Kantian assimilation of sensibility to rationality, and it was precisely this assimilation that Heidegger refused to accept. Our orientation in the world is not provided by reason, on Heidegger's account, but by a very specific worldliness and temporality, one in which reason does not provide a means of escape, or a route to cosmopolitanism. Human existence can only be considered in all its worldly forms, and in so considering it, what we encounter is the sheer historical contingency of our human existence. On Heidegger's account, in place of a rationality that enables us to create the world of scientific enquiry, we find ourselves 'thrown' into a world not of our making, and which we are unable to subject to rational control. It is a world characterized by mortality, care, anxiety, temporality, and our dependence on a history for which we can claim no responsibility.

The advocacy of a return to a primordial state, which he increasingly identified with the Presocratics, is a prominent feature of Heidegger's subsequent work, indicating that, for him, philosophy took a wrong path, not in the Enlightenment, but at its origins, perhaps even in its Socratic form. What he seems to be seeking is in fact something quite different from philosophy, something more like the pre-philosophical forms of thought that we looked at in chapter 1, which have been conventionally characterized as Presocratic philosophy but which, as we have seen, were quite different from philosophy. I have been at pains to point out that the way in which the tasks of philosophy have been identified has changed radically, to such an extent that, for many purposes, there is no continuous substantive trans-historical philosophical enterprise. But at a minimal level, the second-order nature of philosophical enquiry has served to characterize it adequately for our purposes. And it is just this second-order enquiry that is in question in Heidegger, and indeed in the late Wittgenstein, both of whom, in their use of homely practical images like repairing fishing nets, have resort, not to a Presocratic but to pre-philosophical imagery. We are in the domain of cunning and strategy.

I am not at all convinced that we have here a replacement for philosophy, or for second-order enquiry more generally, as Heidegger for one certainly believed. But nor do I know of any compelling grounds for saying that philosophy has completely displaced such approaches: that, whatever route one takes, philosophy provides the ultimate form of understanding.

Conclusion

*What is the significance of science viewed as a symptom
of life? . . . Is the resolve to be so scientific about everything
perhaps a kind of fear of, and escape from, pessimism? A
subtle last resort against—truth? and, morally speaking, a
sort of cowardice and falseness?*

NIETZSCHE, 'SCHOPENHAUER AS EDUCATOR'[1]

The philosophical projects that we have looked at have each
had a substantive aspiration: an account of the good life and
how to live, an account of metaphysics as a discipline that can
stand in judgement over and assess other forms of thought,
and philosophy as a theory of everything. That substantive
aspirations have disappeared in many forms of philosophy
over the last century is illustrated by a remark attributed to
the philosopher J. L. Austin, who, when asked what philosophy was, replied that philosophy was just what philosophers
do. One thing that I hope our enquiry has brought to light is
just how odd such a conception of philosophy is. But the odd-
ness of what we might term 'philosophy without portfolio' is

the least of its problems. Locke famously thought of the role of philosophy as clearing away the rubbish in the way of knowledge, but could it be that a philosophy with no overriding aim has in fact put rubbish in its way? The preoccupation of many French philosophers over the last fifty years with novelty, with aspiring to saying something original above all else, has certainly had this effect. But the way in which analytic philosophy in the same period has trivialized problems so that they have become merely technical, as if one were solving scientific or economic problems, has had a similarly deleterious effect. And the response to trivializing analysis has perhaps been even worse: the promotion of an 'analytical metaphysics' in which philosophical questions are pasted into a scientific framework, reminiscent of the school geometry textbooks passed down from year to year in which the student of the previous year has risen above the geometrical content, as it were, and coloured in the circles and triangles.

Nevertheless, the fascination of philosophers with science—and the Sokal hoax shows that this fascination is not limited to analytic philosophy—is not something that can simply be made to disappear. It is, more than anything else, what shapes current conceptions of the aims of philosophy and how it should proceed. In some crucial respects, this has been true since the thirteenth century, when Aristotelian natural philosophy became our sole source of knowledge about the natural world, and it is the concern with, and ability to engage with, science that has marked out Western philosophy as distinctive since then. The association of philosophy with science not only has a long history, but this association lies at the basis of our modern understanding of philosophy. At the same time, independently of questions of how one conceives the function of philosophy, the understanding of science is something that bears directly on the successful pursuit of philosophy.

The fundamental difficulty is not so much one of philosophy freeing itself from a preoccupation with science, but rather that of freeing science from a particular philosophical model. Scientific understanding of the world has been taken by philosophers since the seventeenth century as primarily theoretical understanding. It shared a theoretical character with the theological conceptions that it complemented or replaced, and in this respect it drew on a tradition that had been shaped by theologians, rather than by those working in optics, astronomy, or mechanics. At its most refined, science on this conception is something that takes the form of basic principles, virtually indistinguishable from philosophical abstractions. Science is not alone in this respect by any means, and John Gray has characterized philosophers' cognate approach to political theory as no longer aiming

> to improve the political reasoning of ordinary citizens. Instead, they see their task as providing a body of principles which can best be interpreted by a court. In this view, best represented in John Rawls' deeply meditated and intricately reasoned, yet supremely parochial and unhistorical book, *A Theory of Justice* (1971), politics is redundant. Philosophers supply principles dictating the scope of individual liberty and the distribution of social goods; judges apply them. Little if anything of importance remains for political decision. Rawls calls his theory 'political liberalism', but it is more accurately described as a species of antipolitical legalism.[2]

As regards science, the root of the problem lies in the reduction of science to scientific theory, an egregious failure to appreciate the internal constitution of science: a complex amalgam of (among other things) theory, engineering, technology, and invention.[3] The conception of science as being essentially scientific theory, with everything else simply an 'application' of science, has in fact never been satisfactory, as the long story of 'experimental natural philosophy' from the seventeenth century testifies, and, since the middle of the nineteenth century, it has been impossible to take such a view seriously outside philosophy. There is now a very significant literature in the history of modern science and engineering that undercuts any idea that the engineering and technology achievements of the twentieth century were simply a matter of the application of scientific theory. Given the intimate relations between science and philosophy, a properly realistic understanding of the former is a prerequisite for a proper understanding of the latter.

The lack of a realistic understanding of science carries over into the idea of physical theory as a model of intellectual progress. Consider developments in the last forty years in physical theory. The 'Standard Model' of elementary particle physics tells us that to understand the interactions between the twelve particles and four forces that it postulates, we need to invoke some twenty free parameters which have values that no theory can predict, and 'constants'—including the number of spatial dimensions, the ratio of fundamental energies, the cosmological constant, the number of electrons and protons in the observable universe—which we are unable to derive from any mathematics or principles of physics, and which are quite contingent features of our universe. At the same time, these features depend on there being more matter than antimatter in the universe, but we have no idea why there is this imbalance. In fact, even if the Standard Model were successful, it could at best only describe just under five per cent of the matter-energy content of the universe, given the amounts of dark matter and dark energy. And the possibility of even this five per cent degree of success is highly questionable, given that the prevailing theoretical account, string theory, describes so many universes (in the region of 10^{500}) that it manifestly lacks any of the predictive power that we associate with a successful scientific theory. One might consider that, in Kuhnian terms,[4] we have hit a period of anomalies, foreshadowing paradigm collapse: hardly something on which we would want to model philosophy. This is not meant as a criticism of physics, but of the starry-eyed view of physics held by many philosophers. Get real, as they say.

In short, if philosophy is to avoid becoming merely a form of air guitar to the music of science, it must be recognized that not only is there is no simple success story that philosophers can emulate or aspire to, but also that there is no model of understanding that philosophy can simply lock on to. Its legitimacy as a model of understanding rests wholly on its own resources: it cannot ride on the back of science or anything else. This requires some serious self-reflection, and above all we need to be able to understand how we got to where we are now. Accordingly, I have set out to trace a route to present conceptions, a route that has turned out to be far more discontinuous than has generally been thought to be the case. This discontinuity should act as an antidote to any complacency about the present state of philosophy. It is not the culmination of two and a half millennia of philosophical thought, and there is little that is perennial about it. Instead, contemporary philosophy is something of relatively recent provenance, and it seems to have lost it bearings. This is not the first time in the history of the subject that this has occurred, and my hope is that if we can recognize the earlier failures, we might be able to learn from them.

NOTES

Classical Greek sources are referred to in the Notes below by standard LSJ abbreviations (available at, e.g., http://www.stoa.org/abbreviations.html).

Introduction

1. Thomas Stanley, *The History of Philosophy* (3 vols, London, 1665–66), i. Preface, n.p.

2. John D. Barrow and Frank J. Tipler, *The Anthropic Cosmological Principle* (Oxford, 1986), 15.

3. Quoted in Susan Blackmore, *Conversations on Consciousness* (Oxford, 2005), 75.

4. Daniel Stoljar, *Philosophical Progress: In Defence of a Reasonable Optimism* (Oxford, 2017), 26.

5. Ibid., 28.

6. Much of the sense of the success of physics depends on an egregious failure to distinguish science from independent developments in engineering, technology, and invention. See Stephen Gaukroger, *Civilization and the Culture of Science* (Oxford, 2020), ch. 10.

7. See, for example, Jonathan Rée, *Witcraft: The Invention of Philosophy in English* (London, 2019).

8. Justin Smith, *The Philosopher: A History in Six Types* (Princeton, NJ, 2016).

9. Pierre Hadot, *Philosophy as a Way of Life* (Oxford, 1995); *What Is Ancient Philosophy?* (Cambridge, MA, 2002).

10. Kuno Fisher, *Geschichte der neuern Philosophie* (6 vols, Stuttgart-Mannheim-Heidelberg, 1854–77).

Chapter One: The Emergence of Philosophy

1. Francis M. Cornford, *From Religion to Philosophy* (London, 1912); *Principium Sapientiae* (Cambridge, 1952); see also Jane Harrison, *Prolegomena to the Study of Greek Religion* (Cambridge, 1903); *Themis* (Cambridge, 1912).

2. See Alexander Nehamas, 'Eristic, Antilogic, Sophistics, Dialectic: Plato's Demarcation of Philosophy from Sophistry', *History of Philosophy Quarterly* 7 (1990), 3–16.

3. Andrea Wilson Nightingale, *Spectacles of Truth in Classical Greek Philosophy* (Cambridge, 2004), 3.

4. François Jullien, *The Propensity of Things: Towards a History of Efficacy in China* (New York, 1995), 124.

5. *Shi* here transliterates the character 勢.

6. See Marcel Detienne and Jean-Pierre Vernant, *Cunning Intelligence in Greek Culture and Society*, trans. Janet Lloyd (Hassocks, Sussex, 1978).

7. G.E.R. Lloyd, *The Delusions of Invulnerability* (London, 2005), 104.

8. Arist., *Metaph.* 982^{b}18.

9. Maria Michela Sassi, *The Beginnings of Philosophy in Greece* (Princeton, NJ, 2018), 67.

10. Arist., *Metaph.* 983^{b}19.

11. Friedrich Nietzsche, *Philosophy in the Tragic Age of the Greeks* (Chicago, 1962), 38–39.

12. Arist., *Metaph.* 982^{a}16–19.

13. See Harold Cherniss, *Aristotle's Criticism of Presocratic Philosophy* (Baltimore, 1935).

14. Pl., *Tht.* 174A–B.

15. Arist., *Pol.* 1259^{a}9ff.

16. Hdt., *Hist.* 1.74–76.

17. Arist., *Metaph.* 985^{a}14–18, 985^{a}4–6.

18. Ibid., 988^{a}20–23.

19. Pl., *Grg.* 465A.

20. Jean Pierre Vernant, *Myth and Thought among the Greeks* (London, 1983), 242–43.

21. André Laks, 'Écriture, prose et les débuts de la philosophie grecque', *Methodos* 1 (2001), 131–51; Georg Wöhrle, 'Zur Prosa der milesischen Philosophen,' *Würzburger Jahrbücher für die Altertumswissenschaft* N. F. 18 (1992), 33–47.

22. See Marcel Detienne, *Les Maîtres de vérité dans la Grèce archaïque* (Paris, 1990). See also Louis Gernet, *Anthropologie de la Grèce antique* (Paris, 1968), and Pierre Vidal-Naquet, 'La raison greque et la cité', *Raison Présente* 2 (1967), 51–61.

23. G.E.R. Lloyd, *Magic, Reason and Experience* (Cambridge, 1979), ch. 4.

24. Arist., *Metaph.* 1005^{b}35–1009^{b}1.

25. Andrea Nightingale, 'The Philosophers in Archaic Greek Culture', in H. A. Shapiro, ed., *The Cambridge Companion to Archaic Greece* (Cambridge, 2007), 169–98: 171–72.

26. A. A. Long, 'The Scope of Early Greek Philosophy', in idem, ed., *The Cambridge Companion to Early Greek Philosophy* (Cambridge, 1999), 1–21: 13–14.

27. Pl., *R.* 354C, 353E.

28. See W.K.C. Guthrie, *The Sophists* (Cambridge, 1971), 51

29. Arist., *Metaph.* 987^{b}1–4.

30. Pl., *Men.* 82B–86A.

31. Pl., *Phd.* 74B–75B.

32. Martha C. Nussbaum, *The Fragility of Goodness* (rev. edn, Cambridge, 2001), 25.

33. Pl., *Euthphr.* 8A.

34. See Rebecca Langlands, *Exemplary Ethics in Ancient Rome* (Cambridge, 2018).

Chapter Two: Metaphysics as a Form of Understanding

1. See Stephen Gaukroger, 'Aristotle on Intelligible Matter', *Phronesis* 25 (1980): 187–97.

2. See idem., *The Emergence of a Scientific Culture* (Oxford, 2006), 77–80.

3. See Harold Cherniss, *The Riddle of the Early Academy* (Berkeley, CA, 1945).

4. Arist., *APo.* 71^{b}18–12.

5. Arist., *Metaph.* 1051^{b}13–17.

6. See Richard Sorabji, *Necessity, Cause and Blame* (London, 1980), and Sarah Waterlow, *Nature, Change and Agency in Aristotle's Physics* (Oxford, 1982).

7. Arist., *Ph.* 196^{a}1–5.

8. There is a good selection of primary sources of Stoic and Epicurean philosophy in A. A. Long and D. N. Sedley, *The Hellenistic Philosophers* (2 vols, Cambridge, 1987).

9. Arist., *Ph.*194^{b}16–195^{a}3.

10. Arist., *SE* 184^{b}1–5.

11. See Stephen Gaukroger, *Cartesian Logic* (Oxford, 1989).

12. Pl., *R.* 514A–520A.

13. See Nightingale, *Spectacles of Truth*.

14. Arist., *de An.* 428^{b}17–25.

15. Ibid., 418^{b}32ff.

16. G.E.M. Anscombe, 'Modern Moral Philosophy', *Philosophy* 33, no. 124 (January 1958), 1–16.

Chapter Three: Philosophy's Loss of Autonomy

1. Arist., *EN* 1095^{a}15–22.

2. John M. Cooper, *Pursuits of Wisdom* (Princeton, NJ, 2012), 3.

3. Pl., *Prt.* 356C.

4. Pl., *R.* 443C–445B.

5. Pl., *Ti.* 89D–90A.

6. Arist., *EN* 1096^{a}11–1097^{a}14.

7. Nightingale, *Spectacles of Truth*, 200.

8. Arist., *EN* 1141^{b}7–12.

9. Ibid., 1139^{a}21–31.

10. Ibid., 1094^{b}28–1095^{a}30.

11. Cooper, *Pursuits of Wisdom*, 149.

12. See John Dillon, *The Middle Platonists* (London, 1977), and R. T. Wallis, *Neoplatonism* (New York, 1972).

13. See Eyjólfur Kjalar Emilsson, *Plotinus on Sense-Perception* (Cambridge, 1988).

14. Pl., *Ti.* 28A.

15. Clement of Alexandria, *Stromateis* I.81.4.

16. See Charles Norris Cochrane, *Christianity and Classical Culture* (Oxford, 1944).

17. See See Juliusz Domański, *La philosophie, théorie ou manière de vivre?* (Fribourg/Paris, 1996), 23–29.

18. Augustine, *Retractions*, Book 1, ch. 13.

19. See Adolf von Harnack, *Marcion: das Evangelium vom fremden Gott* (Leipzig, 1921).

20. See Albrecht Dihle, *The Theory of the Will in Classical Antiquity* (Berkeley, CA, 1982), ch. 6.

21. Augustine, *De civitate dei*, 14.6

Chapter Four: The Creation of an Autonomous Role for Philosophy

1. See Marcia Colish, *Medieval Foundations of the Western Intellectual Tradition, 400–1400* (New Haven, CT, 1997), chs 11 and 21.

2. See Charles Lohr, 'The Medieval Interpretation of Aristotle', in N. Kretzman, A. Kenny, and J. Pinborg, eds, *The Cambridge History of Later Medieval Philosophy* (Cambridge, 1982), 80–98.

3. Nicholas of Autrecourt, *The Universal Treatise of Nicholas of Autrecourt*, trans. Leonard Kennedy, Richard Arnold, and Arthur Millward (Milwaukee, WI, 1971).

4. See Robert Lenoble, *Mersenne ou la naissance du mécanisme* (2nd edn, Paris, 1971).

5. See Stephen Gaukroger, *Francis Bacon and the Transformation of Early Modern Philosophy* (Cambridge, 2001).

Chapter Five: From Natural Philosophy to Epistemology

1. *Descartes: The World and Other Writings*, ed. and trans. S. Gaukroger (Cambridge, 1998).

2. *Oeuvres de Descartes*, ed. Charles Adam and Paul Tannery (2nd edn, 11 vols, Paris, 1974–86), vii. 80.

3. Ibid., x. 439.

4. Ibid., vi. 39.

5. Ibid., vii. 50.

6. Ibid., iii. 695

7. Nicolas Malebranche, *The Search after Truth*, trans. T. Lennon and P. Olscamp (Columbus, OH, 1980).

8. Antoine Arnauld, *On True and False Ideas*, trans. S. Gaukroger (Manchester, 1990).

9. See Descartes, *Principia* II, art. 3.

10. See John W. Yolton, *Perceptual Acquaintance from Descartes to Reid* (Oxford, 1984).

11. See James J. Gibson, *The Ecological Approach to Visual Perception* (Boston, 1979).

12. See Stephen Gaukroger, 'Cartesianism and Visual Cognition: The Problems with the Optical Instrument Model', in S. Gaukroger and C. Wilson, eds, *Descartes and Cartesianism* (Oxford, 2017), 112–24.

13. Locke, *Essay Concerning Human Understanding*, IV.iv.3.

14. Idem, 'An Examination of P. Malebranche's Opinion of Seeing all Things in God', in *The Works of John Locke Esq.* (2nd edn, 3 vols, London, 1722)

15. Locke, *Essay*, IV.iv.4.

Chapter Six: Reason versus Sensibility

1. See Stephen Gaukroger, *Descartes' System of Natural Philosophy* (Cambridge, 2002), chs 7 and 8.

2. Locke, *Essay*, II.xxvii.9.

3. Étienne Bonnet de Condillac, *Traité des sensations* (Paris, 1754), Part I.

4. Jessica Riskin, *Science in the Age of Sensibility* (Chicago, 2002), 21.

5. Denis Diderot, *Réfutation de l'Homme*, in *Œuvres complètes*, ed. J. Assézat and M. Tourneux (20 vols, Paris, 1875–79), ii. 351–52.

6. Idem, *Éléments de physiologie*, ed. Jean Mayer (Paris, 1964), 287.

7. Bernard Mandeville, *The Fable of the Bees*, ed. F. B. Kay (2 vols, Oxford, 1924), i. 355–56.

8. Idem, *Free Thoughts on Religion* (London, 1720), 282.

9. See Stephen Gaukroger, 'Romanticism and Decommodification: Marx's Conception of Socialism', *Economy and Society* 15 (1986), 287–333.

10. Adam Smith, *The Theory of Moral Sentiments*, VII.ii.2.14.

11. Ibid., VII.ii.3.21.

12. Ibid., III.iii.34.

13. Adam Smith, *An Inquiry into Nature and Causes of The Wealth of Nations*, II.2.36.

14. Smith, *Theory of Moral Sentiments*, II.ii.3.3.

15. Jeremy Bentham, *An Introduction to the Principles of Morals and Legislation* (London, 1789).

16. David Hume, *A Treatise of Human Nature*, Book 2, Sect. vii.

Chapter Seven: The Retreat from Philosophy

1. Hume, *Treatise*, Introduction.

2. Ibid., Book 1, Part IV, Sect. i.

3. Ibid., Book 1, Part III, Sect. xiv.

4. See, for example, Nicolas Malebranche, *The Search after Truth* (Columbus, OH, 1980), Elucidation 15.

5. See Charles J. McCracken, *Malebranche and British Philosophy* (Oxford, 1983), ch. 7.

6. John P. Wright, *The Sceptical Realism of David Hume* (Manchester, 1983); Galen Strawson, *The Secret Connection* (Oxford, 1989).

7. Hume, *Treatise*, Book 1, Sect. vii.

8. David Hume, *Enquiries Concerning the Human Understanding and Concerning the Principles of Morals*, ed. L. A. Selby-Bigge (2nd edn, Oxford, 1902), 197n.

9. Hume, *Treatise*, Book 1, Part IV, Sect. vii.

10. Ibid.

11. See Donald W. Livingstone, *Philosophical Melancholy and Delirium* (Chicago, 1998)

12. David Hume, *Essays and Treatises* (2 vols, Edinburgh, 1793), ii. 401–14 (Natural History, Sect. I–III).

13. Ibid, ii. 428 (Sect. VI).

14. Ibid, ii. 439 (Sect. IX).

15. Ibid, ii. 489–90.

16. Hume, *Enquiries*, 38 (Sect. XI).

17. Charles Bonnet, *Essai analytique sur les facultés de l'âme* (Copenhagen, 1760), ch. 3.

18. Ibid, ch. 21.

19. Anne Vila, *Enlightenment and Pathology* (Baltimore, 1998), 38.

20. Théophile de Bordeu, *Oeuvres complètes* (2 vols, Paris, 1818), ii. 669.

21. Louis de La Caze, *Idée de l'homme physique et moral* (Paris, 1755), 363–67.

22. Elizabeth A. Williams, *The Physical and the Moral* (Cambridge, 1994), 45.

23. Vila, *Enlightenment and Pathology*, 183.

24. Johann Georg Heinrich Feder, *Untersuchungen über den menschlichen Willen* (4 vols, Göttingen, 1779–93), i. 350.

25. See in particular his essay on 'the art of thinking', in Christian Garve, *Versuche über verschiedene aus der Moral, der Litteratur und dem gesellschaftlichen Leben* (5 vols, Breslau, 1792–1802), ii. 245–430.

26. Karl Franz von Irwing, *Erfahrungen und Untersuchungen über den Menschen* (2 vols, Berlin, 1777–79), Preface.

27. Immanuel Kant, 'Metaphysik Herder', in *Gesammelte Schriften* ('Akademie' edn, 29 vols, Berlin, 1900–) xxviii. 892.

28. Kant, 'Versuch über die Krankheiten des Kopfes', in *Gesammelte Schriften*, ii. 271.

29. Kant, *Gesammelte Schriften*, xxiv. 37; *Lectures on Logic* (Cambridge, 1992), 24–25.

Chapter Eight: The Search for a Theory
of Everything

1. *Novalis: Schriften*, ed. Paul Kluckholn et al. (6 vols, Stuttgart, 1960–2006), iii. 651.

2. Kant, 'Metaphysik Mrongovius', in *Lectures on Metaphysics* (Cambridge, 1997), 109–284.

3. Kant, *Critique of Pure Reason*, Bxvi.

4. Ibid., A26/B42.

5. Ibid., Axx.

6. See Eckart Förster, *The Twenty-Five Years of Philosophy* (Cambridge, MA, 2012).

7. Immanuel Kant, *Practical Philosophy* (Cambridge, 1996), 47.

8. See Lewis White Beck, *Early German Philosophy: Kant and his Predecessors* (Cambridge, MA, 1969), 288–305.

9. J. C. O'Flaherty, ed. and trans., *Hamann's Socratic Memorabilia* (Baltimore, 1967).

10. See Förster, *Twenty-Five Years*, 48–53.

11. Kant, *Practical Philosophy*.

12. See Paul W. Franks, *All or Nothing* (Cambridge, MA, 2005).

13. Kant, *Critique*, A15/B29.

14. See Frederick C. Beiser, *The Fate of Reason* (Cambridge, MA, 1987), ch. 8.

15. See William Brazill, *The Young Hegelians* (New Haven, CT, 1970), and John E. Toews, *Hegelianism: The Path Towards Dialectical Humanism, 1805–1841* (Cambridge, 1980).

16. See Frederick C. Beiser, *Weltschmerz: Pessimism in German Philosophy 1860–1900* (Oxford, 2016).

17. Emil du Bois-Reymond, *Reden von Emil du Bois-Reymond* (2 vols, Leipzig, 1912), i. 475–78.

18. Ibid., i. 560–61.

19. E. O. Wilson, *Sociobiology: The New Synthesis* (Cambridge, MA, 1975), 562.

20. John Stuart Mill, 'Whewell on Moral Philosophy' (1852), in *The Collected Works of John Stuart Mill*, J. M. Robson (33 vols, Toronto, 1963–91), x. 168.

21. Idem, *A System of Logic* (1872), in *Collected Works*, vii. 163.

22. Willard Van Orman Quine. 'Mr Stawson on Logical Theory', *Mind* 62 (1953), 433–51: 446.

Chapter Nine: Science Assimilates
Philosophy

1. Hermann Cohen, *Einleitung mit kritischem Nachtrag, zur neunten Auflage von Langes Geschichte des Materialismus* (Leipzig, 1914).

2. Idem, *Hermann Cohens Schriften zur Philosophie und Zeitgeschichte* (2 vols, Berlin, 1928), ii. 271.

3. See Gaukroger, *Civilization and the Culture of Science*, which sets out in detail why the project of the unity of science is an ideological one, having no basis in scientific practice itself, but rather presenting one of the greatest obstacles to understanding science and its development. See also idem, *The Collapse of Mechanism and the Rise of Sensibility* (Oxford, 2010), Part IV, on the insuperable problems encountered in trying to unify the sciences in the eighteenth century.

4. Ernst Cassirer, *The Philosophy of Symbolic Forms* (3 vols, New Haven, CT, 1955).

5. Bertrand Russell, 'On Denoting', *Mind*, 14 (1905), 479–93.

6. Ludwig Wittgenstein, *Notebooks 1914–1916* (Oxford, 1960), 82.

7. Ibid., 2–3.

8. Ludwig Wittgenstein, *The Blue and Brown Books* (Oxford, 1969), 18.

9. Idem, *Philosophical Investigations* (Oxford, 1968), § 126.

10. For example, see P.M.S. Hacker, *Wittgenstein's Place in Twentieth-Century Analytic Philosophy* (Oxford, 1996), ch. 5.

11. For a particularly good example of this, see the brilliant deflationary account of philosophical scepticism in Wittgenstein, *On Certainty* (Oxford, 1969).

12. Wittgenstein, *Philosophical Investigations*, 206.

13. Wilhelm Windelband, 'Normen und Naturgesetze', in *Präludien* (2 vols, Tübingen, 1915), ii. 59–98: 67.

14. See Lydia Patton, 'Methodology of the Sciences', in Michael Forster and Kristin Gjesdal, eds, *The Oxford Handbook of German Philosophy in the Nineteenth Century* (Oxford, 2015), 595–606: 603.

Conclusion

1. Friedrich Nietzsche, *Basic Writings of Nietzsche* (New York, 1968), 18.

2. John Gray, review of Alex Callinicos, *Equality*, *Times Literary Supplement* no. 5116 (20 April 2001), 3.

3. See my *Civilization and the Culture of Science*, especially ch. 10.

4. Thomas Kuhn, *The Structure of Scientific Revolutions* (4th edn, Chicago, 2012).

INDEX

A NOTE ON THE TYPE

THIS BOOK has been composed in Miller, a Scotch Roman typeface designed by Matthew Carter and first released by Font Bureau in 1997. It resembles Monticello, the typeface developed for The Papers of Thomas Jefferson in the 1940s by C. H. Griffith and P. J. Conkwright and reinterpreted in digital form by Carter in 2003.

Pleasant Jefferson ("P. J.") Conkwright (1905–1986) was Typographer at Princeton University Press from 1939 to 1970. He was an acclaimed book designer and AIGA Medalist.

The ornament used throughout this book was designed by Pierre Simon Fournier (1712–1768) and was a favorite of Conkwright's, used in his design of the *Princeton University Library Chronicle*.